Anonymous

Waifs and Strays of Celtic Tradition

Volume 4

Anonymous

Waifs and Strays of Celtic Tradition
Volume 4

ISBN/EAN: 9783337284756

Printed in Europe, USA, Canada, Australia, Japan

Cover: Foto ©Andreas Hilbeck / pixelio.de

More available books at **www.hansebooks.com**

THE FIANS.

Waifs and Straps of Celtic Tradition.

Series initiated and directed by
LORD ARCHIBALD CAMPBELL.

Demy 8vo, cloth.
ARGYLLSHIRE SERIES.

VOLUME I.
CRAIGNISH TALES.

Collected by the Rev. J. MacDougall; and Notes on the War Dress of the Celts by Lord Archibald Campbell. xvi, 98 pages. 20 plates. 1889. 5s.

VOLUME II.
FOLK AND HERO TALES.

Collected, edited (in Gaelic) and translated by the Rev. D. MacInnes; with a Study on the Development of the Ossianic Saga and copious Notes by Alfred Nutt. xxiv, 497 pages. Portrait of Campbell of Islay, and Two Illustrations by E. Griset. 1890. 15s.

"The most important work on Highland Folk-lore and Tales since Campbell's world-renowned Popular Tales."—*Highland Monthly.*
"Never before has the development of the Ossianic Saga been so scientifically dealt with."—Hector Maclean.
"Mr. Alfred Nutt's excursus and notes are lucid and scholarly. They add immensely to the value of the book, and afford abundant evidence of their author's extensive reading and sound erudition."—*Scots Observer.*
"The Gaelic text is colloquial and eminently idiomatic. . . . Mr. Nutt deserves special mention and much credit for the painstaking and careful research evidenced by his notes to the tales."—*Oban Telegraph.*

VOLUME III.
FOLK AND HERO TALES.

Collected, edited, translated, and annotated by the Rev. J. MacDougall; with an Introduction by Alfred Nutt, and Three Illustrations by E. Griset. 1891. 10s. 6d.

IAN CAMPBELL, OF ISLAY.

(From an Oil Picture by the late Jas. R. Swinton, painted about 1840—1842).

WAIFS AND STRAYS OF CELTIC TRADITION.

ARGYLLSHIRE SERIES.—No. IV.

THE FIANS;

OR,

STORIES, POEMS, & TRADITIONS

OF

FIONN AND HIS WARRIOR BAND.

Collected entirely from Oral Sources

BY

JOHN GREGORSON CAMPBELL,

Minister of Tiree.

WITH INTRODUCTION AND BIBLIOGRAPHICAL NOTES BY

ALFRED NUTT,

*PORTRAIT OF IAN CAMPBELL OF ISLAY, AND ILLUSTRATION BY
E. GRISET.*

LONDON :

DAVID NUTT, 270-271, STRAND.

1891.

CONTENTS.

PREFACE.

THIS volume has been made over to Lord Archibald Campbell for his Argyllshire Series, in full confidence that every justice the writer requires will be given to himself, and to the book, and in appreciation of his Lordship's ardent and judicious services to Gaelic literature in continuing the work so well begun by J. F Campbell, of Islay ; a work that has broken down the prejudices which existed against Gaelic matters, and has gone far to make them valued and esteemed. Having seen other volumes of this Argyllshire Series, the writer is still more assured, not only by the energy and aptness shown in their preparation, but also by the learned precision and knowledge of the annotations connected with the work. He also considers his Lordship more likely to be acquainted with the best means of forwarding the object desired—that of making these subjects known—than anyone in his remote and uninfluential position.

JOHN GREGORSON CAMPBELL.

MANSE OF TIREE,
   June, 1891.

INTRODUCTION.

THE stories, poems, and traditions which are given in this volume have been gathered entirely from oral sources as opportunities occurred. The labour of collecting them has extended, over well-nigh thirty years, since the coming of the writer to his present charge. This is a personal and, perhaps, too obtrusive a matter to be mentioned; but it is due to the subject to say that the portals of knowledge being, through English, to the boy whose native tongue Gaelic is, and the writer having received most of his training and education in the south, though aware of the names of Finn MacCoul and other ancient heroes of Gaelic times, was as much a stranger to these subjects as any one can be. All that he knew was only fragmentary pieces that were to be found in books; that the Gaelic language was of Indo-European and Aryan race, like Latin or Greek—and it was only gradually that it dawned upon him that, in the language itself and its stores of knowledge there was an abundance of unwritten literature that would bear comparison with any literary composition he had ever fallen in with. Those stores contain Songs, Ballads, Tales, Traditions, Proverbs, Riddles, etc. However it arose, or wherever it came from, there was a mist-like cloud overhanging the Highlands, and Gaelic was in neglect, which is gradually wearing away. It is a matter of much satisfaction that these vapours and clouds, when they disappear, will show a language through which the rays of human knowledge will receive much access of strength.

In this volume, which entirely belongs to the episode of the Fians, there are points which will strike the reader as having their analogy in Greek and Roman tales; thus, the death of Dermid (*Diarmad*) being in his heel is like that of Achilles, who was also said to be vulnerable only in his heel. Cacus, the robber, is also said to have leapt and walked backward into his cave, as Garry does after the burning of "Brugh Farala". In the ancient geographical names of Greece and Rome many place-names are to be found that admit of much explanation from Gaelic, *e.g.*, "Marathon by the sea" is very like *Maranan* Seas or Waves; but the making of this, and similar names, clear to the stranger to Gaelic, requires an explanation of elisions and other points of Gaelic Grammar which is foreign to this work. The resemblance of other Dictionary names is only what might be expected from the affinity between the languages. In their progress westward the Gaelic-speaking race have in Ireland and the Highlands of Scotland come as far west from the original seat of mankind, wherever it was, as early times would admit. Apparent traces and impressions of their progress and divergences can be found from Morocco along the west coast to the extreme north.

The origin of these tales about Fingal and Ossian, etc., cannot well be traced to any resemblance between them and the history and traditions of Rome. The Romish invasion of Britain offers no analogy and no trace. No Roman ever set foot in Ireland, and their attempts at the Grampians, for their own sake, would not be sought by them a second time. Who the first Britons were, or who the first people were who came across the Straits of Dover, if they came that way, and the many subsequent questions as to who the Picts and Scots were, and how the Gaelic language overspread the Highlands, while English remained in the level country, opens a wide field, of which an explanation can perhaps be got by a careful consideration of the Gaelic language and other kindred Celtic tongues of which there are remains still surviving.

The Fian tales are old and purely Celtic, but the human imagination runs in similar grooves all the world over, and the traditions and tales of widely different tribes may in this way bear a resemblance, but this will not admit of any conclusion as to identity.

In passing, it becomes me to mention that those from whom the stories, etc., were heard, were uniformly men of retentive memories, of good intelligence, and so far as could be judged by even the most cynical, men of prudent and respectable character. Many of them did not know a word of English; some might, perhaps, conversationally, but few of them knew it as a written tongue, so that questions agitating the world of letters passed by them without exciting even a passing remark. At one time this class, and all tales, were looked upon as idle and unworthy of attention, only interfering with godliness and sanctity; and though a better state of matters now exists, it cannot but be deplored that the "rigid righteousness" and rigid wisdom have led to the loss of much valuable matter.

In a dedicatory Gaelic letter to an Earl of Argyll in a Gaelic book on prayer, published as early as 1567, by Carsewell, Bishop of Argyle, the Bishop complains that his countrymen were fonder of listening to idle tales about the Féinne or heroes of the time of Fionn Mac-Cumhaill, than of taking any interest in the Word of God. On this subject the writer is indebted for his information to a rare work, "The Gaelic Hymnal" (*An Laoidheadair Gaelic*), published about the year 1836, by D. Kennedy, under the patronage and recommendation of the Reverend Dr. Macleod of Campsie. The same continued to be the case until very recent times, and a person who was about seventy years of age, a few years ago, in giving an account of old Highland habits to the writer, said that when, *e.g.*, the people of a place assembled to build a boundary dyke, some one would observe that they should wait till so-and-so came, and when he appeared, as the day was good and long, one or other would remark that the new comer might tell, before they began, some incident in the history of the Fian bard. The whole party then sat round the storyteller, and listened to his marvellous account. By the time that he was done the sun was drawing westward, and some one would then say it was hardly worth while beginning that day, and that he might tell some other story suggested by the previous narrative. When the second story was finished the sun was well-nigh setting, and the parties separated after agreeing to meet next day, as nothing had been done that day. These were the good old easy days, when the saying, " Hurry no man's cattle," held its ground, and people were not pressed to the same extent as now for the means of living.

In what the writer has to say upon the subject of these heroic tales, he prefers to use the name *Fionn Mac Cumhaill*, and the Host of the Fians (*Feachd na Féinn*). The renderings of Fenian and Fingalian have other ideas attached to them, and the writer's information and belief in the value of the tales as historical or archæological is entirely founded upon them as they exist in popular tradition. It seems to him that in this way they are more free from the embellishments of idle fancy, and in their own proper place subservient to the elucidation of truth.

The Fian heroes are to this day prominent in proverbs and riddles, and sayings and references to them and their actions, occur continually in common every day conversation, although the precise incident to which reference is made may not be known. It is in this way that people speak of Ossian after the Fians (*Ossian an dèigh na Féinne*), and in the riddle, " Fionn went to the hill and did not go ; he buried his wife there and did not bury her" ("*Chaidh Fionn do 'n bheinn, 's cha deachaidh idir ; thiodhlaic e 'bhean ann, 's cha do thiodhlaic idir*"), etc., etc.   Ans.—*Idir* was the name of a dog.

Very prominent among these stories are those referring to Fionn and his dog Bran. This redoubtable dog is referred to in the story of "Ossian after the Fians" (*Ossian an deigh na Féinne*) as having survived all the other dogs of the Fians. It had a venomous or death-inflicting spur on its foot. Fionn's visits to the Kingdom of Big Men. How Fionn's wife fled with his nephew. The death of his nephew *Diarmaid.*   The wars in which he was engaged, etc., etc.

Fionn occupies in Gaelic the position of a model gentleman or nobleman in the original, and best sense of the words. He was not accounted the strongest of the "Fian Host", but was looked up to as ever a kind friend and judicious adviser, wise in counsel, a solver of doubts and difficulties, hospitable to the stranger and poor, a protector of the weak and defenceless, and in every respect trustworthy. The tales of his having visited the Kingdom of Big Men and of his having a long ship (*Long fhada aig Fionn*) are told in various forms, and in many different tales.

The object of the writer has always been in all matters affecting Celtic antiquities to make whatever he deems worthy of preservation as available and reliable to the reader as to himself, without addition, suppression, or embellishment.

The writer himself being unable to write, the work of transcribing this volume has been undertaken for him, in loving memory of one (his widowed mother's only child) who, though of tender years, and partly an alien, said of Gaelic, " I love it best" (*Si Ghailig is docha leums*).

INTRODUCTION.

To all who have any love for the traditions of the Scottish Gael the name of the Rev. J. G. Campbell, of Tiree, has long been a household word, and from them this volume, comprising as it does the gatherings of some thirty years, will be sure of a hearty welcome. If we bear in mind that these tales and ballads are taken from one section only of Gaelic tradition, and have been selected from a very small district, we can form some idea of the richness and vigour with which that tradition still flourishes in the Gaelic-speaking portions of Scotland. As each fresh collection comes before us it is impossible not again to ask the question whence come these old-time tales and songs? what is their place in the history of Gaelic thought and fancy? what relation do they bear to the stories and legends of other races?

Mr. Campbell holds what may be called the traditional and patriotic view—what the Gaelic folk tells to-day it has told from immemorial times, and, as we listen to the living peasant or fisherman, we catch glimpses of, we hear far-off tidings from,

> "The old days which seem to be
> Much older than any history
> That is written in any book."

But many scholars would by no means admit that we are justified in doing this. Gaelic folk-lore has, as a rule, been noted within comparatively recent periods, and the temptation for many persons is apparently irresistible to conclude that it is equally recent. The question is a complicated one, and cannot be answered in a rough and ready fashion. Indeed, whilst so many of the elements of the problem are not clearly before us, owing to the fact that by far the larger portion of Gaelic heroic legend still remains unpublished, it is impossible to give any answer that is not necessarily a provisional one. All that we can do at present is to see how far the evidence at our disposal carries us, and to draw from it principles which may guide us in the investigation of the unexplored, or only partially explored, tract which must be examined before we can hope to reach any definite conclusions.

Roughly speaking, the record of Gaelic mythic and heroic legend reaches continuous and unbroken from pre-Christian days unto our own time. The oldest MS. evidence takes us back to the eleventh century, and many of the texts of that date approve themselves, even to the most cautious and sceptical of scholars, as very much older. As a rule we owe the preservation of Gaelic history and Gaelic legend in the Middle Ages to the clergy, and, unless we believe that many of the monks and abbots, to whom we owe the oldest Irish MSS., amused themselves by inventing pagan beliefs and fancies, we must admit that texts which are substantially pagan reach back to pagan times. Taking native Gaelic legend in its entirety (excluding merely the Christian hagiological elements) we can distinguish five strata—the mythological and pseudo-annalistic—the Ultonian (of which Conchobor and Cuchullain are the chief personages)—the Fenian, or Ossianic—the *post*-Fenian historical—and the living folk-tale. Now it is quite true that the MS. evidence for the first, second, and fourth of these strata or classes is, on the whole, much older than for the third; whilst, as for the fifth, 95 per cent. of the evidence belongs to this or the preceding century. To certain minds the conclusion seems inevitable that the order in which this MS. evidence comes before us, represents the order in which these various manifestations of myth- and legend-creating impulse assumed shape in the consciousness of the Gaelic race. But there is something to be said on the other side.

The moral and intellectual level of the men to whom we owe the preservation of Gaelic legend in the Middle Ages may be little, if at all, superior to that of the folk of to-day; but it was certainly much higher than that of the folk of their day. Not only did they exercise selection in what they committed to the memory of their pupils, or to the vellum leaves which formed the proudest treasure of a monastery or a chieftain's court, but they were necessarily and inevitably indifferent to whatever did not come within certain well-marked limits. Again leaving the Christian element out of consideration, these limits, as far as the native literature was concerned, may be said to have been conterminous with the mythical, historical, and customary antiquities of the tribe or clan. Whatever could exalt the pride or strengthen the pretensions of the clan chieftains, the clan wise men, or the clan brehons, that would be eagerly sought after by the clan story-teller—that would be cherished and recorded by the clan scribes. Thus it has come about that such a large proportion of the MS. space is taken up by genealogies; that legends, obviously mythical in their origin, have put on a quasi-historical form and connected themselves with the fortunes of special clans; that topographical legends are so carefully noted; that the rights and customs, whether of the tribe or the individual, are set forth with such minuteness. What room was there for the folk-tale in the ideal library of an Irish chieftain, which is what the great MSS. of Irish antiquity aimed at being? The argument *ex silentio* would be invalid, even if it were rigorously correct, and it is not. Even from Irish mythic and heroic legend as it has come down

to us we can recover the outlines, or we can distinguish
the essential features of many a folk-tale current to this
day among the Gaels of Ireland and Scotland. I will
note but a few examples : The three-fold gaming against
a supernatural antagonist who loses twice but wins the
third time, imposes a heavy task upon the hero, or
claims from him some object he holds dear—this theme,
so frequent in Gaelic tales, is as old as the seventh
century, at least, as it is found in the *Tochmarc Etain*,
the wooing of Etain by Mider, a prince of Faery ; the
combat of the disguised hero against the evil beings to
whom a princess is exposed, his rescue of her and his
discovery by means of a ring—this theme is as old as
the eleventh century, at least, since it is found in the
second redaction of the *Tochmarc Emer*, or Cuchullain's
wooing of Emer ; the theme of the bespelled being, who
can only get his spells lifted if he induce the hero to
fulfil a task, is as old as the tenth century, at least,
since it is found in the oldest part of Cormac's Glossary ;
the theme of the exposed child must be as old as the
ninth or tenth century, since it forms a part of the hero-
tale which tells how Connaire Mor was slain by over-sea
pirates ; the theme of the skilful companions is found in
the Seafaring of the Three O'Corras, a tale which goes
back to the seventh century. I am quoting from Irish
sources alone. I could easily extend the list if I made
use, for purposes of comparison, of those Welsh
Mabinogion which are certainly older than the outburst
of the Arthurian romance, *i.e.*, older than the twelfth
century. But Campbell of Islay has already done this
in the fourth volume of the *West Highland Tales*. I
will only add to what he says the expression of my
conviction that Welsh romance of the eleventh and
twelfth centuries was influenced by—perhaps is largely
derived from—older Gaelic romance. It may be said
that the examples I have cited are the starting-points

B

of the modern tales. Even if this were so I could
still point out that a long period is postulated during
which the folk-tale must have lived on without being
recorded, which is all I contend for ; but I do not
believe for one moment that it is so. On the contrary,
the way in which these themes occur in the heroic
legends I have mentioned, shows that they must have
been commonplaces familiar both to the story-teller and
to his hearers. In other words, the mythical and heroic
sagas of the Irish Gael, sagas recorded in writing from
the seventh to the fifteenth centuries, pre-suppose a
background of traditional fancies, beliefs, and conceptions of the same *essential* character as those still
current. I underline the word essential, as I do not for
one moment intend to deny that changes have taken
place in the mass of tradition, that some things have
utterly died away, others been profoundly modified,
much again been added.

It is necessary to insist upon this view of the facts,
because distinguished scholars have a way of treating
the date of transcription as equivalent to the date of
origin. Thus M. d'Arbois de Jubainville, in his *Essai
d'un catalogue de la littérature épique de l'Irlande*, often
adds the designation "conte moderne", solely it would
seem because only modern MSS. exist. I by no means
deny the existence of heroic, or simply fairy tales to
which the term modern may be properly applied, *i.e.*,
which are the outcome of a deliberate and individual
artistic effort on the part of a writer living within the
last two centuries. It is by no means the least remarkable feature of Gaelic legend that it has retained its
vital power down almost to the present day ; thus,
almost within the memory of living men, fresh com-
binations of the old materials have won popular favour
and swollen the mass of folk-literature. I only say that
the fact of recent transcription does not suffice to range

a tale in this category. In some cases I venture to
think that Mons. d'Arbois de Jubainville is decidedly
in error, *e.g.*, when (p. 88) speaking of the *Ceithcirnach
Caol riabach*, "the slim swarthy fellow", of which the
oldest Irish MS. is dated back by him to 1789,
and of which there are two fragmentary versions in
Campbell (*West Highland Tales*, vol. i), he says, "Ce
conte a pour base des événements de la fin du XVIe
siècle." Now the tale tells how the storyteller of
the King of Leinster was helped out of a great per-
plexity by Angus of the Brugh. I have some difficulty
in believing that Angus, the son of the Dagda, the wisest
wizard of the Tuatha Dé, turned the wife of the head
ollamh of the King of Leinster into a hare and played
divers practical jokes on divers Irish chieftains about the
year 1600. The ground for Mons. d'Arbois's statement
probably lies in the fact that one of these chieftains is an
O'Connor Sligo, who was placed at the end of the 16th
century. As a matter of fact his date is 200 years earlier,
and Dr. Hyde has taken the year 1362 as a *terminus a quo*
for dating the version of the "Slim Swarthy Fellow"
which has come down to us (*Beside the Fire*, p. xxix).
He grounds this opinion upon the fact that the episode
in which O'Connor Sligo figures and which belongs
to the year 1362, is common to all the versions,
Scotch as well as Irish. But I am by no means
sure that this fact is enough to warrant the conclusion.
It only proves to my mind that the tale, *as we have it*, is
younger than the day of O'Connor Sligo; it does not
prove that an older version may not have existed
before his day. There is a well-known English mumming play in which St. George, as champion of England,
has to encounter and overcome a series of enemies.
Among these, in some south-country versions is Bony.
It would be incorrect, I think, to say that the mumming
play was based upon events of the early 19th century,

incorrect also, even if every version mentioned Bony,
to assume that the play as a whole took shape after
1815.

The most exaggerated form of the contention I am
demurring to with which I am acquainted is due to
an American scholar, Professor W. W. Newell, who, in
No. xii of the *American Folk-Lore Journal* (p. 84), speaks
of "folk-tales like Campbell's, and those lately printed
by Curtin, a large class of which are Irish only in name,
being simply literal translations of, or trifling alterations
of a common European stock". It is interesting to find
that in America Ireland is looked upon as being outside
the "common European stock." Professor Newell is a distinguished scholar, but he seems to me to have stated the
question is an altogether inexact manner. It is necessary
to state emphatically that if we look to the incidents and
themes which form the staple of the vast majority
of folk-tales, these can be traced back on Gaelic soil as
far, in some cases farther, than amongst other European
races. It is quite true that collections of tales were made
—even printed—in Italy 250 years, in France 120 years,
in Germany 30 to 40 years before such collections
appeared in any part of Gaeldom. But if it is seriously
urged that the Gaelic folk-tale corpus is to be traced
directly to the collections of Straparola (16th century), of
Basile (17th century), of Perrault (late 17th century), of
Musäus (late 18th century), and Grimm (early 19th century), there will I think be little difficulty in showing the
utter baselessness of such a contention. I by no means
deny that Gaeldom has shared in the general give and
take of folk-tale and folk-lore, which has gone on all over
Europe, but the word "translation" describes this pro-
cess, in my opinion, most inaccurately.

Hitherto it will have been noticed that I have drawn
my evidence for the long continued existence on Gaelic
soil of a considerable body of folk-tales from outside the

Ossianic or Fenian cycle. But Mr. Campbell's volume is primarily concerned with this cycle, which forms indeed the most interesting and important monument of Gaelic folk-fancy throughout the last 1000 years. It cannot but strengthen the contention for the antiquity of the folk-tale corpus to find that this group of heroic tales has held its ground so long and so vigorously, whilst the written record, being so much fuller in the one case than in the other, we are enabled to verify for the hero-tale group what we can only surmise for the folk-tale group. All investigation into the nature and origin of traditional literature among the Gael must therefore start with an accurate knowledge and a searching criticism of the Ossianic cycle. It was with the object of obtaining a guiding principle in accordance with which a number of isolated facts could be classified that I put together my notes in the second volume of this series on the development of the Ossianic saga. As a matter of fact, the task I there essayed had not been essayed before, and in spite of shortcomings, of which I am more conscious than anyone else can be, I venture to think that these notes may be found useful by others. I do not propose to go over the same ground again, but will merely emphasise what seemed to me then, and still seems to me, the chief conclusion to be drawn from the facts which I set forth, namely, that from the earliest date to which we can trace it, the Ossianic saga is romantic rather than historical; in other words, it narrates to a very slight extent events which ever actually happened, or which ever would happen. Since the appearance of Mr. MacInnes's volume a new theory has been propounded respecting Finn Mac Cumhal himself, and respecting the proper place of the Fenian stories in the history of Irish literature. This theory, due to Professor H. Zimmer of Greifswald, is urged with all the learned

professor's wonted acuteness, subtlety of thought, and
exhaustive knowledge of early Irish literature. I gave
a brief sketch of this theory in the *Academy* for Feb. 14
last. This sketch I here reprint with some slight modi-
fication. I would, however, earnestly urge upon all who
care for these subjects not to rest content with my bare
summary, which necessarily fails to do justice to Professor
Zimmer's argument, but to read for themselves the
original article, the title of which will be found at the
foot of this page.[1]

The historical conditions which form the basis of Prof.
Zimmer's argument are, briefly, as follows : In 795 Norwegian
Vikings appear for the first time upon the coasts of Ireland,
which they assail and harry for more than half a century. At
first they only plunder and sail away ; but soon they fix themselves in the land ; seize upon strategic points, ally themselves
with the native kings (who eagerly seek their aid in the inter-
minable conflicts which every Irish chieftain waged with all
his neighbours), marry native women (who greatly appreciated
their stature and comeliness), and become half-Irish. In the
early years of the ninth century a Norwegian leader, Thorgils,
seeks to found a Norse kingdom, but fails and is slain. The
political organisation of Ireland is not seriously affected by the
Norsemen. It is otherwise with the next batch of invaders—
the Danish Vikings—who appear in the middle of the ninth
century, seize and hold Dublin both against Irish and Norwegians, whom they defeat with terrible slaughter, and found
a Danish kingdom, which has imitators in the South and West,
plays its part in the ceaseless warfare that rages between the
head-king of Ireland and the under-kings, and which is at times
the most powerful political factor in the island. The Danes
remain heathens until the middle of the tenth century, when

[1] *Zeitschrift für deutsches Alterthum.* Vol. 53. H. Zimmer,
Keltische Beiträge, III, weitere nordgermanische einflüsse in der
ältesten überlieferung der irischen heldensage ; ursprung und
entwickelung der Finn-(Ossian-)sage ; die vikinger Irlands in Sage;
geschichte und recht der Iren.

Anlaf, son of Sitric, invades England, is conquered by Eadmund, and submits to baptism in the year 943. Christianity furthered the assimilation of Celt and Scandinavian, as did likewise the political events of the late tenth and early eleventh centuries, when the Munster chief, Brian, wrested for a time the head-kingship of Ireland from the North-Irish chiefs, with the aid of the Danish Vikings, and then turning against the latter, inflicted upon them the defeat of Clontarf, which, however slight in its immediate effects, yet marks the termination of the period of invasions. The later raid of Magnus Barelegs (A.D. 1103) was an isolated event, standing in no real connection with the invasions of the ninth and tenth centuries.

Such is the historical background to the Fenian saga. Prof. Zimmer first examines the fifteenth century account of Finn, which represents him as the head of a standing militia engaged chiefly in protecting the coasts of Ireland. He has little difficulty in showing that at the period assigned to him (second and third century, A.D.) Ireland was exposed to no invasions, and that texts of the tenth and eleventh centuries which deal fully with the history of that period know nothing of any standing militia. Moreover, the texts of the older Ultonian heroic cycle, redacted in the seventh century, revised and interpolated down to the tenth century, although they contain numerous traces of the influence exercised upon them, by both the classical and Christian culture which blossomed forth so richly in Ireland in the seventh and eighth centuries, and by the Norse mythic and heroic tales of a later period, yet show no sign of any such institution as that pictured in the later Fenian texts. Nor is any mention made in the Book of Rights, a compilation of the late tenth century, of the elaborate code of rights and privileges of the Fenians as we know them from the fully developed Fenian saga.

Irish texts of the eighth-twelfth centuries repeatedly present the word *fiann*, plural *fianna* (also *fénnid*), in the sense of "warrior", "warrior band". Later texts specialise the meaning, referring it to the warrior bands of Finn and Goll, the Fenian militia. The word *fiann* is a loan-word from the Norse ; it is the Norse *fiandi*, plural *fiandr*—"enemy". In illustration of the contention a passage is quoted from the *Orgain brudne da Derga*, an Irish hero-tale, the text of which as we have it goes back to the tenth century. Ingcel and his fellow-pirates are attacking the house in which the high-king of Ireland is passing the night. "Up, *fianna*," says he to his men; "let us attack the house." When they draw near, the king, hearing a noise, asks who is there. "Fianna," answers one of his champions. The Norse Viking was thus the enemy *par excellence*, he was also *par excellence* the brave enemy, the warrior whose valour roused the admiration of the puny (*schmächtig*) Irishmen. From thence to "mercenary", "chieftain's suite", "fighting force of the clan", the transition is easy. Examples of all these various meanings are given, and it is shown that the word occurs in passages where Norsemen are either mentioned or where their presence may be suspected. In the form *Fēne* the word likewise came to specifically denote one of the races inhabiting Ireland. This took place when the original connection between the words *fianna* and *fēne* and the Scandinavian population had died out of the popular mind. Thus a verse in Fiacc's hymn to Patrick, which runs thus, "he [Patrick] preached thrice thirty years to the heathen bands of the Fene", was taken in the sense that *Fēne* was an old generic name for the population of Ireland. But how comes a name originally applied to Norse Vikings to appear in an early hymn to Patrick? The apostle of Ireland certainly never preached to the Norwegians. No, but the tenth-century Irishmen thought he did. Prof. Zimmer quotes several texts, of which I shall mention the most important presently, in support of this statement. But why did they believe this? The answer to the question is suggested by the consideration of the Patrician documents in the *Book of Armagh*. Ever since the beginning of the eighth century Armagh had striven to push her claims to primacy; she had valiantly stood on the side of Rome in the struggle against the particularist usages of the Celtic Church (reckoning of Easter and special form of tonsure), and had not hesitated to forge a series of documents in furtherance of the Roman claims. Prof. Zimmer hints that the primacy was the price Rome paid to Armagh for this support. But the pretensions of Armagh were not finally accepted by the Irish Church until the middle of the ninth century, and we can follow the stages of the conflicts in the Annals. In the tenth century a new danger arises : the Danish king is baptised in England ; the Danish Christian community looks to Canterbury rather than to Armagh. The old device is resorted to, and a series of pious fabrications of the last quarter of the tenth century represent Patrick as having converted the ancestors of the Danes. The device met with the success that attended any more than usually outrageous perversion of the truth in the Middle Ages generally, and in Ireland specially. Armagh triumphed ; but her very triumph led to oblivion of the facts. In the eleventh century, when the mythology and heroic history of Ireland were thrown into chronological form, the Irish antiquaries were puzzled by the statement that Patrick had converted the *Fene ;* they had forgotten all about the Danes, to them the *Fene* were one of the early races of Ireland, and they romanced about them to the top of their bent. But by this time, as we shall see presently, Finn and his men had been transferred back into the third century. The connection of *Fene* with Finn was by this time well established. But the Irish antiquaries of the eleventh century knew that Patrick was later than the third century ; they got over the difficulty by feigning that some of the *Fene* had lived long enough to be converted by the apostle of Ireland. Thus arose the fable of the supernaturally prolonged life of Ossian and Cailte.

Let us now turn to a tenth-century text which brings together Patrick and the *Fene.* " Loegaire's Conversion" states that Patrick codified the customs of Ireland with the help of eight other commissioners, two with himself to represent the Church (Benen, Cairnech) ; three representatives of the kingly power (Loegaire the head-king, and the under-kings of Ulster and Munster) ; and three others, Dubthach, head bard of Ireland, Fergus the poet, and Rus mac Tricim *sui berla feni,* " a knower of speech of the feni." This Rus mac Tricim is a Rus Tryggvasonar, and the *berla feni* is Norse. This fable corresponds to a fact. The Senchus Mor, the most considerable codification of early Irish custom which has come down to us, is no purely Irish text of the fifth-sixth centuries, but a late tenth-century codification of Irish, Norse, and Norse-Irish custom, which came into existence when the Scandinavian invaders had welded themselves into the political and social life of Ireland.

So far has the word "fiann" carried us. Now for the earliest accounts of Finn himself. These date from the tenth century, and figure him as the chief of a Viking band, strong in the possession of the strategic position of Almu, allying himself now with this now with that native chief, making love early and often, playing such rough practical jokes upon his followers as to tie up one naked to a tree all night because he had deemed it too cold to go out when told (an interesting testimony to the antiquity of the special Teutonic form of humour), son probably of a Norse father and an Irish mother, and endowed with the seer's gift. As early as the second half of the tenth century he figures as a personage of the second and third centuries. How did this happen ? The circumstances of the times in which the historical Finn (the semi-Viking semi-Irish chief) lived must have been like those of the third century, so like as to induce confusion in the minds of the tenth-century Irishmen who had no correct idea of the past.

Now at the end of the second century Ireland is equally divided between Mug Nuadat and Conn Cetchathach. In the middle of the ninth century Fedlimid mac Crimthain is the recognised king of Southern Ireland (*leth Moga*, Mogs's half). The record of his struggles with the Northern kings, Niall and Maelsechlainn, recalls that of the second-third century head-kings, Art and Cormac mac Airt, against Southern Ireland. Indeed, it may be assumed that the tenth-eleventh century accounts of the second-third century wars were influenced by the real history of the ninth century. In one instance this can be proved. A late tenth-century North Irish poet decks out the legendary North Irish third-century king, Cormac mac Airt, with traits derived from the historical South Irish bishop-king of Cashel, Cormac, slain in 903. Again, in one of the oldest tales about Finn, his father, Cumall, carries off his mother Murni, daughter of Tadg mac Nuadat.

Now Ailill Aulom, a celebrated legendary king of the early
third century, is a son of Mog Nuadat (mac Moga Nuadat);
whilst Tadg mac Cèin is a prominent figure in the Leinster
legendary history of the late third century. Tadg mac Nuadat
reminded the Irish story-tellers of both these earlier personages,
who were separated by nearly two generations—hence he was
sometimes dated as if he belonged to the one, sometimes as if
he belonged to the other generation, a fact which explains the
uncertainty that prevails in the earliest Fenian texts about
Finn's alleged date, and his being made to live over a period
of some 150 years. Finn is thus brought down to the period
of Fedlimid mac Crimthain, *i.e.*, to the early eighth century;
and we find at this date a Caittil Find who was slain in Munster
in 856 by Imar and Olaf, kings of the Dublin Danes. These
had appeared in Ireland a few years previously, and their hand
had been laid as heavily upon their Norwegian predecessors
as upon the native Irish. The Norsemen—now after two
generations half-Irish—made common cause with the natives
against them. Caittil Find was their chief leader; his defeat
and death in 856 marks the triumph of the Danish invaders,
who were to rule in Dublin for three centuries. About Caittil
Find himself—half-Norse, half-Irish—gathered every floating
story, every characteristic trait that the Irish knew of in connection with the Norsemen. His fight against the Danish
overlord, when transferred back into the third century, becomes
the fight of the Fenian militia against the head-king of Ireland.
But, it may be objected, Find is no Norse name. No, it is the
Irish translation of *hviti*, "white". This nickname of his
had been taken by the Irish for his proper name, and translated
by them, and as the form it thus assumed in Irish, Find, is a
frequent element in many Irish names, *e.g.*, Findbar, Findlog,
etc., the recognisable part of the name, "Find", persisted, and
the unrecognisable part, Caittil, died out. Thus the twelfth-
century scribe of the *Book of Leinster* fragment of *Cogadh
Gaedhel* substitutes for the unintelligible word *Caittil* the Irish
word *caur*, "hero", in the passage describing Caittil's defeat
by Olaf. Many of the Vikings of the first invasion, who came
mostly from the Hardangerfiord, had *hviti* as their name or

nickname. Indeed, the predominance of the name "white" struck the fancy of the Irish, and they called the over-sea visitors *findgenti*, "white strangers". Later, when the Danes appeared, and straightway came to blows with the Norsemen, they were distinguished as *dubhgenti*, "black strangers".

The after development of the Fenian saga is conditioned partly by its semi-Norse origin, partly by the fact that the later bards borrowed scenes, incidents, and traits from the older Cuchulain cycle, and wove them into the new heroic epos. One instance may suffice. In the Cuchulain cycle Ulster defies the remainder of Ireland: Cuchulain, single-handed, holds at bay all the forces of the South and West. In the Fenian saga Ireland takes the place of Ulster, and success-fully withstands the onslaught of the King of the World and his motley tribe of allies. Through all, too, pierces the original heathen character of the eponymous hero of the saga. But South Ireland was already Christian in the third-fourth centuries, so that conscious heathen practices, definitely recog-nised and described as such, could no more have occurred there in the ninth century than in the Germany of the twelfth or thirteenth century. Another testimony this to the imported nature of Fenian legends. The most distinctive trait of heath-enism associated with Finn himself, and the one which seems to have impressed the Irish the most vividly, is his divinatory power, and the magic practices with which it was accompanied. From one of the oldest Finn stories, dating back to the tenth century, we learn the names of these practices, *imbas forosnai*, *teinm laegda*. This latter cannot be explained in Irish; it is the old-Norse *teinar laigðir* = "the thrown staves", and this method of divining the future may be compared with the casting of "surculi" described by Tacitus in chap. x of the *Germania*.

One other point may be cited. Lochlann has hitherto been referred to Norway, and explained as "lake-land". But ac-cording to Prof. Zimmer, the oldest form is *Lothlind*, gen. *Laithlinde*, and it is an Irish rendering of Låland, the island whence came the first Danish Vikings. At first it designated the Danes' country alone, and received the extended meaning of Scandinavia generally at a comparatively late period.

The arguments against the theory are of two kinds, (1) the purely philological ones, (2) the historical ones. Prof. Zimmer lays great stress upon his philological explanation of the word "fiann". But every one of his contentions has been traversed by Mr. Whitley Stokes, a philologist of the highest reputation and authority, as was indeed lately evidenced by his being made the recipient of the most valued honour that can be bestowed upon a scholar—corresponding membership of the French Institute. But Mr. Whitley Stokes did not confine himself to philological arguments, which only an expert can appreciate. He likewise challenged the German professor's explanation of the Irish phrase *teinm laegda*, and declared that the proper Irish form is *teinm laido*, that the signification is quite different from that asserted by Prof. Zimmer, and that the phrase can have nothing to do with a Norse *teinar laigðir*, which, moreover, is a purely hypothetical form, and cannot be instanced from any Norse writings.

Further historical arguments in disproof of the theory have been brought forward by Prof. Kuno Meyer and Mons. H. d'Arbois de Jubainville. Those of the latter have great interest in view of the bearing of Prof. Zimmer's revolutionary theory upon the proper interpretation of the Irish Brehon laws which have hitherto been regarded as one of the most archaic bodies of Aryan custom in existence, but which, if the Greifswald scholar is right, can no longer pretend to that position. Mons. d'Arbois de Jubainville has made a long and profound study of Irish law; it is not too much to say all Celtic scholars, save, perhaps, Prof. Zimmer, regard him as the leading authority upon the subject. His opinion carries, therefore, the greatest weight. Now, the hypothesis treats *Féne*, a designation of the Irish race, in whole or in part, as a development of the word "*fiann*", which denotes primarily the invading, then the settled Norsemen and

Danes. It is hardly too much to say that this development could not have been completed before the first
quarter of the tenth century. All texts, therefore, in
which the word *fēne* occurs, would, in their present form,
be no older than the middle of that century. But Mons.
d'Arbois de Jubainville shows that, whilst the *Senchas
Mor*, as we now have it, is a compilation of comparatively
recent date (possibly as late as the tenth, more probably
of the eighth, century), it is based upon and often repro-
duces verbally much older texts. Among the very
oldest portions the word *Fēne* occurs several times, and
in a connection which absolutely forbids the late date
which Prof. Zimmer's theory postulates. Again, Mons.
d'Arbois de Jubainville urges a much earlier date for
Orgain bruduc da Derga than that allowed by Prof.
Zimmer; he would put it back to the seventh century,
and he looks upon the word *fiann*, which is used in it, as
belonging to the oldest portion of the story, and consequently as existing with the signification "warrior" long
prior to the middle of the ninth century.

The force of these objections can be appreciated by
all. I would merely add that others, like myself, have
doubtless felt the improbability of the starting-point of
the whole hypothesis—that invaders, namely, should de-
scribe themselves as enemies, and that the inhabitants of
the invaded country should appropriate this foreign word,
and by a progressive series of favourable significations
come at last to use it as a designation of themselves. It
may further be noted, with respect to Prof. Zimmer's
theory, how Caitill Find came to be known in Irish
legend as Find simply, that the antagonist of Caitill,
Olaf, the Dublin Dane-king, invariably bears the nickname *hviti*, the white one, in the Norse sagas, yet he is
never called Find by any Irish authority. Where, know-
ing that the nickname existed, we find that it was not
translated, ought we not to look askance at the supposi-

tion of translation in a case where we have not one jot
of evidence that the nickname ever did exist?

It is far from my wish to prejudice a question which
only Celtic experts can decide. I have essayed to set
forth the arguments *pro* and *con*, fairly and clearly. But
it may not be out of place to add a few remarks which
can hardly fail to suggest themselves to the careful student
of the Ossianic cycle. Whoso, for instance, met this
cycle for the first time in the following pages could not
but be struck with the insistence laid upon the oversea
element. Finn and his men are always repelling Lochlann raiders, or themselves paying hostile visits to the
King of Lochlann, and carrying off his treasures or his
women. Now, it is certain that nothing of the kind
happened in the third century—the period to which the
Irish annals assign Finn. Whether Prof. Zimmer is
right or wrong in claiming Cumhal's son as a half-
Viking, none the less is it certain that a large portion of
Ossianic cycle reflects conditions which only obtained
during the Viking period, *i.e.*, as far as Ireland is concerned, from the end of the eighth to the beginning of
the twelfth century, when the last Norse raid, that of
Magnus Bare Legs, took place. But this was an isolated
event, and, substantially speaking, the close of the Viking
period in Ireland may be said to be marked by the battle
of Clontarf, at the beginning of the eleventh century.
Now, why, if the historic basis of the cycle is furnished by
events of the third century, do we nevertheless find that
the majority of the texts reveal a state of affairs which
cannot be older than the ninth century? Here Prof.
Zimmer's theory would seem to be more in accord with
the facts of the case than the one previously current.
But, on the other hand, it must be noted that the texts
in question invariably picture Finn and his men in
standing antagonism with the Lochlann folk. How
does this agree with Prof. Zimmer's view? True, his

Finn is only half a Viking ; true, he falls fighting against
the Danish invader; still he has Viking blood and Viking
ways, and it hardly seems likely that Irish legend would
represent him as the defender *par excellence* of Ireland
against oversea raiders. I submitted this difficulty to
Prof. Zimmer, who answered in effect that I was arguing
from one section only of Fenian texts. The quarrel of
Finn and the Lochlannach is, he says, a special feature of
the North Irish and Highland texts, to be accounted for
by the presence of Lochlannach in North-west Scotland
as late as the fifteenth century, and by their conflicts with
the Celtic population. It is necessary to follow up this
hint, as it compels some sort of classification in the existing body of Ossian texts, and such classification is the
indispensable preliminary to a sound criticism of the
cycle.

Roughly speaking, the Fenian or Ossianic texts may
be divided into two classes, those vouched for by
MSS. which reach back beyond the middle of the
twelfth century, and those for which we have only much
younger MS. authority. Of the former I need only
repeat again that their presentment of Fionn is fully as
romantic as that of the later texts. I have referred to
the majority of these texts in my notes to vol. ii of
this series. The second class comprises by far the
larger number of Fenian texts. Roughly speaking, it
admits of a threefold division : (1) Prose texts, of which
the *Agallamh na Senoraib*, or Discourse of the Elders,
is the most important, and which are at least as old as the
beginning of the fifteenth century, as they are found in
MSS. of that date. (2) A body of ballad poetry which is at
least as old as the end of the fifteenth century, as it is
largely extant in the *Dean of Lismore's Book*, a West
Highland MS. of the early sixteenth century, and which
has maintained itself orally in Gaelic Scotland down to
the present day. Most of the texts in the present volume

belong to this class. (3) A similar body of ballad poetry found in Irish MSS. of the last and present century. The second and third sub-classes are largely alike, but by no means entirely so ; certain episodes and incidents are to the best of my knowledge and belief only found in the Scotch Gaelic, others only in the Irish Gaelic texts. Of many texts common to both, the Scotch MS. authorisation reaches two centuries farther back than does the Irish.

Sub-classes 2 and 3 differ profoundly from sub-class 1. Not only are the episodes, the incidents, the themes different, but the whole colouring and setting, the whole tone and temper are unlike. Are we then to conclude that some time between the beginning of the fifteenth century, when the *Agallamh na Senoraib* form of the Fenian legend is vouched for by several MSS., and the end of the same century, when the ballad form appears fully developed in the book of the Dean of Lismore, the legend was profoundly modified in form (from prose to verse), in subject-matter, and in temper? Or are we to look upon the ballad as possibly of equal antiquity with the *Agallamh na Senoraib* form, and as owing its peculiarities to having developed in a different part of Gaeldom, among different historical conditions? Again, must we look upon the Irish ballads as an offshoot from the Scotch ballad stock? This would seem to follow if we pursue Professor Zimmer's argument to its legitimate conclusion.

One way of settling the question would be by a careful comparison of those ballads which are found substantially in the same form in both Scotland and Ireland. This is one of the tasks which await future students. Another way is to examine the differentia between the *Agallamh na Senoraib* and the ballads. I have already touched upon this subject (MacInnes, (p. 411), and I would here only emphasise one point.

In *Agallamh na Senoraib* the witness to the departed
glories of the Fenian band is Caoilte, in the ballads Oisin.
Now Caoilte is on excellent terms with St. Patrick,
for whom he has a proper and becoming respect. It
is quite otherwise with Oisin. The aged hero is perpetually reviling the saint, perpetually comparing past
heathendom with present Christianity, greatly to the
disadvantage of the latter, perpetually making the most
unorthodox remarks.

> " I would take more delight in the bound of the buck,
>   Or in looking at badgers between two glens ;
>   Than in all that thy mouth promiseth me,
>   And all the joys I would get in heaven beyond"—
>
> (Oss. Soc., iv, 41.)

says the defiant old pagan in the Irish version, whilst
in the Lismore one the corresponding passage runs—

> " Didst thou hear the hounds and the sounds of the hunt?
>   Thou wouldst rather be there than in the holy city."
>
> (Lismore, 19.)

Now, is this temper a creation of the fifteenth
century? a specific Scotch-Gaelic graft on the legend
trunk? It may be so, but it seems to me to require a
deal of proving. Again, one can hardly fail to be
struck by the kinship of tone between the Gaelic poems
ascribed to Oisin, and the Welsh ones ascribed to
Llywarch Hen. In both cases the reputation of poet
is simply due to the semi-dramatic nature of the composition. Both Oisin and Llywarch Hen were regarded
as fit personages in whose mouths to place sentiments
of a particular cast, and later ages finding this or that
elegy or battle piece assigned to the Gaelic or Welsh
prince naturally considered them as being the authors
of the same. Oisin and Llywarch are both old and
feeble, the last survivors of a mighty generation,

savagely rebellious against the slings and arrows of outrageous age, bitterly mindful of the pride and lust of their youth.

> "Wooden crook ! is it not the spring,
> When cuckoos are brown, when the foam is bright,
> And I, lack a maid's love ?
>
> *　　*　　*　　*　　*　　*
>
> What I loved when a youth are hateful to me now,
> A stranger's daughter and a gray steed.
> Am I not for them unmeet ?
> I am old, I am lonely, I am decrepit and cold.
> After lying on fair rich couches,
> I am miserable, thrice bent !" (Skene, *F. A. B.*, 328.)

Thus the Kymro complains—

> " No soft wooing, and no chase
> In both of which I took delight.
> Without the battle-march or fight,
> Alas, how sorrowful life's close." (*Lismore*, 5.)

Or again :

> " Feeble this night is the power of my arm,
> My strength is no more as it was ;
> No wonder though I should mourn,
> Poor, old relic that I am." (*Lismore*, 13.)

answers the Gael.

Now the Welsh poems are assuredly far older than the fifteenth century, and it seems more reasonable to hold that this kinship of situation and temper between the two literatures is due to some special impulse which affected alike the bards of Gaeldom and those of Wales, than to look upon it as a simple coincidence. But this impulse could hardly have stirred Ireland two or three centuries later than Wales.

One thing finally should be noticed. If the ballad-poetry be a late and specifically Northern Gaelic deve-

lopment, then the Highland *savants* of the last century
were right, and "Ossian" (meaning thereby the ballads
partially known to and used by Macpherson) was Scotch
rather than Irish.

What I have now said, and what may be found in my
notes to Mr. MacInnes' volume, will suffice, I hope, to
give some idea of the complexity and interest of the
questions connected with the Ossianic cycle. The notes
at the end of this volume are intended to be of use to
such as wish to pursue investigation for themselves.
They chiefly consist of references to M. d'Arbois de
Jubainville's list of Irish sources, and to Campbell of
Islay's *Leabhar na Feinne*, in which the entire corpus of
Scotch-Gaelic Fenian ballad-poetry is reproduced. The
materials thus lie ready to the hand of the student.
Will the Gael of Scotland leave the task of elucidating
and interpreting the heroic epos of their race to German
scholars? I have spoken of Professor Zimmer; let me
now mention such men as Professor Windisch, as Kuno
Meyer, as Max Nettlau, who are labouring unweariedly
in the field of Celtic research. Labouring unweariedly,
not because it is their business; each of those scholars
has other and arduous duties to perform first, but with
that ardent zeal for knowledge which is the crowning
glory of Germany. And all this while the academic
world of Scotland (with but few honourable excep-
tions) stands by idle, and neglects its birthright. Men
who have but a tithe of the work, but triple and quad-
ruple the remuneration of these German scholars, are
content to let this noble and inspiring subject of study
pass out of their hands—hands of sons—into those of
strangers. It is, indeed, characteristic of this country
that, when Lord Archibald Campbell sought assistance
in the task of preserving the traditions of his race, he
sought it not from professional scholars, but from hard-
working ministers of religion; characteristic also that

the most extensive, the most important, the most valuable series of researches which have appeared in Scotland in this department of study are due to a country gentleman, Campbell of Islay.

Let us look at the matter in another way. There is but one other race of modern Europe which has preserved to the present day an heroic epos reaching back into a far distant past. I allude to the Finns, and to their noble mythico-heroic poem, the Kalewala. Contrast the loving care with which official and academic Finland has cherished the Kalewala, the scientific thoroughness with which every variant has been noted, the recognition of the epic as an object of national pride, national solicitude, with the treatment of the Ossianic ballads in Scotland—a contrast all to the discredit and disgrace of the richer and more illustrious people.

And yet who shall say that the Fenian hero-tales are unworthy the care, the study which every other European race has bestowed upon its national traditions ? Let us not forget that for hundreds of years these tales were the delight and solace of our forefathers, that they spring from the heart's blood of the race, that they have become bone of the bone, flesh of the flesh of the Gael wheresoever he has fixed his dwelling. Simply consider the cold, abstract scientific value of an oral tradition which is still quick and flourishing. So long as men live the tale of Troy divine will be to them both a delight and a wonder, an imperishable source of beauty, and a problem the fascination of which may not be gainsaid. The great Karling may perchance live longer as the white-bearded emperor of the Chanson de Roland than as the heir of the Cæsars. And the German songs proudly vaunt, and not without reason, that the praise of Siegfried and Dietrich shall never die from out men's mouths. Of Arthur, too, the same boast was made. But all these mighty epics, although they form a part of humanity's most precious treasure, are yet dead in a certain sense ; they have faded out of the folk-consciousness, we know of them from books alone. But if every book in the world were to perish we could find the tale of Finn and his men still entire in the memories of men who know nothing of books, whose culture is due solely to oral tradition.

Here, then, is means of verifying the hypotheses that have been put forth so freely concerning the genesis and development of heroic tradition ; here, and here alone in Western Europe can we study the physiology of tradition from a living specimen instead of from anatomical plates. Gaelic Scotland has at length organised the song- and letters-loving tendencies of her children, as the Kymry of Wales did long since. Let the first task of the Scotch Eisteddfod be to promote the criticism of the one living hero-cycle of Western Europe, the tales of Finn MacCumhal and the Fian band.

ALFRED NUTT.

NOTE.

In giving the Tales collected by the Reverend J. G. CAMPBELL. to the public, I must not omit to express the warmest thanks for services rendered by Mr. DUNCAN MACISAAC, of Oban, who has been an invaluable aid to us in getting the work ready for the Press. He has assisted us in every way, and been of the very greatest use in the Gaelic portion; a prompt, able, and an enthusiastic and willing worker at what I feel will not be labour lost in rescuing the Tales of our beloved land from oblivion.

ARCHIBALD CAMPBELL.

THE FIANS.

PREVIOUS to written history, and indeed outside of the literary world, there was to be found among the Celtic races a profusion of traditions and tales which may be said to have been a closed book to the rest of the world. Songs and traditions exist among all races, but among the Celtic tribes, whose wealth of imagination and general intelligence are known, or with which they are at least credited, there existed an abundance of legends and tales and poetry which it is very desirable should be laid hold of. The position which these tales and poems occupy is difficult to fix. They are not pure imagination, and it would not be safe to look upon them as historical truths. In the early period of history, as in the infancy of the individual, the power of credence is unlimited, and the most extraordinary stories pass unchallenged : ogres, giants, and people of strange shapes and marvellous powers are readily believed in. When the field of imagination is entered upon there is no obstacle in the way which the mind cannot get over.

There is a saying, with which the writer has fallen in, in Skye, that the oldest ballad is the "Lay of the Red" (*Dan an Deirg*), as the oldest history known to the Celts was the history of Connal Gulban, and the oldest poem the "Lay of the Great Fool", and the greatest praise the praise of Loch Key.

"Every ballad to the Ballad of the Red,
Every history to the History of Connal,
Every lay to the Lay of the Great Fool,
And every praise to the Praise of Loch Key."

1

" *Gach Dan gu Dan an Dèirg,*
Gach Eachdraidh gu Eachdraidh Chonaill,
Gach Laoidh gu Laoidh an Amadain Mhoir :
'S gach Moladh gu Moladh Loch Cè."

(See *Nicolson's Proverbs*, p. 189.)

Perhaps even older than these is the fairy song, or
lullaby ascribed to the fairies, and reaching at least
to pagan times ; indeed, probably as old a ditty as
we have in Gaelic, in which the following passage
occurs :—

" My cause of merriment, soft and sweet art thou,
Of the race of Coll and Conn art thou.
My cause of merriment, soft and sweet art thou,
Of the race of Conn art thou.

" My soft cause of merriment, my soft rushes,
My lovely rock plant,
Were it not for the charm that is on your foot
We would lift you with us.

" Of the race of Coll and Conn art thou,
My cause of merriment, soft and sweet art thou,
My soft cause of merriment
My knee has brought up,
Were it not for the burn on your foot
We would lift you with us."

" Mo mhire bhog bhinn thu,
Siol Cholla 's Chuinn thu,
Mo mhire bhog bhinn thu,
Siol a chinne Chuinn thu.

" Mo mhire bhog, mo luachair bhog,
Mo chneamh an creig,
Mar bhi an sian th' air do chois,
Gu'n togamaid leinn thu.

"Siol Cholla is Chuinn thu,
Mo mhire bhog bhinn thu,
Mo mhire bhog,
Mo ghlùn a thog,
Mar bhi an losgadh th' air do chois,
Gu'n togamaid leinn thu."

This lullaby attracts attention not only by its weird and
beautiful music, resembling the wild night-wind about
the house or in neighbouring trees, but also by its
allusion to the race of Coll and Conn, which are not
commonly to be met with ; in fact, till a person becomes
acquainted with the heroes of Ossian's time, he will be
unable well to understand these allusions. At one time
the tales of the Fian heroes were common all over the
Highlands, but are now only to be fallen in with in
some localities. The fairy lullaby is here given to illus-
trate the antiquity and prevalence of the stories which
are collected in this volume. With greater facilities of
making one's self acquainted with different parts of the
Highlands, it is very likely that a good many more of
the same kind might be fallen in with. The writer can
only say that he has endeavoured to make the best of
such material as he has met with, and that it is here
given without addition, subtraction, or alteration of any
kind. There are many questions of interest as to
the date, antiquity, and origin of these stories and
poems, but they have been avoided, and it is as free to
the reader to form his opinion as it is to the writer.
Tales of this kind are denominated, in popular lore,
"Tales of Fionn, Son of Cumhal, and the Fian Host"
(*Naigheachdan air Fionn MacCumhail agus Feachd na
Féinne*), and the matter to which they refer was so much
the subject of talk that it became a saying, that if the
Fians were twenty-four hours without anyone men-
tioning them they would rise again. They are lying, it

is said, in the boat-shaped mound called Tom-na-h-iubhraich, which for some years past has been used by the town of Inverness as a burying-ground ; others say they are lying in Glenorchy, Argyleshire ; and there is a story that when they were last seen it was by a person who chanced to enter the place where they are lying. When he struck a chain that was suspended from the roof, the Fians rose upon their elbows, and their big dogs began to bark. The intruder was so much frightened that he ran away. As he was going out at the door he heard a voice calling—

> "Evil and ill-guided man,
> Who leaves us worse than when found."

> "A dhuine dhona dholaich
> 'S miosa dh' fhag na fhuair."

The tenacity of popular tradition is shown by the fact of these compositions being still to be fallen in with in widely separated parts of the Highlands and Islands, though rare and much mutilated. Of the versions which the writer has been able to fall in with, or has seen in print, this is particularly noticeable ; the history of Connal has fallen to pieces, so that it may now be classified among the fireside tales (*Sgeulachdan*). The Lay of the Great Fool is, from its character and incidents, apparently a fragment of Druidic times. It contains stories of enchantments and allegories of a different type from any now current, or to be found within the fields of literature. The Ballad of the Red contains one verse which is of much value, from the old-time reference which it contains. It was heard from a person who had heard the ballad from his mother, a native of Jura, perhaps forty-five or fifty years ago, and this was the only part of the poem he could remember. The story of the Red was to the effect that the Red was married, and was in doubt whether his wife loved

THE INTRUDER.

[To face p. 4.

him or not. He was induced to appear as if killed in
the chase, and he was taken or carried home "on a
shutter" and laid out as if dead. His wife sat beside
the body, and then crooned or sang the "Lay of the
Red". The noticeable verse was—

> "I see the hawk, I see the hound
> With which my love hunted;
> Since well he loved the three,
> Let us be laid in the grave with the Red."

> "Chi mi un t-sheobhag, chi mi 'an cù
> Leis an deanamh mo rùn 'n t-sealg
> On a b' ionmhuinn leis an triuir
> Carair sinn san ùir le Dearg."

(See *Nicholson's Proverbs*, p. 415 ; Gillies' *Collection*, p. 301.)

This verse is of more than passing interest, as it
points to a time when those in high estate were wont to
hunt with hawk and hound, and even it may be to a
time when *suttee* was practised, and the wives of great
men were buried along with them, as is still done in India.
In ancient sepulchral mounds which antiquaries have
fallen in with, the grave is about three feet in length,
and the hero was placed apparently in a sitting position.
Smaller bones have been found in a grave adjoining the
sarcophagus, and it is impossible to say whether they
were the bones of a slenderer human being or those of a
dog.

An earlier stratum of legend than that commemorating
the Fenian heroes is preserved orally in the Highlands,
as specimens of which may be cited the stories of Conlaoch and Cuchullin, and of Deirdre.

CONLAOCH AND CUCHULLIN.

In the poems published by Macpherson Cuchullin figures as one of the characters, but in the tales and traditions about him which are still to be found floating, he does not figure as one of the Fian or Fingalian band. The popular tale told of him is that he lived at Dunscaith (*Dunsgàich*), in the district of Sleat, in Skye. Some say that he was apprenticed to a smith in the locality, and was taught all the arts of war (*air fòghlum cogaidh*). Here he left his wife, and told her that the child to be born to her, if a male child, was to be named Conlaoch, was to be trained in feats of arms, and when of age was to go to Ireland, and not tell his name to anyone except under compulsion (*bheireadh air 'ainm innse*), or tell it in spite of himself (*bheireadh 'ainm dh' aindeoin dheth*). He himself, Cuchullin, went to Ireland, and was matchless in prowess. There was one feat which seems to have consisted of throwing javelins (*gath builg*) across water, at which no one at all ventured to compete with him. When Conlaoch was of age he went to Ireland, and there was a meeting of nobles, at which no one could equal him in arms. He was asked his name, but refused, even though the one who was sent to him complimented him upon his stature.

"Long and fair is your side, warrior."

"Is fhada briagha do shlios a churaidh."

One who was tutor to Cuchullin told him of this, and Cuchullin himself went to Conlaoch, who, refusing to confess his name in any other way, was challenged to a trial of skill in javelin-throwing (*gath builg*). A match was fought between them, but in this Cuchullin mastered him, and Conlaoch, who knew his father,

though his father did not know him, threw the spear
with the blunt end foremost (*an coinneamh na h-carraich*),
but Cuchullin threw his point foremost (*an coinneamh a
roinne*). Conlaoch was wounded and fell, and when
Cuchullin stooped over him to ascertain his name,
Conlaoch said :

> " ' I am Conlaoch, the son of the Dog,
> The rightful heir of Dun Telva,
> The loved one left in the body
> In Dunscaith to be taught.'

> " ' My curse, son, upon the mother
> From Dunscaith to the tower of learning ;
> It was the love that was in her heart
> That has now left my heart-strings(?) so red.'

> " ' Ill was your recognition of me,
> Noble, haughty, loving father,
> When I threw aslant and feebly,
> The spear wrong end foremost.'

> " ' Alas ! alas ! and another alas !
> It is not the alas that is to-night the burden,
> But the spoils of my son in one hand
> And the war weapons in the other.' "

> " ' Is mise Conlaoch mac-nan-Con,
> Oighre dligheach Dhùn t-sealbha,
> An rùn a dh' fhàgadh am broinn,
> An Dùn-sgàich ga fhoghlum.'

> " ' Mo mhallachd, a mhic, air a mhàthair,
> O Dhùn-sgàich gu Dùn faoghlum ;
> 'Se an rùn bha na cridhe
> Dh'fhàg mo liantan cho dearg.'

> " ' 'S olc an aithne rinn thu orms',
> Athair uasail uaibhrich ghràdhaich,
> Nuair thilginn ort gu fiar fann,
> An t-sleagh an ceann a h-earraich.'

"'Och nan och ! is och eile !
Cha-n i'n och an nochd an eire,
Faoibh mo mhic san darna làimh
'S na h-airm san làimh eile.'"

The dead body of his son was carried by Cuchullin
to the shelter of a tree, and for many days no bird
dared to perch on the tree, or any man to come near;
he ate no food. At last a crow or raven was observed
to settle on the tree, and then people knew that
Cuchullin was dead.

DEIRDRE.

The story of Deirdre, whose name figures in Macpherson as Darthula, is to be found in a fragmentary
state in many parts of the Highlands and Islands. Of
the fragments of the poems on the subject which have
been gathered and preserved, many are of the highest
poetic merit. A form of the tale which was got in
Barra is given in the *Transactions of the Inverness
Society*, vol. xiv, p. 241. That which the writer has
fallen in with is, in the main, to the same effect.
Deirdre was the daughter of the harper of an Irish king,
and a very pretty child. When she was nearing woman-
hood, a young man, Naos, took her away. He was
accompanied by his own two brothers. The king, who
had intended her for himself, when he heard of their
flight, sent for his Druids, who raised a thick wood in
their way, which they said the fugitives could not get
through. Naos, however, and his two brothers cut their
way through the wood, and, accompanied by Deirdre,
fled out of the kingdom. At this point popular imagination in the prose tales gets full swing, and the fugitives
are represented as having gone to Scotland, etc., and
the story ends with the death of the three brothers,

and ultimately her own self-inflicted death, when she
found that Naos had been killed by the king. The
ample freedom of popular imagination is well shown in
the version of the tale already referred to as having
appeared in the *Transactions of the Gaelic Society of
Inverness.* The *Amhuisgean,* which figure in it, are not
mentioned in any other version of the story that has
appeared in print or been heard of by the writer, and it
is possible may have been worked into the story from
some other popular tale.

OF the tales and poems still current, and introducing
us to the endless tales of the Féinne or Fingalians, is a
lay commencing with :

> " Conn, son of the Red, filled with heavy wrath,
> Coming to avenge his father's death without reservation,
> On the great nobles and worthies of Ireland."

> " Conn Mac-an-Deirg air a lionadh le trom fheirg,
> Tighinn a dhioladh bas Athair gun fheall,
> Air uaislibh 's air maithibh na h-Eirinn."

The tale is one of the superhuman strength of Conn, and
the victory over him by *Goll MacMorna*, and is evidence
of the wisdom with which Finn had welded together
the originally widely inimical parties of which the Fian
band was made up.

The history of the Fians, or body of strong men to
whom that name is given, may be said to extend as
far back as either history or tradition does. They, the
Féinne, were said to be in two parties, Clanna Mòlum
and Clanna Baoisgne, and Fionn was leader over them
both. They followed the chase, both in Ireland and
Scotland. Oscar and Dermid were also leaders. According to one account there were 9,000 perfect heroes
(*naoi mile gaisgeach glan*) in the Féinne, and their
work was to guard women from the giants, and
no spells or enchantments could ever lie upon the
Fians (*cha do luidh geasan air an Fhéinn riamh*).
Hence their continual success. They were no stronger
than other people, but the excellence of their bards
made them excellent. The best known, and those
regarding whom the tales and ballads are most popular among the Celtic race, are those of the time of

Fin MacCoul—*Fionn MacCumhail.* The stories about
this leader and his band were so universal and popular
in the Highlands, that their prevalence was made a
standing joke against Highlanders, and the great
strength and valour ascribed to the band were made fun
of. Thus Dunbar, who lived before the end of the
fifteenth century, speaks of the Celtic hero:

> " My fore grandsire hecht Fin MacCoul,
> Wha dang the deil and gart him yowll,
> The skyis rainit when he would scowll,
> He troublit all the air.
> He gat my grandsyr Gog Magog;
> Ay whan he dansit the warld wald shog,
> Five thousand ellis gaed till his frog,
> Of *Hieland* pladdis, and mair."

This latter saying is of value as proof of the antiquity
of tartan. Other Scottish poets also make mention of
Finn MacCoul, somewhat in a similar slighting manner,
the most ancient of these being Barbour, who, in a
poem called " The Bruce", written about 1380, compares
the defence made by the Bruce at Dalree to that made
by Fingal against Gaul.

The antipathy between Celtic lore and that current
in educated circles in the south culminated on the
appearance of Macpherson's *Ossian*, which professed
to be poems found floating in the Highlands, and
resembling the poems of Homer and Virgil. The
questions of the authenticity or genuineness of these
poems were warmly controverted, and Dr. Johnson
went to the Highlands, as Walcot says, " to eat Macpherson midst his native North". Without entering in
any way on the questions at issue, it is beyond doubt,
and open to the judgment of everyone, that the poems
which Macpherson published contain much that is
deserving of attention as good poetry. To those who are
conversant with ballads still to be found among the

people, the name of Ossian, or the bard of the Fians, to
whom the ballads are attributed, is worthy of all the
admiration given to him.

The heroes mentioned in the lay, which tells of the
greatest strait in which the Fians ever were (*Teanntachd
mhòr na Féinne*), seem to have been principally leaders of
tribes who in time were incorporated with the Fian band.
When Manus, King of Lochlin, collected all his forces,
and the battle of the Hill of Howth was fought (*Latha
cath Beinn Eudainn*), the heroes who were prominent
for their prowess and strength were Oscar, the son of
Ossian, grandson of Fionn himself, and incomparably
the most powerful man of the party ; Goll, leader of the
Clanna Morna ; Ceutach, leader of the Colla men ;
Dermid, nephew of Fionn, and the only son of his
twin sister, whose story is widely spread, and known
from his having fled with his uncle's wife, and his having
slain the wild boar that Grey Eyebrows had in her possession of pigs :

"The old grey wild boar, that was ever working mischief,
  That Grey Eyebrows had in her possession of pigs."

"Sean torc liath bha riabh ri olc,
  Aig Mala Liath air sealbh mhuc."

Among their poets we hear of *Ferghus Fillidh* (Fergus
Poet), chief spokesman and ambassador of the warlike
band, and whose designation still survives in, and perhaps
was derived from, the common word *fillidh*, a poet.
Others whose names occur are MacRedhinn, who gives
his name to the sound that separates Skye from the mainland. When the Féinne were hunting in the Isle of Skye,
and observed a dark-coloured, low-lying smoke from the
dwelling in which they had left their wives, they hurriedly
swung themselves on their spears across to the mainland,
and came to Brugh Farala, which they found, with all its

inmates, consumed by fire to ashes; MacRedhinn fell into the sound, which now bears his name, Kyle Rea (*Caol Redhinn*).

> "Every man swung himself by his spear-head point,
> And they left MacRedhinn in the sound."

> "Leum gach fear air barr ceann sleagha,
> 'S dh' fhag iad MacRedhinn sa Chaol."

Garry (*Garai*), whose watchfulness had detected the manner in which the women kept themselves in good condition, when hunger and the loss of the chase had made the men themselves become feeble and spare, and who was the cause of Brugh Farala's being burnt, was discovered, caught, and executed. His death being at his own request, he chose to have his head cut off by *Mac-a-Luin*, Fionn's sword, while his head rested upon Fionn's thigh. As the redoubtable sword at one blow could cut clean through every obstacle put before it, and never required a second blow, Fionn's thigh was carefully guarded by seven divots of lea ground full of coarse fibre, and the sword not only cut off Garry's head, but pierced Fionn himself, till blood spouted from the wound.

> "More numerous than the dewdrops on the grass
> Were the ends of arteries cut on Fionn's thigh."

> "Bu lionmhoir na driùchd air feur
> Ceann cuisle gearrte an sleasaid Fhinn."

During their season of activity, and in the prime of their strength, the band seems not only to have engaged in conflicts and in the chase, and listened to the songs of bards, but also to have engaged in agricultural pursuits. It was when so employed that the Norsemen came upon them in the Very or True Hollow of Tiree (*Fior Lagan Thiridhe*), which is said to have been in the district now called Kilmoluag.

The derivation of the word *Fëinne*, the Fian host, is

uncertain; it is a collective noun, and though those of
whom popular tradition makes most mention were those
under the leadership of Fin MacCoul, a similar band
seems to have existed in the days of Coul (*Cumhal*),
his father, and to have been driven to take refuge in
caves and other places, when disbanded by an opposing
force. That their enemies were the Northmen does not
seem a tenable supposition. That in very early times
there was intercourse between the Celts of Ireland and
the Lochlinners, or people of the far east, is a creed
tenable enough, but many of the best stories on the
subject have an air of post-Ossianic times.

Of places in the Highlands which have names derived
from the heroes of the Fians are to be mentioned Loch
Oscair, in a small islet near Lismore. Dermid is said
to have slain the wild boar in several places. The pin-
fold of Dermid (*Buaile Dhiarmaid*), where Grey-Eye-
brows had her pigs, is said to be in Scorr, near Portree,
Skye; and Dermid's cave (*Uaimh Dhiarmaid*) is said to
be the Big Cave (*Uaimh mhòr*) in Kenavara hill, Tiree,
facing the Atlantic.

Brugh Caorainn is said to be in Braes, in the parish of
Portree, Skye and Brugh Dhubhain in Glendale, in the
same island. The big stones on which their kettle
(*coire*) rested, four or five in number, are still seen
between the manse of Kensilair and Scoirinish, and
Ossian is said to "sleep in his narrow glen" in more than
one locality. In the poem of the "Owl" (*Comhachag
bhochd na Sroine*), which is said to have been composed
near Loch Treig, in Lochaber, the bard mentions as
places within view from where he was sitting, *Srath
Ossian nam Fian* (the strath of Ossian of the Fingalians); and popular tradition associates the Fians with
almost every wonderful natural feature. The cave in
Staffa is *Uaimh Fhinn*, or Fingal's Cave; and the parallel
roads of Glenroy are known as the Roads of the Ossianic

Heroes (*Rathaidean nam Fian*). There is in Kilmuir, in Skye, a trap dyke, or seeming wall, that runs up an almost perpendicular incline, called the Wall of the Fians (*Garadh na Feinne*), and in more than one hill in Skye, from which magnificent views are to be got, there are places called the Chair of Fionn; but it is a question among the common people whether the name means a sitting-place in the hill (*Cathair 's a bheinn*) (the Chair in the Hill), or the sitting-place of Fionn (*Cathair suidhe Fhinn*). In *Beinn Iadain*, in Morven, there are steps in the rock near the summit popularly known as *Ceumanan Fhinn*, or Fingal's Steps.

FIONN MacCoul, or, as he is better known since the
appearance of Macpherson's works, Fingal, the son of
Cumhal, was a posthumous son. Cumhal (*Cumhail*), the
father, was an Irish chief of high estate, and was driven
from his seat by the quarrels in which the chiefs of that
time seem to have been engaged. In the heat of battle
he (Cumhal) entered the house of the Ulster smith and
asked for a drink of water. The smith's daughter was
the only one in, and she gave him the drink if he himself could take it out of the only vessel she had at hand.
This vessel had seven or nine crevices or pipes (*feadain*),
which had to be kept closed with the fingers, and
the question was warmly debated at one time, among
reciters of these tales, whether it was not a kind of reed
or pipe through which a person had to draw the water,
the hole of the pipe which was in the mouth forming
one of the orifices of the vessel which had to be kept
closed. While he was taking a drink the water spouted
out through one of the holes, and the smith's daughter
began to laugh. He threw the dish from him. On
returning to battle, while lying wounded and under foot,
he was slain by Black Arky, the fisherman (*Arcai Dubh
Iasgair*), who came and offered, for an exchange of
swords, to carry him to a safe place. When he got
Cumhal's sword he thrust it in from behind and killed
him with his own weapon. A report had spread abroad
(*bha e san tairgreachd*) that a son of Cumhal would
avenge his death, and regain the superiority that had
been lost by the death of Cumhal himself. The enemy,
having heard of this, sent people to watch, so that, as
under Herod Agrippa's decree, every male child born
within the boundaries of the estate for the next nine

months was slain. In the words of the reciters of these tales, the daughter of the Ulster smith became "heavy and fruitful, spotted and speckled, what did not increase in the day grew at night (*dh' fhas i trom torach breac ballach, na nach d' fhas san latha dh' fhas e san oidhche*), and at last she drew near her confinement." A sister of Cumhal, named Speedy Foot (*Los Lurgann*), succeeded in introducing herself among the watchers; some say that she killed the midwife and took her place. The first-born was a male child, and Speedy Foot put a lump of fat (*gainne saille*) in his mouth, which kept it from crying out, then tied it to his big toe (*ordag a choise*), so that if the lump she tied should at any time be so drawn as to interfere with his breath, the spasm of the child to withdraw the obstruction would make him kick, and so remove it. In this way the cries of the child were hushed and all obstacles to its safety were removed. A female child was then born, and she, Speedy Foot, found a way of removing the first-born out of the way, and taking him to her brother, the joiner-smith (*gobhan saor*), the best smith that ever lived. His dwelling was in the Ulster wood. She asked him to make a house for her in one of the trees, on which, when the house was finished, no stroke of adze or axe (*buille thàil no thuaidh*) was to be seen, so that no one could tell there was a house there. He made the house, and having carefully looked over the whole appearance of the tree, she asked him if anyone could make out now if there was a house there. He made one or two additions to the construction in the tree, and said that no one now could make out that there was a house there. "If," said Speedy Foot, "there is no one that knows my secret but yourself, there will be no one," and she scraped his head off (*Mur 'eil fear ruin orm ach thusa cha bhi na's fhaide, agus sgriob i dheth an ceann*). In this house she continued to live with her infant charge till he grew to be a good stripling, and taught

him feats of swimming, leaping, and running. The way
in which she taught him running was by giving a switch
of hawthorn (*squab dreaghain*), with which to run after
her round a tree. She herself had a similar bunch of
hawthorn in her own hands. With these they chased
each other round the tree, and when she overtook
the boy she belaboured him behind the feet with
her bunch of briers, until at last he could run round
the tree so fast that he belaboured her with his own
branch, and he did not leave a particle of flesh and
blood (*ribe fuil no feola*) on her legs with his broom of
thorn, while she could never overtake him. She then
taught him to leap by digging a hole in the ground,
which was gradually getting deeper, till at last he could
spring up a wall from a hole which reached to his
breast. She taught him swimming by throwing him in
the water, until he could at last swim over nine waves
and be ashore before herself. All that was now wanted
was a suitable name for him, and she went with him to
a lake where the children of those who had been the
enemies of his father were disporting themselves, their
parents looking on. Speedy Foot told him to go out
and avenge his father's death. He did so, and every
child that he fell in with he put under water and kept
there, till at last he was observed by those ashore, who
cried out, "Who is the Fair White one that is ever drowning the children?" ("*Co Fionn Ban tha sior bhathadh
nam mac?*") "May you enjoy your name," said Speedy
Foot; "your name from this time will be *Fionn* (Fair)".
In this way the son of Cumhal (*Cumhail*) received his
name. She then took him on her back and fled with
him to the Ulster wood. Getting tired, she let Fionn to
the ground, and he, taking her by the shanks, placed
her on the back of his neck and took her through the
woods, heedless of her outcry and mindless of anything
but escape from the pursuers. When he got out of the

wood there was a lake in front of him, and he had
nothing left of Speedy Foot but the shanks (*an da
lurgann*); these he threw out on the loch, which derives
its name from the occurrence—Loch Lurgan.

Another account of this latter incident is : The Clanna
Mòlum and their children were now in the place where her
young charge ought to be, and on a Sunday she went and
found the children bathing in front of the palace and the
old people looking on. By her advice the child went out,
and catching a child of the Clanna Mòlum in each hand,
dived, and drowned them. The Clanna Mòlum then said :
" *Co am Fionn bàn tha sior bhàthadh nam mac?*" *Los
Lurgann* leapt forward, and said : " *S'e sin a th' ann Fionn
MacCumhail ic Luthaich 'ic Threin 'ic Fhinn ic Airt, 'ic
àrd òg rìgh Eirinn*" (He is Fionn, the son of Cumhal, son
of Looäch, son of Trein, son of Finn, son of Art (Arthur),
son of the young high King of Erin). She then hastily
took up Fionn, who had now got a name, and ran with
him through the wood till she was tired. Fionn then
caught her by the ankles (*caol na coise*), and throwing
her across his neck, ran so fast that he did not observe
his heavy burden becoming lighter. When he got out
of the wood he had only the shins (*cnaimh an da
lurgann*). He threw them out on the loch, called Loch
Lurgan to this day. He was now friendless, without a
home or any place to go to. He went to a river near
at hand, and falling in with a fisherman, he asked him
to make a cast for his luck (*air a shealbhaich-san*). The
fisherman did so, but the fish that was caught was so
good that he kept it to himself. Fionn then asked him to
make another cast for him, and this time also the fish
(salmon) proved so good that the covetous fisherman
told him he must prepare the fish on the other side of
the river, and allow no spot to be burnt or blister to rise
upon it. Fionn saw a piece of the fish-skin rising. He
put his hand upon it to press it back into its proper

place, and in doing so he burnt himself, and put his
finger in his mouth. This made him acquainted with
his wisdom tooth (*deud fios*), which is so frequently
mentioned in popular lore. This tooth, when pressed
by his finger, gave him knowledge that made him a
solver of questions. On this occasion he acquired the
knowledge that Dark Arky (*Arcai Dubh Iasgair*) was
the one who had slain his father; and when Arky came
to where he was, he asked him what was the death
of Cumhal. Black Arky told him: "He roared like a
yearling calf, and broke wind like a gelding when my
spear went slanting through his back" ("*Ciod bu bhas do
Chumhail?*" "*Raoiccadh e mar ghamhuin's . . . e mar
ghearran's mo shleagh siar troimh fheaman*").

A fuller account is: Fionn then went home, and hunger
was tormenting and pinching him severely (*ga ghualadh
's 'ga ghreadadh*). He came where Black Arky (*Arcai
dubh Iasgair*) was fishing on a rock, and asked him to
make a cast for his benefit (*air mo shealbhaich*). He did
so, and caught a salmon (*bradan*), which is a royal fish
(*iasg righ*), and refused to give it up. This occurred
three times. The fourth fish was given to Fionn, but
Arcai told him that, when roasting it, if he allowed a
spot to rise upon it his head would be made a foot and
shinty ball of (*ma thig ball loisgte air 'se do cheann is ball
cois is iomanachd dhomh*). Fionn kindled a fire, and as
he roasted the salmon a spot (*ball donn*) began to rise on
the fish. He was hungry, and he put his finger on the
spot to keep it under, burnt himself, and put his finger
in his mouth. He then found out how Black Arky
killed his father, and said, "That is just the death I am
going to give you" ("*Sin direach am bas bheir mise
dhuitsa*"), and taking Arky's fishing-rod, broke it against
his knee; with this piece of the rod he knocked down
Arky, and then killed him. Being free to shift for
himself by means of the knowledge to be gained through

his wisdom tooth, he learned that his mother was the ugliest woman in all Ireland (*an boirionnach bu ghraunda bha'n Eirinn*). He wandered away, and before long came to the house of the Ulster smith. Being in need of a sword to make his way in the world, his mother, the smith's daughter, who came to recognise him, and to whom he told his troubles, said that her father would make a sword for him of so fine a temper that it never would require a second blow. This was the celebrated sword of Fionn, the son of Cumhaill, that never left a remnant from its blow (*Mac-an-Luinn nach d'fhag riabh fuigheal beum*). She warned him to be careful not to enter the smithy, where her father was to be at work upon the sword. The material he was to use would be iron and coals from a place that was not good (*le gual 's le iaruinn a aite nach robh math*), and the sword was to be tempered in the blood of the first living creature that entered the smithy, the blood of man, woman, or dog (*fuil mic, mna, na madaidh*). When the sword was nearly finished, Fionn's mother, by a slight opening of the door, managed to get a dog to enter the smithy, and in a while Fionn himself entered and got the renowned sword.

Another account is: By putting his finger under his knowledge tooth (*mhear fo dheud-fios*), of which he now learned the virtue, he became aware that the ugliest woman in Ireland was his mother. He went to the house of the Ulster smith, and when his mother saw him, she said, a third of her hearing was now come back to her. She advised him to hire himself to the smith, who was swordmaker to the Clanna Mòlum, and kept a roomful of swords, and to take no payment but a sword (*air am bi* MAC-A-LUIN *mar ainm, nach fàg fuigheall beum, thig a gual 's a iarunn a àite nach 'eil math g'a dheanadh*). The night he made this sword the smith shut himself up in the smithy,

saying that if he returned he would thrust (*adhartaich*)
the sword into whatever first entered the smithy in the
morning. The door was agape (*braoisg*) in the morning,
and Fionn, by his mother's advice, threw in a little
dog (*measan*), into which the smith thrust the sword.

Having got this prized weapon, he went in search of
his father's men. He found them driven to take refuge
in caves by the shore, and the news of Cumhal's son
having appeared spread like wildfire. From cave to
cave the word passed, "What was foretold has come
true" ("*Thainig am fàth fìor, thainig am fàth fìor*"). The
men were all overgrown with hair and beard, and, if all
tales are true, Fionn shaved them and dressed them
with the sword, *Mac-a-Luin*. Or, as another account
says: Fionn went for service to the Clanna Mòlum; his
mother gave him a bag of apples and three pins (*deilg*).
When he entered the palace they said to him, "*Biatachd
abhul, oganaich, b'àill leinn fhaotuinn uait*" ("Food of
apples, youth, we would fain get from you"). He had left
the bag at the door, and told them to bring it in themselves and take their pleasure (*taitneachd*). One after the
other of the Clanna Mòlum went out, and not one could
move the bag (*cha chuireadh iad ceige ann*). At last
Goll said: "*Miagh uile agus iorghuidh oirbh nach tugadh
sibh a stigh e, ged a bhiodh a sheachd urrad fhein do
thalamh 'slaodadh ris*" ("The shadow of evil and evil
wishes be upon you that would not bring it in, though
seven times its own weight of earth was sticking to it").
He went out himself, broke three of his ribs, and came
in roaring (*donnalaich*). Fionn went out and took it in
on the point of a twig, and this was the first terror he
struck into Clanna Mòlum. Then the palace (*teamhair*)
took fire, and was burning at its two ends, and in the
very middle (*lasadh san da cheann 's an teis-meadhoin*).
Fionn stuck his three wires (*na tri deilg*), one in the
middle and one at each end, and the fire went out.

This was the second terror. His father's men had fled to the cave on the shore, where they lived on shell-fish (*maorach*). Fionn went for them. He found one at home cooking for the rest, and he, when he saw Fionn, cried out: "The prophecy has come true" ("*Thainig am fàth fìor*"), and for some time no other word could be got from him. Fionn shaved them all with Mac-a-Luin, gathered the cows, etc., belonging to the Clanna Mòlum, and killed a wether (*molt*). The first of the rest who came to the cave, when he smelt the sheep instead of *samh 's aile a' mhaoraich* (the smell and odour of shell-fish), called out: "The prophecy has come true" (*Thainig am fàth fìor*). Making them take an oath on his sword, Fionn went up with them and displaced Clanna Mòlum.

Thus, when Fionn came upon his father's men in their poverty and solitude in the caves by the sea, his first action in obtaining superiority over them and evincing that "he was a worthy son of a worthy father", was by bringing a bag of apples which he left, and which by enchantment or secret sleight could not be lifted off the ground. One after another of the men in the cave was sent to bring the bag in, but they could make nothing of it either individually or as a body. One by one they failed to lift it from the ground. Finn (Fionn) himself then went out, and took in the bag, suspended from his little finger. This at once put him in the forefront, and even made him master of the whole band.

The tale is also told as follows:—Cumhal was driven by the Lochlinners to a castle in a loch in Ireland. He had long arms (*bha gavirdeanan fada aige*), and no one could overcome him while under armour. The Lochlin men planned to send a beautiful woman to a grassy islet (*eilein feoir*) in sight of the castle. She was to walk where Cumhal would see her, and at last he would swim to where she was. He was then to be killed by Black Arky, the fisherman (*Arcaidh dubh Iasgair*), who was to hide himself among the grass till he got his opportunity. This was done, and then Lochlin obtained possession of all Ireland, and the Féinn were driven to take refuge in a cave by the seashore, where they were pressed with want and anxiety.

Fionn's mother was taken care of, and if her offspring were a boy he was to be killed. When her time was come (*far a glùine*) she had first a girl, and word was sent out to the watchers surrounding the house that such was the case. Before long a boy was born, and Speedy Foot (*Luaths Lurgann*), the sister of Cumhal, caught him in her apron. She put an arrow-like lump of fat (*gàinne saille*) in his mouth and went away with him. She was the best jumper, the best swimmer, and the best runner of all Ireland (*leumadair 's snamhadair 's ruitheadair na h-Èirinn*), and if she got three yards of market measure (*slat mhargaidh*) ahead no man or horse in Ireland could overtake her.

Another version is : *Los Lurgan* was Fionn's father's sister. When Cumhal was killed, those who usurped his place gave orders that if the child to be born to his wife was a male child he should be slain. She had twins, a boy and a girl. Speedy Foot (*Los Lurgann*) fled with the boy, and got her half-brother (?) to cut out a board between bark and peel (*eadar chairt is rùsg*) to make a house for her in a tree, and on his finishing the work, so that no one could now find out her refuge, she said : " I see a fault (*"Chi mi meang"*); he bent down, and she swept off his head to make her concealment complete. They lived on the chase and game (*sealg 's sithionn*). She taught Fionn all kinds of feats of strength, till at last he excelled herself. In running she could barely touch his heels with a thorn-brush, and he could switch her back. She could swim over nine waves, and though at first he could swim only over five, he at last could

swim over nine. She then thought him qualified to
avenge his father's death. They came to a loch where
a number of children were swimming. Fionn went out
among them, and every one he caught he kept his head
under water and drowned him. A woman who was
looking out at a window said: "Who is the Fair White
one who is ever drowning the children?" (" *Co Fionn bàn
tha sìor bhathadh nam mac?*")

Los Lurgann said: " May you enjoy your name; you
will be called Fionn always after this, and you were
without a name till now" (" *Gu meall thu t-ainm 'se
Fionn bhios ort as a dheigh so, 's bha thu gun ainm gus a
so*"). Fionn, son of Cuval, son of Looach, etc., son of the
high King of Ireland. (*Fionn MacCumhail ic Luthaich
ic Threin*, etc., *ic Ard Righ Eirinn*). The people
gathered to attack him, and he fled. He caught his
aunt by the feet, threw her on his back, and fled through
a thick wood, never looking behind him. Feeling his
burden getting light, and looking round, he found he
had only the two legs left. He threw them out on a
loch, which ever since has borne the name of *Loch
Lurgann.*

Fionn went on and met the Ulster smith (*An
Gobhain Ultach*), who asked who he was. He said,
" A good servant in search of a master" (" *Gille maith
ag iarraidh maighstir*"). He engaged himself for a
year and a day with the smith, and his wages were to
be a sword that was to fit his hand (*claidhe fhreagras
do'm laimh*). The smith never had one who could ply
the hammer like him. Fionn knew by his knowledge
tooth (*dend fios*) his mother was in the house and his
twin sister, for Fionn was only one of twins (*leth dhuine*),
and her likeness to him was often noticed, though all
were in ignorance of the relationship. At the end of
the year the smith told him to go to a pile of swords
lying in the smithy and choose one for himself. Every

one he tried he shook and sent it in shivers. The smith made a heavier one, but it went the same way. He asked him, "Who are you, that a sword would not fit you which would fit another person?" "That would fit me from mine and from coal, that would fit another person." ("*De'n duine thusa nach foghnadh claidheamh dhuit mar a dh' fhòghnadh do neach eile?*" "*Dh' fhoghnadh sin domh a mein's a gual, mar a dh' fhòghnadh do neach eile.*") "The face of your evil and your mischance be on you. I wish I never saw you." The smith said he must remain up all night to make the sword. His mother said to Fionn, the sword was to be tempered in the blood of a man, a woman, or dog (*fuil mic, mna, no madaidh*), and that she would know when the last strokes were being given to the sword, and he was to take the dog, a female one, and throw it in at the smithy door. He did this, and the smith killed the dog with the sword. Fionn entered and got the sword (*Mac-an-Luin*) that left no remnant of its blow (*Mac-an-Luin nach d' fhàg fuigheal beum*), and struck off the smith's head. When he came out and went to take leave of his mother, she said she would not have long to live now. Fionn said it was past that now, and went away.

Feeling hungry, and seeing a fisherman at a river fishing salmon, he asked him to make a cast for his benefit (*air a shealbhaich fhéin*). He did so, and caught a large fish, which he refused to Fionn, but said he would give him the next one. He caught a still bigger one, which he also refused (some say he tried seven times, and gave the seventh to Fionn). He promised the next, but on its proving still larger, he told him that he was going to have a sleep, and Fionn was to take the first and roast it on the salmon spear (*air iarunn a chroinn mhordha*), and if he allowed any of the skin to rise (*bolg*) he would have his head. When roasting the fish a

swelling came on a spot of the skin. Fionn put his
finger on it to press it down, and burnt his finger. He
put it in his mouth to cool, and then knew that the
fisherman was the man who had killed his father. He
went and asked him what kind of death Cüal had (*as
before*). "That is a kind of death I cannot give to you,
but I will do worse"; and he tore him asunder.

He went in search of the Féinn, and he found them in
a cave by the sea-side, living on shell-fish, and overgrown with hair and beard (*fionnadh 's feusag*), and having
seven pins or skewers in their garment with want.
There was a prophecy among them that Cüal's son
would come yet, and an old man taxed him with being
Cüal's son, saying that "a third part of my strength and
eyesight has come back to me", and told him to hide
himself at first, or else they would devour him with kindness for very joy. (*Thainig trian do'm neart's do'm
shealladh air ais dhomh; cuiridh mi'm falach thu neo
ithcadh iad thu le toilinntinn.*) When they saw him
first, they saw him one by one. Fionn shaved them with
Mac-a-Luin, and they scoured their arms, and again took
the kingdom.

Fionn had a daughter, who, it is said, was very handsome. When the Norsemen landed, the Féinn were
horrified by their number, and Fionn's daughter went
and offered herself to the King of Lochlin, with a dowry
of a hundred horsemen, etc., etc., on condition of his
turning away in peace. He said it could not be done,
as his men were sworn to conquer the country, but he
would spare her and her father. She said it was not
fear, but desire of peace, made her come. In the battle,
the Féinn, for the first and only time in their history,
went one day back.

After this we do not hear much of Fionn till he
appears as leader of the whole band of heroes to whom
the name of Fians or Fingalians is given. They seem to

have followed the chase wherever venison was to be found, both in Ireland and Scotland. The tales told of them are both numerous and entertaining. Some tell of deep and sad sorrow; some refer to feats of strength and activity, and in all of them *Fionn* (Finn) figures as a man of great wisdom and sagacity. Belonging to this part of the history of the band is the tale of how Fionn got his wonderful dog Bran, and how he was in the House of the Yellow Field, without leave to sit down or power to stand up, and about his long ship, in which, as we hear in later stories, he visited the Kingdom of Big Men.

When the Fian bands were in full order and activity, the companies of which the host was made up were seven, in addition to the company of Morna (*seachd cathanan gnathaichte na Fèinne 's cath chlanna Morna*). The most prominent of these embattled hosts was the Clanna Baoisgne, of whom Fionn himself was one; and frequent mention is made of the Clanna Morna, whose leader was Goll MacMorna. Though the Clanna Morna were at first at war with Fionn's men, and in the time of Cumhal were open enemies, yet by the wisdom of Fionn they became safe and reliable friends. The *Collaich* under Ceutach, the son of their former king (*Ceudach mac righ nan Collach*), and their history and position in the Fian band, forms an episode by itself, and seems to have been a subject of much talk.

II.—OSCAR.

EACH hero had a separate story or adventure ascribed principally or peculiarly to himself; thus, Oscar, who is said to have derived his name from his grandfather asking, when he fell in battle, "Is there a voice left in him?" ("*Bheil an t-oscar ann?*"), was the son of Ossian and grandson of Fionn, the company which he commanded being of importance, and his banner ranking next to that of Fionn. The banner of Oscar's company was called the *Sguab Ghabhaidh* (the Terrific Sweep or Broom), of which it was said, that when the news of fight came to headquarters there was no inquiry but as to the fate of this banner, the *Sguab Gàbhaidh* (the Terrible Brush or Sheaf).

> "That is no other than the Terrific Brush,
> The banner of strong, heroic Oscar;
> When the fight of chosen men was reached,
> The only inquiry was for the Terrible Sheaf."

> "Cha 'n i sud ach an Sguab-gabhaidh,
> Bratach Oscar chrodha laidir;
> Nuair a rigteadh cath nan cliar
> Cha b' fhiu a fioraich ach an Sguab-gabhaidh."
>
>   (*Gillies*, p. 311.)

In the versions of "Lays about the Fians", it is said of it that it never went a foot backwards, till the heavy grey earth trembled; but in other versions the same is said of the banner of Goll, leader of the Clanna Morluin. In the opinion of many, Oscar is the one heard of in the tale of "How Goll Killed his Mother", and with whom he disputed about the marrow-bone. According to some, Oscar's first name was The Bent One of Bones (*Crom nan Cnamh*). He grew big and gawky,

and no one thought he would prove so strong. He took
the marrow-bone from Goll, and being a tall, idle lad, of
no account, for this reason, as well as out of regard for
his father's position, he was never asked to any of the
contests in which the Fian band were engaged. One
day, when they were engaged in one of these frays,
Oscar, finding himself left alone, went out to where the
combatants were, and being destitute of any other
weapon, lifted a beam, or big log of wood, and laid about
him with such good effect that the enemy was routed,
and Oscar was ever after regarded as the best hero of
the Fians (*ceud làmh fheum na Fèinne*); and in a version
of the Greatest Strait in which the Fians ever were, it is
said of him :

> "The like of Oscar, my son,
> Was not to be found here or there."

> " Ach samhuil d' Oscair mo mhac sa
> Cha robh aca bhos na thall."

His father's cousin, Diarmid *donn* (the auburn-haired),
was the third best hero of the band (*treas lamh fheum na
Fèinne*), and it is observable that in all the tales and
traditions, both about Oscar and Diarmid, they are mentioned as having lived together on terms of very kindly
relationship and fast friendship. Diarmid, as being the
older of the two, taught his cousin's son feats of arms
and skill. He taught him to play on the *tailcasg*—
chess or backgammon.

The celebrity of this hero may be inferred from his
name being still used in the Western Islands as the first
or Christian name of a person ; thus, *e.g.*, there was very
recently in Tiree a man who went by the name of
Tearlach Oscair, or Charles, the son of Oscar, and he
also occurs as the name of fairy lovers in tales of super-
stition. The adjective *Oscara* (Oscar-like) is applied to
the human voice, and denotes a strong, loud, and power-

ful voice. The death of Oscar is recorded in the following hymn (*Laoidh*), as it is called, which was taken down word for word from the dictation of the late Roderick Macfadyen, Scarnish, Tiree, in October 1868, now nearly twenty years ago. Macfadyen was then about eighty years of age. He said he had learned it from his father, who died when he himself was only fifteen. He told the writer at the same time that old men, when they repeated these Ossianic hymns, put off their bonnets from a feeling of reverence, with which the sensitive reader will readily sympathise. One is, as it were, in the presence, not only of a master mind in the poem, but also in the presence of the deepest sorrow.

The battle of Gavra was ever memorable among the Celts both of Ireland and Scotland, and as a tale of "Old and happy far-off things, and battles long ago", was as much the subject of talk as any battle of modern times is among the races whom it affects. It is said that two men out at night sheep-stealing, or some predatory occupation, had their attention drawn to two gigantic figures on the hills on opposite sides of the glen in which they were. One of these giant figures said to the other, "Do you hear that man down below? I was the second door-post of battle at Gavra (*an darna ursainn chath a b'fhearr an Cath Gabhra*), and that man knows all about it better than I do." Gavra seems to have been somewhere in the north of Ireland, although its exact locality, as far as the poem is concerned, is a matter of conjecture. Oscar, suffering from a mortal wound, could not have been carried far on spears, and the ships of his grandfather having come in sight before his death, Gavra could not have been far from the seaboard.

There are several names in the poem which, on comparison with other versions in print, call for correction, although it has been deemed best in this case to give the poem exactly as it was taken down. To the archæ-

ologist it is of importance to have the exact words of
the reciter, without suppression, or emendation or alteration. Cairvi is called in other versions Cairbre ; and in
the quarrel between him and Oscar, in all the versions
as well as this one, the spears are called spears of seven
and nine *seang* (slimness), but the explanation which
the writer heard elsewhere, at Lochowside, leaves no
doubt that the word should be *seun* (a charm). The
charms were on the spear-shaft of Oscar, and on the
spear-head of Cairbre. The usurper naturally thought
that if he got Oscar's charmed spear-shaft along with
the charmed spear-head he himself had he would be
invincible.

Putting all the materials together in a natural junction,
the story seems to run that Cairbre, a strong, powerful
man, having usurped the sovereignty of all Ireland, and
finding the Fians unsubmissive to any but their own
leaders, took what in olden times seems to have been a
too common way of bringing an enemy to subjection.
He invited their best hero to a feast, which, according
to the fashion of the times, consisted of plentiful libations
of strong drink—a rare and much prized luxury in those
days—and finding himself failing in his object, he picked
a quarrel, which led to the battle of Gavra.

There are stanzas and expressions in this poem that
point unmistakably to heathen times—the charms upon
the weapons of war, the fay woman (*beanshith* pre-
dicting the death of those about to be slain, the introduction of the ominous raven as a sign of evil, and other
expressions, show that the poem was composed not
only in troublous times, but during the prevalence of
heathen beliefs and customs. It was pointed out by the
reciter that Oscar was the first who was buried without
his clothes. The last verse could not be explained by
him, nor is there satisfactory explanation to be found in
any version of the poem.

The incident of the quarrel between Oscar and Cairbre has been worked by Macpherson into the poem of " Temora", but a comparison of the hymn or poem with the epic will readily enable the reader to judge who the true poet is. The short, sharp words in this composition are those of angry men, compared to the lengthy speeches of the epic, and altogether there is about this poem an air of genuineness that removes it from the suspicions which have been urged against the genuineness of the other.

THE BATTLE OF GAVRA, OR, HYMN OF OSCAR.

I will not call my music my chief (effort), (1)
Tho' Ossian were fain, (2) he could to-night,
Since Oscar and the stalwart (3) Cairvy
Have fallen in the fight at Gavra.

Word came down to us,
To hardy Oscar of the Féinne,
To go to a feast with his Fians,
And he would get tribute (4) according.

The handsome Oscar who shunned not an enemy.

* * * * * *

[Three days previous to the fight, Oscar, who, in his grandfather's absence, was leader of the Féinne, was invited to a feast with Cairbre.]

Three hundred men of might
Went with him, attendant on his will and want.

[On the way a fairy woman met them, and Oscar said to her :]

Weird (5) woman that washest the garments,
Make for us the self-same prophecy,
Will any one of them fall by us,
Or shall we all go to nothingness?

3

There will be slain by thee, she said, nine (6) hundred,
And the King himself, be wounded to death by thee,
And the choicest man that falls on thy side
All his lifetime has come.

[They reached Cairbré's house, where three days were
spent in drinking.]

We got honour, and we got meat
As ever we got before,
To be joyfully entering in,
Along with Cairbré into his palace. (7)

The last day of the drinking
Cairbré cried with a loud voice,
"Exchange of spear-shafts, I will have from thee,
High brown-haired Oscar of Alba."

"Whatever exchange of spears you want,
Red-haired Cairbré of ship-harbours,
Often I and my spear were with thee
In time of battle and hard conflict.

"But exchange of shaft, without exchange of head,
It were unjust to ask that of me.
The cause of that request is
That I should be without Feinn or father."

"Though the Feinn and your father were
As well as ever they were in life,
I would require for myself
That what I asked, I should get."

"If the Feinn and my father were
As well as they were in life,
Scarce would you get here below
The breadth of your house of Erin."

Hatred filled the heroes full,
As they listened to the controversy :

Fierce words, half and half
Between Cairbré and Oscar.

Lasting words these, lasting words,
The red Cairbré would give:
"That envenomed spear in thy fist
For it shall be thy speedy death."

Other words against these
The stalwart Oscar gave,
That he would put the spear of nine enchantments
Where his beard and hair met.

Lasting words these, lasting words,
The red Cairbré would give
That he would put the spear of seven enchantments
Between his kidneys and navel.

We took with us next day
As many of the Feinn as were of us,
We took with us our host and multitude
To the north side of Erin. (8)

When we happened there
In a confined gorge, in a narrow glen,
Cairbré cried with a high voice,
"Martial sounds (9) are advancing to meet you."

There came upon us, but not for succour,
Five-score of bowmen;
These fell there under Oscar's hands,
And disgrace (10) went to the King of Erin.

Five score of fierce Gaël,
That came from a rough, inclement land,
These fell there by Oscar's hands,
And disgrace went to the King of Erin. (11)

Five score of men-at-arms,
That came from a rough land of snow,
These fell there by Oscar's hands,
And disgrace went to the King of Erin.

Five score red Cairbrés (12)
That resembled Cairbré of the people,
These fell by Oscar's hands,
And disgrace went to the King of Erin.

The five who nearest were to the King,
Whose duty was heroism and lofty deed,
These fell there by Oscar's hands,
And disgrace went to the King of Erin.

When the red Cairbré saw
Oscar ever hewing the people,
The envenomed spear (13) in his hand
He threw it to meet Oscar.

Oscar fell on his right knee,
With the envenomed spear through his body,
And gave the next throw,
To the meeting of hair and beard.

[Then the people of Cairbré said to his son :]

"Rise Art, and grasp your sword,
Stand in your father's place,
If death is not lying in wait for you,
You will be deemed to us a son of good fortune."

He gave the next throw upwards,
And to us the height seemed sufficient,
And he threw down by the correctness of his aim
Art, son of Cairbré, at the next throw.

The people of Cairbré, so firm was their struggle,
Put a helmet on a post, (14)
So that they might win the field of battle,
When they saw Oscar in sore pain.

He lifted a thin hard slate
From the earth beside the bank,
And smashed the helmet on its post—
'Twas the last deed of my noble son.

"Lift me with you now, Fians,
What you never did before;
Take me to a clean hillock,
But take off my dress." (15)

We lifted with us the handsome Oscar,
On the tops (16) of our lofty spears,
And we gave him gentle carriage
Till we came to the house of Fin.

We heard in the beach to the North,
Shouts of people and clang of arms,
And our heroes gave a sudden start
Before Oscar grew cold in death.

(*Oscar loquitur*)—

"Evil betide thee, son of many virtues, (17)
You will lie a second time;
These are ships of my grandfather,
And they are coming with succour to us."

We all blessed Fin;
If we did he gave not blessing to us,
Tears of blood flowed from his eyelids,
And he turned his back upon us.

(*Fin loquitur*)—

"Worse, my son, were you off,
That day we were at Dun-Skaich, (18)
When geese (19) would swim upon thy breast,
It was my hand that healed thee."

(*Oscar loquitur*)—

"My healing is not by growth, (20)
Neither will it be ever done;
The spear deep in the right hand side
Wonts not that it can be healed."

(Fin loquitur)—

    " Worse, son, were you off,
    The day we were in Dundalk,
    Geese would swim upon thy breast,
    It was my hand that healed thee."

(Oscar loquitur)—

    " My healing is not by growth,
    Neither can it ever be done,
    Since the sevenfold charmed spear
    Is between my kidneys and navel."

(Fin loquitur)—

    " Wretched, it was not I that fell
    In the fight of sunny, scanty Gavra,
    And you were east and west,
    Marching before the Fians, Oscar."

(Oscar loquitur)—

    " Though it were you that fell
    In sunny, scanty Gavra's fight,
    One sigh east or west
    Would not be heard in pity for you in Oscar. (21)

    " No man ever knew,
    A heart of flesh was in my breast,
    But a heart of the twisted antler (22)
    That has been covered with steel.

    " But the howling of dogs beside me,
    And the wail of old heroes,
    And the weeping of the crowd of women by turns,
    'Tis that that pains my heart."

(Fin loquitur)—

    " Beloved of my beloved, beloved of my beloved,
    Child of my child, white skinned and slender,
    My heart is leaping like the elk, (23)
    And it is my utter sorrow, Oscar will not rise.

"The death of Oscar, that pains my heart,
The champion of Erin, great is his loss to us,
When saw I my time
One so valorous behind a sword-blade?"

Wife would not weep for her own husband,
And sister would not weep for brother,
As many of us as were round the dwelling
We all were weeping for Oscar.

'Tis I would give in very truth,
The dark raven of my unreason,
The five of us who were round the board
That the hero's wound had closed in health. (24)

CATH GABHRA, NO LAOIDH OSCAIR.

Cha 'n abair mi mo thriath (1) ri m' cheol,
Ge oil (2) le Oisian e nochd,
Oscar is an Cairbhi calma (3)
Thuiteam ann an Cath Gabhra.

Thainig fios thugainn a nuas,
Dh' ionnsuidh Oscair chruaidh na Feinne
E dhol dh' ionnsuidh fleadh le' Fhiann
'S gum faigheadh e cis (4) da réir.

An t-Oscar aluinn nach d' ob naimh[1]
Tri cheud fear treun
Dh' imich leis, freasdal da thoil 's da fheum.
*   *   *   *   *   *
A bhaobh (5) a nigheas an t-eudach,
Deansa dhuinne 'n fhaistneachd cheudna,
An tuit aon duine dhiu leinn,
No 'n d' theid sinn uile do neo-ni."

---

[1] They then reached Cairbre's house, where the three days
were spent in drinking.

" Marbhar leats' (ars ise) caogad (6) ceud,
'S gonar leat an righ e fein,
'S a raogha nam fear a laigheas leat,
A shaoghal uile gu'n d' thainig."

Fhuair sinn onoir, 's fhuair sinn biadh,
Mar a fhuair sinn roimhe riamh,
Bhi subhach a' dol a steach
Maille ri Coirbhi an Teamhair (7).

An latha mu dheireadh de'n òl
Ghlaodh Cairbhi le guth mòr
" Iomlaid sleagha (cruinn) b' àill leam uait,
Ard Oscair dhuinn na h-Alba."

" Ge be 'n iomlaid sleagha th' ort,
A Chairbhi ruaidh nan long phort,
S' tric bu leat mis' agus mo shleagh
'N àm cath agus cruaidh chòmhraig.

" Ach malairt croinn gun mhalairt cinn
B' eucorach sud iarraidh oirnn ;
'S e fàth an iarrtuis sin,
Mise bhi gun Fheinn gun athair."

" Ged do bhiodh an Fhéinn is t' athair,
Co math 's a bha iad 'sa bheatha
Cha b' uilear leamsa dhomh fhìn
Gach ni dh' iarrainn gum faighinn."

" Na'm biodh an Fhéinn is m' athair,
Co math 's a bha iad 'sa bheatha,
'S gann gum faigheadh tu bhos,
Leud do thighe do dh' Eirinn."

Lion fuath na laoich làn
Ri éisdeachd na h iomarbhaigh,
Briathran borba, leth mar leth,
Eadar an Cairbhi 's an t-Oscar.

Briathran buan sin, briathran buan,
A bheireadh an Cairbhi ruadh :

" An t-sleagh nimhe sin ad dhòrn
'S ann uimpe bhios do luath-bhàs."

Briathran eile an aghaidh sin
A bheireadh an t-Oscar calma,
Gu'n cuireadh e sleagh nan naoi seang
Ma choimeachd fhuilt agus fheusaig.

Briathran buan sin, briathran buan,
A bheireadh an Cairbhi ruadh,
Gu'n cuireadh e sleagh nan seachd seang
Eadar àirnean agus imleag.

'S thugadh leinnan la'r na mhaireach,
Cho liona da 'n Fhéinn 's a bha sin,
Thugadh leinn ar feachd 's ar sluagh,
Gus an taobha tuath de dh' Eirinn (8)

Nuair a tharladh sinn ann,
Am bealach cumhann an caol ghleann,
Ghlaodh Cairbhi le guth àrd,
Loinnearachd (9) a' teachd' nar còmhdhail.

Thainig oirnn 's cha b' ann gu'r cobhair,
Coig fichead do dh' fheara bogha,
Thuit sid air laimh Oscar thall,
'S chaidh masladh (10) gu righ na h-Eirinn.

Coig fichead Gaidheal garg,
Thainig a tir uamhainn ghairbh,
Thuit sid air laimh Oscar thall,
'S chaidh masladh gu righ na h-Eirinn (11)

Coig fichead de dh' fhearabh feachd
Thainig a tir ghairbh an t-sneachd,
Thuit sid air laimh Oscar thall,
'S chaidh mosgladh gu righ na h-Eirinn

Coig fichead Cairbhi ruadh (12)
Bu chosmhuil ri Cairbhi 'n t-sluaigh,
Thuit sin air laimh Oscar thall,
'S chaidh masladh gu righ na h-Eirinn

A chòigear a b' fhaigse do 'n righ,
G'am bu dual gaisge agus mor ghniomh,
Thuit sid air laimh Oscair thall,
'S chaidh masladh gu righ na h-Eirinn

Nuair a chunnaic an Cairbhi ruadh
Oscar sior-shnaidheadh an t-sluaigh,
An t-sleagh nimhe (13) bha' na dhorn
Thilg e sud an comhdhail Oscair.

Thuit Oscar air a ghlun deas
'S an t-sleagh nimhe roimh chneas,
S thug e 'n ath urchair a null
Ma choimeachd fhuilt agus fheusaig

An sin thuirt sluagh Chairbhi ri Mhac :

" Eirich, Airt, is glac do chlaidheamh,
'S dean seasamh an àite t'athar,
Mur 'eil an t-eug ort a' brathadh,
Measar dhuinne gur mac rath thu."

Thug e 'n ath urchair an àird
'S ar leinne gum bu lèoir a h-àird,
'S leagadh leis aig meud a chuims'
Art Mac Chairbhi air an ath urchair.

Sluagh Chairbhi bu gharg gleachd,
Chuir iad Cath Gabhra (14) mu cheap ;
Chum 's gum faighteadh leo buaidh làrach,
Air faicinn Oscar gu cràiteach.

Thog e leacag thana chruaidh
Thar na talmhainn, taobh a' bhruthaich,
'S bhriste Cath-Gabhra mu cheap ;
'S e gniomh mu dheireadh mo dheagh mhic

" Togaibh leibh mi nise, Fhiann,
Ni nach d' rinn sibh roimhe riamh,
Thugaibh mi gu tulaich ghlain,
Ach gum buin sibh dhiom an t-eudach" (15)

Thog sin leinn an t-Oscar àluinn
Air bharraibh (16) nan sleagha àrda,
'S thug sinn da iomrachadh grinn,
Gus an d' thàinig sinn tigh Fhinn

Chuala sinn air traigh mu thuath,
Eubhach sluaigh is faobhar arm,
'S chlisg air gaisgich gu luath,
Mu'n robh Oscar a' fàs marbh.

" Marbhaisg ort, a mhic nam buadh, (17)
Ni thu breag an darna uair,
Loingeas mo sheanar a t' ann,
Is iad a' teachd le cobhair thugainn."

Bheannaich sinn uile do dh' Fhionn
Ma bheannaich, cha do bheannaich dhuinn ;
Shil na deòir fhala o rosg,
'S thionndaidh e ruinn a chùlaobh

" Is miosa, mhic, a bha thu dheth
An latha sin bha sinn 'n Dun-sgàthaich, (18)
Nuair shnàmhadh na geòidh (19) air do chneas,
'S e mo lamh-sa rinn do leigheas."

" Mo leigheas cha 'n ann le fàs, (20)
'S ni mò nìtear e gu bràth,
'N t-sleagh dhomhain 's an taobh a deas
Cha dual gu'n deantar a leigheas."

" Is miosa, mhic, a bha thu dheth
An la bha sinn an Dundealgain,
Shnàmhadh na geòidh air do chneas
'S i mo làmh-sa rinn do leigheas."

" Mo leigheas cha'n ann le fàs
'S ni mò nìtear e gu bràth,
O na tha sleagh nan seachd seang,
Eadar m' àirnean agus m' imleag."

" 'S truagh nach mise a thuit ann
An cath Gabhra grianach gann,

'S tusa bhi 'n ear 's an iar,
'G imeachd roimh na Fianntai, Oscair."

" Ged bu tusa thuiteadh ann
An cath Gabhra grianach gann,
Aon osna 'n ear no 'n iar
Cha chluinnteadh', gad iargain aig Oscar. (21)

" Cha d' fhiosraich duine riamh
Cridhe feòla bhi am chliabh,
Ach cridhe de chuinn a chuir (22)
'N dèis a chomdachadh le stàilinn.

" Ach donnalaich nan con ri m' thaobh.
Agus bùireadh nan seann laoch,
'S gul a' bhannail mu seach,
Sid an rud a chràidh mo chridhe."

" Laogh mo laoigh thu, laogh mo laoigh,
Leanabh mo leinibh, ghil, chaoil,
Mo chridhe leumadh mar lon (23)
'S mo chreach lèir nach eirich Oscar.

" Bàs Oscair a chraidh mi 'm chridhe,
Treun fear Eirinn, 's mòr g'ar dìth,
C' àite am faca mi ri m' linn
Aon cho cruaidh riut air chùl loinn."

Cha chaoineadh bean a fear fhéin,
'S cha chaoineadh piuthar a brathair—
Na bha sin uile mu 'n teach
Bha sinn uile caoineadh Oscair.

Mise bheireadh seachad fhéin
Fitheach dubh mo mhi-cheill
A chòig tha sinn mu'n chlàr
Ach sùil fir a bhi' ga shocadh. (24)

NOTES.

(1) *Triath* (chief) means the poet's best effort or masterpiece. In his effort the poet has marvellously succeeded, but, on comparison with other ballads or poems ascribed to him, there is evidence of a higher and more far-reaching stretch of the poetic mind. These evidences, few in number as they are, fortunately, are out of reach of the spuriousness ascribed to the works published by " Macpherson".

(2) *Oil.* It is a matter of discussion what *oil* means. In this recitation there is no doubt as to the meaning being the same as *Ged bu thoil le*, although " It is the will of the poet", but in the common conventional expression, *Ge b' oil leat* (in spite of you), it is doubtful but that there is a verb *oil* which might convey a meaning directly opposite. Very possibly it conveys an idea that the will of the person addressed is of no consequence as to the result.

(3) *Calma* implies the confidence of superior strength, and it is noticeable that strong people are not usually so fiery and cross-grained as weaker people.

(4) *Cis*, tribute. The Fians, as already pointed out, were not tributary to any king of Ireland, and the usurper, when he brought the whole country under one sway, naturally sought the friendship of these warriors. They must have been a powerful band when three hundred brave men were detached as bodyguard of their leader's grandson.

As to the stanzas which are here awanting, it was endeavoured by the writer to supply the failure of the reciter's memory by quoting to him from other copies of the poem in preservation in Campbell of Islay's book of the Fians. but unsuccessfully. The utmost that could be got from him was, that such expressions might have been, but he did not remember them.

(5) *Baobh*, an evil woman, hence a common name applied to witches. *Gheibh bao' guidhe ach cha n-fhaigh h-anam tròcair*, an ill woman gets her wish, but her soul gets no mercy. The word here does not imply more than that the woman was not of mortal race. From the poem it cannot be inferred that there is any island or special place for the souls of the departed, as is commonly asserted to have been the old pre-Christian faith. The poet's view is entirely confined to the present visible world, as it is also in the Mosaic teachings.

(6) *Caogad.* This word is not in common use, though it frequently occurs in Ossianic ballads. Nine is given as its most probable meaning. Nine as the multiple or cube of three is a mystic number, and occurs frequently.

(7) *Teamhair* denotes the place better known in modern times as "Tara's Halls". Its locality is not definitely fixed; all that can be safely inferred is, that it was the abode of the high king of Ireland (*Ard righ Eirinn*). "Where once the Harp of Erin the soul of music shed."

(8) At this stage the words occur in other poems connected with this battle : "*Bha sinn an oidhche sin gun chobhair thall sa bhos aig taobh na h-amhuinn*" (We were that night without succour on this and that side of the river). The river denoted is perhaps the Bann, where probably also Finn MacCowal, when a stripling, killed *Arcaidh dubh iasgair* (dark Arci the fisher) who had slain his father, *Cumhail.*

(9) *Loinnearachd,* martial music and the tramp of armed men.

(10) *Masladh.* It was a matter of doubt to the reciter, as it has been to every commentator, whether the word should be *masladh* (disgrace), or *mosgladh* (warning). Either is suitable.

(11) Here occurs in other versions, "*Mungan MacSeire a bha san Ròimhe chomhraigeadh e ciad claidheamh glas.*" The introduction of this champion, though the slaying of him is creditable to Oscar, is inadmissible as part of the original poem ; it savours too much of the Middle Ages.

It was a common saying, in all old tales (*sgeulachdan*), that a redoubtable warrior had " The combat of a hundred men on his hands". In the north-west islands, *Domhal Mac Iain ic Sheumais,* who fought the battle of Carinish in Uist, is the last who is said to have had the combat of a hundred men on his hand (*comhrag ceud*).

(12) *Coig fichead Cairbhi ruadh.* The men were called Cairvi by the reciter, and were probably men resembling the king in personal appearance and dress, kept for the purpose of misleading the enemy in the heat of the conflict. A ruse of the same kind is alluded to in Shakespeare, in *Henry IV*, Act V, Scene 3, at the battle of Shrewsbury—

> "*Douglas*—And I do lament thee in the battle thus,
> Because some tell me that thou art a king.
> *Blunt*—They tell thee true."

(13) *Nimhe* means deadly piercing, or death inflicting. There is no evidence that the Celtic tribes used poisoned weapons.

(14) *Cath Gabhra.* A helmet (?). The reciter had here *Cath Gabhra* (the battle of Gavra), which he explained as being "The king's dress", but did not know why it was so called. The word is probably *Cathbharr*, given in Lhuyd's Dictionary in his *Archæologia* as a helmet, quoting it from Plunket, one of the oldest Irish Glossaries. It is easily resolvable into Cath-bharr, a war head-piece. *Ceap* means a block, a pillar, or post, shoe-maker's last, round which or upon which anything is placed.

(15) *Eudach,* clothes. Some say this was a shirt of chain-mail (*eididh cruadhach*), but the reciter said, probably with more correctness, that the whole of Oscar's dress was stripped off previous to his burial. This also more agrees with the fay woman having been seen washing his clothes, the sight of which, previous to that vision, not having been an omen of evil. "*Gus an d thainig an diugh an aoibh sin cha b' olc a tional.*"

(16) *Air bharraibh* here evidently means on crossed spears, not as *barr* commonly means, on the points.

(17) *Mhic nam buadh,* gifted one. The saying is probably that of Oscar, on word being brought to him that sounds were heard on the beach. He thought they might be part of the deceitful plans laid by Cairbré for the destruction of the Fians.

(18) *Dùnsgàthaich* is said to be in Sleat in Skye, and that it was there that Cuchullin left Conlaoch his son, whom he afterwards killed, in ignorance of his identity. The poems referring to it have the appearance of being ante-Ossianic. *Dundealgain* is given in Lhuyd's *Archæologia* as Dundalk in Ireland.

(19) *Geoidh.* Geese swimming on the breast of the wounded hero means excessive loss of blood. In other versions. notably that in Gillies' collection, the phrase occurs (cranes would swim on thy breast) [*Shnambadh na corran roimh d' chneas*], denoting a gaping wound. *Curra* or *corra,* a heron, or ungainly bird, is also employed to denote birds in the same sense in which it occurs in jail-bird (*Corracha margaidh*), *i.e.,* market herons, birds or people who haunt markets or places where they are likely to find employment, though that employment may not be of much responsibility or pay. It is the word used in the Gaelic Scriptures to denote the "Fellows of the baser sort", whom the Jews at Thessalonica stirred up to annoy the Apostles. It is also said to denote children born in adultery, who, in all probability, have no one to look after them. *Aithris an darna curra air a churra cile* is an expression meaning the reproach of one worthless woman of another, much the same as *Aithris bradaig air breugaig, i.e.,* the thief's reproach of the liar.

(20) *Fàs.* It is not quite clear what this expression means, whether it is *le fàs* (by gradual growth), *i.e.*, healing, or *ri fas* (it is not destined to heal).

(21) *Gad iargain aig Oscar.* It was said by the reciter that this expression was to lessen the grandfather's grief by a pretended indifference on the part of the dying hero.

(22) *Chuinn a chuir.* The reciter did not know the meaning of this expression, but explained it as *ungadh ghlain* (clean anointing). It is quite a rational explanation that it is *Cuibhne-chuir*, a twisted antler, than which not even a stone is more unfeeling. If covered with iron, as in the text, nothing more incapable of emotion can be conceived.

(23) *Lon* was another word the reciter did not know the meaning of. He thought that in this case its common meaning was excessive love or desire or appetite, and meant that " Fin" had an overpowering love for his grandchild. It is a common Gaelic expression (*Co luath ris na luin*) [as swift as deer], and the expression likely means that the speaker's heart was beating swiftly or violently. Some say that *luin* is a form of *lothain*, a leash of deerhounds, but in this case more probably it denotes some kind of deer, perhaps an elk or some other animal of the deer kind.

(24) The translation here given is but guess-work. The main objection to it is that the gloom of sorrow and unreason are not in Gaelic represented by the blackness of the raven. The knowledge with which that bird is credited (*Fios fithich*) is not that of the "shadow of coming events", but the almost instinctive knowledge that the bird has of prey or carrion (*Fios fithich gu roic*), upon which it feeds with more relish than on prey that has been killed. There is no instance within the range of Gaelic literature, so far as the writer knows, in which the bird is credited with a knowledge of future events. *Coigead* in this stanza is not a word in conventional use. *Coig* is the common numeral five, and following the analogy of *fichead, triochad,* which is given in Lhuyd's *Archæologia,* as meaning thirty, it may mean fifty, but the indication is not certain. *Socadh* is the word used when wood, which has shrunk through dryness, is put again in water and becomes tight ; thus, when a boat which has been long exposed on the beach is again launched, and the water has had due effect upon it, the wood recovers itself and the boat is said to be seasoned (*air a socadh.*) *Chlàr* may mean bier.

III.—GOLL,

WHO was the leader of the Clanna Morna, seems to have ranked as the second best hero of the Fian band. The name given to him in the lays is Goll of Blows (*Goll na Beumanan*), very probably derived from his skill as an expert and powerful swordsman. It is said of him that he never fell in the combats of men (*an comhrag dhaoine*), and that he was squint-eyed, whence his name (*Gol-shùil*), which is said to be contracted into Goll. He had the *cis-chnàmh*, or right to the marrow-bones. Goll is mentioned in the "Lay of the Banners" (*Duan nam Brataichean*) and also in the "Lay of Conn, Son of the Red" (*Conn Mac an Deirg*).

Goll's great stature is noticed by Dunbar in one of his poems, in which he calls him

> "My fader meikle Gow MacMorna,
> Out of his moderis wame was schorne :
> For littleness was so forlorn,
> Siccan a kemp to beir."

It is noticeable how this hero, so powerful in after life, was so small and dwarfish at birth. Of his mother it is said, that when she grew old she lost her teeth, and her son claimed marrow-bones for her benefit. This is told in the following story :

"THANKS TO GOLL, HE KILLED HIS MOTHER."

The growing lad who opposed him in the story, is called Coireal of Bone (*Coireal o Cnàimh*), but, from his strength and youth, the probability is that the one denoted by the story is Oscar, and one good oral authority

4

on tales of this kind said it was Oscar. Coireal is not
mentioned in any other tale known to the writer. The
story is given as it came to hand.

Coireal was the son of a daughter of Fionn, and when
he was a soft growing lad he bade fair to be the strongest
and most powerful of the Fian band. Goll's mother was
aged, and had lost her teeth, and the biggest bones were
kept for her, and she lived on the marrow. Coireal was
mortified that he had to give every bone that had marrow
in it to the old woman. One day he got a large bone
which he refused to give up. Fionn was afraid to offend
Goll, and his judgment was, that a hole should be made
in a plank of wood and the bone set in it, that Goll
should pull the one end and Coireal the other ; whoever
drew the bone through the hole would have the right to
it. This was done, and it was likely that Coireal would
have the bone. He pulled Goll's hand to the mouth of
the hole. Fionn then said that the bone must be turned,
and the thick end given to Goll. They did so, and at
long last Goll took with him the bone. He drew the
bone and threw it at Coireal in order to kill him dead
Coireal saw it coming, and bent his head out of the way.
The bone struck the old woman and killed her. "Thanks
to Goll", said Coireal, "he has killed his mother." Hence
the proverb, "*Tapadh le Goll, mharbh e mhàthair.*"

'. Is e mac nighean Fhinn a bha ann an Coireal, 'se b' ainm
dhà Coireal o cnàimh 's nuair bha e 'na bhogbhalach bha
choltas air gur h-è duine bu làidire 's a b' fhoghaintich' a bhiodh
san Fheinn. Bha màthair Ghuill sean, agus air call a fiaclan,
agus bha na cnaimhean bu mhotha air an cumail air a son, agus
bha i tighinn beo air an smior. Bha Coireal air a ghualadh
gum feumadh e h-uile cnàimh sam biodh smior thoirt do 'n
chaillich.

Latha bha sin fhuair e cnàimh mòr agus dhiult e thoirt
seachad. Bha eagal air Fionn corruich a chur air Goll, agus
'se bhreth thug e, gum biodh toll air a chur ann an déile fiodh,

agus an cnàimh air a chur ann agus gu 'n slaodadh Goll an darna ceann, agus Coireal an ceann eile, agus co sam dhiu bheireadh an cnaimh a mach roimh 'n toll, gum biodh an cnàimh leis.

Rinneadh so, 's bha choltas gum bitheadh an cnàimh aig Coireal; thug e lamhan Ghuill gu bial an tuill, Thuirt Fionn an so, gum feumadh an cnàimh a thiunndadh agus an ceann garbh thoirt do Gholl. Rinneadh so 's mu dheire thall thug Goll leis an cnàimh. Thug e 'n tarruing ad air a chnàimh, agus thilg e air Coireal e, los a spadadh. Chunnaic Coireal e tighinn, 's chrom e cheann as an rathad. Bhuail an cnàimh a' chailleach, agus mharbh e i. "Tapadh le Goll," orsa Coireal, "mhàrbh e mhàthair," agus is ann uaith sin a thainig an sean-fhocal.

Dearmaid was, as already said, the only son of Fionn's twin and only sister. He had a beauty-spot (*ball seirc*) on his face, and it was said that no woman ever saw it but fell in love with him. He was himself the third best hero of the Fians (*Treas lamh feum na Fèinne*), and is spoken of as being very good-looking, and an ardent admirer of the fair sex; the common name given to him is the "Yellow-haired Dermid of women" (*Dearmaid Buidhe nam ban*), besides being bold and courageous. On the day of the battle of Gentle Streams (*Amhuinn nan Sruth Seimh*) he raised his visor, and Grainne, his uncle's wife, who was looking at the combatants, saw the beauty-spot and fell madly in love with Dermid. In his old age Fionn had married Grainne, daughter of the Earl of Ulster, which then formed one of the five parts of Ireland. "The daughter of the Earl of Ulster" (*Nighean Iarla choig Ulainn*), or, as some say, "The daughter of *Cormac* of Cuilin" (*Nighean Charmaig o Chuillin*). She seems to have been a woman of small size, and not over nice in her selection of lovers. Dermid long continued indifferent to her allurements, and placed her under spells (*fo gheasaibh*) that she was not to appear before him either by night or day, clothed or unclothed, on foot or on horseback, in company or without company. She, however, went to a fairy woman (*bean shith*), and got garments made from mountain down (*Canach an t-sleibh*). She came with this garment on, riding on a he-goat in the dusk of the evening, when it was neither light nor dark, and thus it could not be said that she was clothed or unclothed, on foot or on horse-back, in company or without company, and consequently

was deemed free from the spell laid upon her. Her
attentions at last came to be a persecution, and Dermid
consulted his uncle, the solver of questions (*Fionn fear
fuasgladh cheist*), that he might know what to do. The
question which he put to Finn was, "Is it best to bear
reproach, or decay?" (*Co dhiu 's fhearr guth na meath?*)
Fionn's answer was, " Do not decay while you live, my
sister's son" (*Na meath 's tu beo mhic mo pheathar*).

Some time after this Dermid went off with Grainne,
but where he passed the night he left unbroken bread to
show that he was still blameless. It was while on this
flight, with the Féinne after them, that the incident
occurred of Dermid's being up a tree, when Oscar and
Conn or Goll were down below playing at *tailcasg* (see
note). When Oscar was likely to win, some say through
Dermid dropping a berry on the spot on which he was
to play, his opponent said, " The faithful teaching of
Dermid causes Oscar's ready play" (*Teagasg dhileas
Dhiarmaid, rinn cluich calamh Oscair*). Oscar replied,
" Though you don't like that man, we loved him well"
(*Ged nach toil leatsa an duine sin bu toil leinne e*).
Dermid after this fled to a cave in the hills. Locally, a
cave in Kenavarra Hill, in the west end of Tiree, is said
to have been the cave in question. This, however, may
be merely the tendency of every place to localise
tradition. It is said that, when climbing the hill, a voice
called to him, " Dermid, take the hill slantwise" (*Dhearmaid fiar am bruthach*) ; to which he replied, " How can
I do that when Thin-man is after me?" (*Ciamar ni mi
sin dar tha Caoilte as mo dheigh?*) In the cave, a night
of mist and storm came on, so wild that Dermid would
not venture out of the cave under the most urgent
necessity (*cion-modh*). He accordingly went to the
furthest off end of the cave. Unfavourable as the night
was, *Ciuthach mac-an Doill*, whose name is probably a
slight difference of *Ceathach mac-an Doill* (Mist, son of

Darkness), came in from the western ocean in a coracle
with two oars (*curachan*), and having drawn it into the
cave, he was about to embrace Grainne, when Dermid
slew him. When Grainne was returning to the sheltered
part of the cave, she made a remark, that she had been
for so long a time with the third best hero of the Fians,
and he had not been so bold to her. Next day, when
they started on further flight, he left broken bread behind
him. When he was caught and brought back to the
Fians, Fionn, who could not bring himself to kill his
sister's son, and besides that, like Achilles, Dermid could
only be killed by the heel, sent him to hunt the wild
boar. His death lay in *bonn du na coise*, or fore-part of
the heel, and after the boar was slain, Fionn made him
measure the animal with his foot.

> " Dermid, measure the boar,
>   How many feet from nostril to heel?"

> " Dhearmaid tomhais an torc,
>   Co meud troigh o' shoic gu shail?"

It was found to be sixteen feet, and no harm came of
that measurement. Fionn then asked him to measure
the boar against the bristle (*an aghaidh a chuilg*), in
hope that one of the bristles might inflict a death-
wound. Dermid did so, and one of the bristles penetrated the fore-part of his heel (*bonn du na coise*), where
his death lay. As he grew faint, a drink from the hands
of his uncle Fionn would have revived him, and Fionn,
from an adjoining well, was going to give him a drink.
When he thought of his nephew he raised his hands full
of water, and when he thought of Grainne he allowed
the water again to fall on the ground. While he was
thus wavering Dermid died. " Is not this", said Fionn
to Grainne, "the sorest cry that ever you heard?" (*An
glaodh 's gort chual tu riamh*). "No," she said, "but
the cry of Ciuthach under the soft hands of Dermid"

(*Glaodh Chiuthach o lamhan boga Dhiarmaid*). It was then that Fionn became aware of the blamelessness and long-enduring suffering of Dermid.

In another version of Dermid's flight with Grainne, it is said: When Dermid fled with Grainne there was fresh snow on the ground. He turned his shoes backward, and the Féinn in pursuit, thinking the dogs were going the wrong way, were killing them. Wherever Dermid passed the night he left unbroken bread (*aran slan*) to show his guiltlessness. At last they came to a cave, and when resting in it a giant (*Ciuthach*) came in with a string of fish (*gad éisg*). He then began disporting himself (*deasachd*), and Grainne said to Dermid, "That is different from being a lump on the side of the cave" ("*Cha b' ionnan sud sa bhi air tom taobh na h-uamha*"). On this Diarmaid killed Ciuthach. Grainne put her feet in a pool of water, and some of it splashed on her. She said, "I am so long a time going with the third best hero of the Fians, and he never approached so near" ("*Tha mi 'n uiread so ùine air falbh le treasa làmh fheum na Féinne, 's cha d' thainig e riamh co dlù sud orm*"). Then Dermid left broken bread behind him. Bran was sent after him, and he was caught. It was then he was sent to kill the boar, and Fionn made him measure it against the bristles. It was thirteen feet of good measure (*tri lamhan deug de dheagh thomhas*).

There is also another version of the incident, to the effect: On the night of Fionn's marriage with Grainne the Feinn were at Kennavara. The bones thrown out at the door from the feast set the dogs fighting. They went out to separate them, and it was then Grainne saw Diarmad's beauty-spot (*ball seirc*), which no woman could see without falling in love with him. She wanted Diarmad to run away with her, but he would not. At last, seeing she would otherwise have his life, he came to Fionn and asked him (*as per former story*). He did this thrice, and at last receiving the same replies, he ran away with her to the Big Cave (*Uamh mhor*). It was winter time, and he was there under hiding (*air chomhach*). One day of snow and sleet he went to the door of the cave, when the *Ciuthach mòr* came in with his boat from the sea, and drew it in on a shelf in the cave. He and Diarmad played *tailcasg* and *Ciuthach* won. As his prize he asked the woman. Diarmad said that he would have, who had the sharpest blade and hardest edge (*is géire lann 's is cruaidhe faobhar*). He took off the Ciuthach's head. Every night he put a cold stone between himself and Grainne. In the spring Manus and his men came. The Féinn gave the war-cry (*gaoir-chath*). Diarmad said, "I am under oaths and vows where I hear that to answer it" ("*Tha mionnan is boidean orm, far an cluinn mi sid gum freagair mi e*"). Fionn and Manus fought hand to hand on Trai-Bhi, and were out to the waist (*ionad a chrios*) in the water. Diarmad went to the rescue and saved Fionn. When the strife was over, order was given to make a circuit round him and make a captive of him. He jumped over Fionn's head and made for the hill. "Dermid, take the hill aslant." "That is difficult for me, and Thin-man after me." ("*Dhiarmaid fiar am bruthach.*" "*Is deacair sin domhs', agus Caoilt' as mo dheaghaidh.*") He was caught, and Fionn by his knowledge tooth (*deud fios*) knew his death could only be by his sole (*bhas am bonn du a choise*). He was then sent against the wild boar in Ben-nevis. In two or three days he killed it. Fionn said to him, "You are tired" ("*Tha thu sgith*"); but when he remembered Grainne, he made him measure the boar against the bristles. "You are wounded, Dermid. With what can you be healed?" ("*Tha thu goirt a Dhiarmaid. De dheanamh do leigheas?*") When Dermid died Fionn said to Grainne, "That is the hardest cry you ever

heard" ("*Sid an glaodh is cruaidh chuala tu riamh*"),
and she said no, it was that of Ciuthach. The innocence
of Dermid was thus discovered, and Grainne was buried
alive.

This encounter with the wild pig is given in the following lay, which was taken down from the recitation of
John Sinclair, Barrapol, an old man of about eighty
years of age, who said he learned it in his youth from
Peter Carmichael, Tiree, who was at that time an old
man. It was written down in the summer of 1881.

THE LAY OF DERMID.

Listen shortly if you care for a hymn
Of the company to be deplored,
Grainne and hospitable Fionn,
And the son of Dui'ne of noblest gifts.
The glen, and the glen beside it,
Where sweetly sounded the voice of deer and elk,
And the Fians often were
In keen pursuit, east and west, with dogs.
As we sat on the blue Ben Gulban,
Whose summits are the loveliest beneath the sun,
Often the streams were made red
By the Fians hunting the deer.
They prevailed, and great was the deceit,
On the son of Dui'ne of ruddy hue,
To go to Ben Gulban to hunt
The boar, that was difficult for weapon to subdue
"Dermid," she said, "do not answer the hunt,
And do not frequent the deceitful hill-top;
Be not near to Fionn MacCumhal,
As he is lamenting the loss of his wife."
"Grainne, dearest of women," he said,
"Do not make your consort, men's disgrace.
I would answer the sound of the hunt,
Despite all the men of the Fians."

They awoke the monster from its sleep,
The troop of heroes up the glen,
Listening to the noise of the Fians
As they came in their eagerness
High above where it lay.
They let loose their good hounds,
Fionn's, and the huntsmen's hounds,
And they the white boar mangled,
Until its brain was turned.
Son of Dui'ne—man of strength,
If your mighty deed will be successful,
Be mindful of your arm,
For it is under it that peace will be done.
The son of Dui'ne of favouring weapons,
On seeing the monster,
Taking it from his own gentle fair side,
He thrust the spear into the wild beast's heel.
He drew a shaft from his white fair hand
To thrust it into its body.
And the shaft was broken in three,
Without any part going into the boar.
He drew his old sword from its sheath,
Since it was victorious on every field,
And he slew the great wild beast,
And escaped from it himself uninjured.
Sadness came upon hospitable Fionn,
And he threw himself westward on the hillock,
That the son of Dui'ne of favouring weapons
Should escape unhurt from the boar.
After being some time silent,
He said, and evil was the saying,
" Dermid, measure the boar,
How many feet from snout to heel?"
He did not refuse Fionn's entreaty,
And regretful to us was his coming.
He measured the boar along the spine.

The son of Dui'ne of weighty step ;
" Sixteen feet of sure measure
In the spine of the wild pig."
" That is not it at all," said Fionn ;
" Measure it again, Dermid,
Measure it against (the bristle) minutely,
You will be rewarded accordingly,
The choice of sharp-edged new war-weapons."
He measured, and it was no fortunate effort,
The son of Dui'ne of mighty step ;
The rough venomous bristle penetrated
The sole of the hero, who was strong in fight.
" One drink from your cup, Fionn,
Good king, to succour me ;
Since I have lost my energy and substance
Alas ! I am wretched, if you don't give it'.'
" I will not give you a drink,
Neither will I quench your thirst ;
Little you ever did for my benefit,
Much more you did to my loss."
" I never did you any harm,
Here or there, east or west,
But going with Grainne in secret
Appearance, taking me under spells."
Then fell wounded,
The son of Dui'ne of twined locks,
The most enduring hero of the Fians,
On the south-west hillock.
Powerful to attract women,
Son of Dui'ne of highest gifts.
Of love-making there is no mention
Since the earth has covered his face.
There was blueness and greyness in his eye,
There was smoothness and beauty in his cheek,
There was strength, there was valour in the hero,
And these were free from death's breast.

We buried in the same hillock,
When settling the wild pig,
Grainne, daughter of Cormac o Coolin,
The two dogs and Dermid.

LAOIDH DHIARMAID.

Eisdibh beag ma 's aill leibh laoidh
Air a chuideachd chaoidh so a craidh,
Air Grainne is air Fionn fial,
'S air Mac o Duimhne a b' fhearr buaidh.
An gleann sin, 's an gleann ri thaobh,
Far am bu bhinn guth feidh 's loin,
Far 'm b' tric a bhiodh an Fhéinn
Sear 's siar gu dian le 'n coin.
'Nar suidhe dhuinn air Beinn Ghulbainn,
A 's aille tullaichean tha fo'n 'n Ghrein,
Is tric bha na sruthain dearg
Aig an Fhéinn a' sealg nam fiadh.
Dh' iomair iad, 's bu mhor a 'cheilg,
Air Mac o Duibhne 'bu dearg lith,
'Dhol a bheinn Ghulbainn a shealg
An tuirc, 'bu deacair 'airm a chlaoidh.
"A Dhiarmaid (ors ise) na freagair an fhaoghaid,
'S na taghaill am fireach breugach,
'S na bi teann air Fionn MacCumhail,
O 's caoidheadh leis bhi gun cheile."
"A ghaoil nam ban, a Ghrainne (ors esan),
Na toill thusa nair' ad chéile,
Fhreagarainn-sa guth na seilge
A' cheart aindheoin fir na Féinne."
Dhuisg iad a 'bheisd as a suain,
Na freiceadan shuas air a 'ghleann,
An eisdeachd ri gairich nam Fiann
'S iad gu dian os a cionn.
Leig iad ris na deadh ghaothair,
Gaothair Fhinn, 's fir na seilg,
'S gu 'n d' rinn iad mhuc bhàn a liodairt,

'S gus 'n robh h-eanchain air tionndadh.
Mhic o Duibhne a thréuin,
Ma 's e gu 'n deid do euchd leat,
Bi thusa cuimhneach air a laimh,
So an t-sith fa deanntear leat.
Mac o Duimhne nan arm aigh,
Air faicinn dha an uile-bheist,
O shlios thaobh-gheal shamhach thlàth,
Chas e 'n t-sleagh 'an sail an tuirc.
Tharruing e crann o 'n dorn gheal bhan
A chum a shathadh 'na chorp.
'S bhristeadh leis an crann 'na thri,
Gun aon mhir a chur san torc.
Tharruing e an t-sean lann as an truaill,
O' si buaidh buaidh gach blàir,
'S mharbhadh leis an uile-bheist,
'S thearuin e fhein uaipe slan.
Luidh sprochd air Fionn fial,
'S leig se e fhein siar air a 'chnoc,
Mac o Duimhne nan arm aigh
Dhol as slan air an torc.
Air dha bhi tamull 'na thosd,
Labhair e 's gum b' ole r' 'radhain,
" Dhearmaid tomhais an torc
Co mhiad troidh o shoic gu shàil ?"
Cha do dhiult e achanaich Fhinn,
'S b' aithreach leinn a theachd o' tigh
Thomhais e 'n torc air a dhruim,
Mac o' Duimhne an trom troidh ;
" Sia troidhean diag de dh' fhior thomhas
Ann an druim na muice fiadhaich."
" Cha 'n e sin idir an tomhas, ors Fionn,
Tomhais e rithist a Dhiarmaid,
Dhiarmaid tomhais e rithist an aghaidh gu mion.
Geibheadh tu do dhuais da chionn,
Raoghadh nan arm roinn-gheur ùr."
Thomhais e 's cha bu thuras àigh,
Mac o Duimhne an trom troidh ;

Tholl am bior-nimh bha garg,
Bonn an laoch, bu gharg 'san trod,
" Aon deoch as do chuaich, Fhinn,
A dheadh righ gu mo chobhair ;
O 'n chaill mi mo bhladh 's mo bhrigh
Ochan 's truaigh mi mar d' thoir."
" Cha d' thoir mise dhuitsa deoch,
Cha mho chaisgeas mi t-iotadh,
'S beag a rinn thu riamh do 'm leas ;
'S mo gu mor a rinn thu 'm ainleas."
" Cha d' rinn mise cron ort riamh,
Thall na bhos sear neo siar ;
Ach imeachd le Grainne fo bhraid,
Tuar 'gam thoirt fuidh gheasaibh."
Thuit e sin fuidh chreuchd,
Mac o Duimhne nan ciabh cleachd,
Sar fear fulanach nam Fiann,
Air an tullaich siar fo dheas.
Cumhachdach gu mealladh bhan,
Mac o Duimhne bu mhor buaidh ;
Air suiridhe cha do chuireadh duil,
Bho 'n chaidh an ùir air a ghruaidh.
Bha guirme, bha glaise 'na shuil,
Bha mine bha maise 'na ghruaidh ;
Bha spionnadh, bha tabhachd san laoch,
'S bha sid saor o cneas bais.
Dh' adhlaic sinn air an aon tulaich,
An àm suidheachadh na muice fiadhaich,
Grainne nic Chormaic a' Chuillinn,
Da Chuilean, agus Diarmaid.

The immense size of the wild pig slain by Dermid,
and whose bristle was subsequently the cause of his
death, exceeds the size of any animal of the kind now
known. Probably, the size having been measured with
the foot, the hide of the animal must have been spread
on the ground, and, according to the lay, its measure
was taken from the very snout to the very heel of the

animal. In this way the height of the animal, as well as its length, would be taken into account. Its measure was not merely from head to tail, but also from snout to forehead, and from the root of the tail to the extremity of the foot on to the ground.

The precise colour of Dermid's hair is not always described by the same adjective. He is commonly called *buidhe*, or yellow, but he is also very commonly called *Diarmaid donn*, auburn, or brown shading off to yellow, as in the following verse, an Anacreontic verse by William Ross, one of the most popular of modern Gaelic bards :—

"About Fionn I would lilt a song,
 And of Auburn Dermid I fain would sing,
 But melody my harp will not raise
 But one on the love of maidens."

"Air Fionn gun togainn fonn,
 'S air Diarmaid donn bu mhath leum seinn,
 Ach duan cha tog mo chlarsach
 Ach dan air gradh nan caileagan."

Some say that the wound which caused Dermid's death was made by the bristle entering beneath his great toe (*fo ordag a choise*). Neither are reciters uniform as to who Grainne was the daughter of. That she was the daughter of the Earl or Jarl of Ulster has been here adopted from its having a preponderance of evidence in its favour, and being at least intelligible. In the poem above given she is called the daughter of Cormac of Coolin, which may be some other place different from Ulster (*Ulainn*).

V.—CAOILTE.

THE fastest runner among the Fianns was *Caoilte*, or
Thinman, whose name at first was *Daorglas* or *Gerglas*
(intensely grey). When at full speed he was said
to appear as three individuals, and this appearance he
presented when he returned with the arms on the day
of the "Battle of Sheaves". Some, however, maintain that the appearance of three was caused by the
height to which he lifted his feet when running.
Neither supposition is possible, but the story that Bran,
or Fionn's dog, when at full speed had the appearance of
a dog at every opening (*aig gach beallach*) presents the
same marvellous idea. It was said that a fairy sweetheart gave Thinman (*Caoilte*) a belt, telling him to put it
on, and not be afraid of any man :

> " Put the belt round your sides,
>   Son of Ronag, beloved of men,
>   And avoid not son of woman or mother,
>   That will come or has come on earth,
>   For hatred, for deliberation, or doughtiness."

> " Cur an crosan mu d' thaobh
>   Mhic Rònaig a ghaoil do dh' fhearaibh
>   'S na seachainn mac mna' no mathar
>   Thig no thainig air thalamh,
>   Air fhuath, no air athadh, no air eabhonadh."

The principal occasion on which this hero figures is in
"The Lay of the Magic Smith", when his swiftness or
activity led to the change in his name. The ballad, or
lay, is commonly called *Duan na Ceardaich*, or "The Lay
of the Smithy", and is as follows :

One day that we were on the rush covered plain,
Two fours, two folds, was our company,
Oscar, Derglas, and Diarmid,
Fionn himself was there, the son of Cumal.

There was seen coming towards us
A tall man on one leg,
One top eye in his forehead,
Always making straight for the son of Cumal.

Ugly was the coming of the Big man,
Ugly it was and deformed,
With his darksome helmet of skin, that did not grow
    twined.
Barely weaved and deeply red with rusted spots
(With his excessively large helmet
On his bare garments that had become ugly).

" Whence have you come, man ?
Or are you a clothier to shape skins ?"
" I am not a clothier to shape skins,

But I came to put you under spells,
Since you are a people engaged in warfare.
That you follow me an easy-going company
Westward to the door of my smithy.

Lon Macliven is my name,
I am the best warrior in this part of the country.
King ! it is a pity of the woman who reared me,
Myself and my other two brothers."

Var. [Edmond Tosny is my name,
If you knew me very well,
And I do smith work
To the Norse King in Spylie."]

" Where, wretch, is your smithy ?
And will we be the better of seeing it ?"

5

" See you it if you 're able,
And if I am able you won't !"

They then became four companies,
Like five out on a bare expanse ;
One company of these was the smith,
And another company was Derglas.

Lon made off like the swift spring wind,
Over the dark glens of the hill,
And we could only see with difficulty
Portions of skirts about his heels.

Var. [The smith would only take one step
Over every glen and desert.]

Fionn was behind at that time,
And a few nobles of the Fians,
As we descended to the bottom of the glen,
And ascending to the windy pass.

Then was heard the blowing of bellows,
And with the utmost difficulty a smithy was found.

" Delay a little," said the smith ;
" Don't close before me," said Derglas,
" Do not leave me here alone,
Westward, in the door of the smithy."
Var. [In a narrow place here alone.]

There were seven smiths joyfully at work,
Seven men ugly and unshapely.

The smith had seven hands,
Seven tongs broad and light,
Seven hammers knocking out sparks,
And Thinman could fully answer them all.

One of the smiths then spoke,
A grim and frowning man.

" What thinman is that, fearless one,
Who is stretching out fire for steel-making ?"

Then said Fionn, the solver of questions,
The man who did not require teaching,
" He will not bear this name without it being spread ;
Derglas was his name till now."

Thinman, the watcher of the smithy,
Had the deepest part of the fight,
And redder than the glow of coals from oak
Was his hue from the result of the labour.

Feud, Fàrd, and Faondail,
At your slender hand, son of the smithy,
And the long eastern sea (*muileartach*) that Dermid had,
Many a man in its time it killed.

DUAN NA CEARDAICH.

Latha dhuinn air Luachar Leòthaid
Da cheathra da chro air buidheann
Oscar, is Daorghlas, is Diarmad,
Bha Fionn fhéin ann 's b'e Mac Cumhail.

Chunnacas a' tighinn' nar còiribh
Aon fhear mòr, is e air aona chois
Aon suil mhullach an clàr aoduinn
'S e sior-dheanadh air Mac Cumhail.

Bu ghrannda tighinn an oglaich mhoir
Bu ghrannda sin 's bu duaichnidh
Le clogada ciar-dhu craicinn nach [dh'] fhas dualach,
Air mhaol bhearta 's air dhearg ruadh bhrig.
[Le clogada ceanna mhor ceutach
Air mhaol cididh a d' fhas duaichnidh.]

" Co as thaine tu, dhuine,
No 'n culaich thu gu cumadh chraicionn?"
" Cha chulaich mi gu cumadh chraicionn."

5 ²

Ach thainig mi g'ur cuir fo gheasaibh,
O 'n a 's luchd sibh tha freasdal armachd,
Sibh g'am leantuinn buidheann shocrach,
Siar gu dorsaibh mo cheardach.

Lon Mac Liòbhunn is e m' ainm
'S mi gaisgeach is fearr an taobh-sa
Righ ! gur nearachd bean a dh' araich mi
Mi fhein 's mo dha bhrathair eile."

[Eamunn Toisneadh b' e m' ainm
Na'm biodh agaibhs' orm beachd sgeula,
'S gum bithinn ri obair gobhainn
Aig righ Lochlin ann an Speula (*Spaoilidh*).]

" C'ait, a thruaill, am bheil do cheardach,
No'n fhearrda sinne (dol) g'a faicinn ? "
Faiceadh sibhse sin ma dh' fheudas
'S mu dh' fheudas mise cha-n fhaic sibh.

Chaidh iad sin' nan ceithir buidhnean
Mar choig a muigh an a Cuimrig
B'e buidheann dhiu sin an gobhainn
'S bu bhuidhean eile dhiu Daorghlas.

Thug Lon as, mar ghaoth luath earraich,
Mach roimh ghleannaibh dubh an t-sleibhe
'S cha 'n fhaiceamaide ach air eiginn
Cirb da eididh air a shailteann.
Var. [Cha deanadh an gobhann ach aona cheum
Thar gach glinne is fasaich.]

Bha Fionn air roinne (dheiridh) 'san uair sin,
'S beagan de dh' uaislibh na Féinne
Tearnadh le ùrlar a' ghlinne
Direadh ri bealach na gaoithe.

Chualas an sin builg' gan seideadh,
'S fhuaradh cheart air eiginn ceardach.

" Foiseadh beag ort," thuirt an gobhainn,
" Na druid romham," arsa Daorghlas,

" Na fàg mise so 'nam aonar
Siar mu dhorsan do cheardaich. "
Var. [An aite teann 's mi nam aonar.]
Bha seachd goibhnean ann ri mire
[Seachdnar] de dhaoine duaichnidh mi-shealbhach

Bha seachd làmhan air a' ghobhain,
Seachd teanchraichean leothar eatrom,
Seachd uird a bha ga spreigeadh
'S cha bu mhiosa fhreagradh Caoilte.

Labhair an sin fear de na goibhnean
Gu grimeach, agus gu gruamach,
" Co 'm fear caol tha sid gun tioma
Shineas a mach teine cruadhach."

" Sin," thuirt Fionn, fear fuasgladh cheiste
Lamh nach teagaisgear gun fhuathas,
" Cha bhi 'n t-ainm so air gun sgaoileadh
Bha Daor-ghlas air gus an uair so."

Caoilte fear faire na ceardaich
Sgial deirge 'n truid aige
'S bu deirg e na gual daraich
A shnuadh ri tarruing (toradh) na h-oibreach.

Fead agus Fàrd agus Faondail
Ri da làimh chaola mhic na ceardach
'S a' mhuireartach fhada bha aig Diarmad
'S ioma duine riamh a mharbh i.
Var. ['S an lamh (lann) fhada bha aig Diarmad,
Is iomadh latha riamh a dhearbh e.]

Another version of " The Lay of the Smithy" is as
follows :

One day that we were in the hunting hill,
We saw a sight from the east,
A big warlike hardy man,
And hateful to us was his coming our way.
With his black bundle of swarthy skin

With the bare part streaked and mottled red.
His cap about his bare deeply wrinkled scalp,
That was sharp, and he himself is forbidding.
One top eye in his forehead,
And ever making straight for the son of Cumal.
Then spoke Mac Cumal,
" Let not the man pass.
Put yourselves shoulder to shoulder,
And keep away the sallow-looking man.
Knowledge of your surname we would wish to have,
Since you have happened to come our way,
So that we may again tell a sure tale
Of what your object may be."
" Una, the daughter of Vulcan, was my mother,
The one woman who had most children,
And, O King! 'tis pity of the woman who reared
Myself and my other two brothers.
Lon Mac Livin is my baptismal name,
I am the best warrior in these parts,
And I will put you under spells,
Since you are a people who attend to warfare,
That you follow me an easy-going company,
West, to the door of my smithy."
" In what place is your smithy,
Or will we be the better of seeing it ?"
" Let you be finding it,
For if I can you will not find it."
Lon set off like a north wind in spring
Over the tops of the hills,
And he would only take one step
Over each red desert glen.
Going past the hillock,
The company came close upon each other ;
One of these was the smith,
Another company was Derglas ;
Fionn then was behind,

And a few of the nobles of the Féinne.
" Open quickly," said the smith.
" Close not before me," said Derglas.
" Leave me not here alone,
In a narrow place by myself."
" Youth of fairest look !
Confident am I of the speed of your feet,
And rise up quickly
To let the wandering youth in.
I never thought that Fionn ever had
One who would show his face in my house ;
May you enjoy your name Thinman,
You will not be called Derglas from this hour."

DUAN NA CEARDAICH.

Latha dhuinn bhi 'sa bheinn-t-seilg,
Chunnacas sealladh leinn bho 'n ear,
Fear mor colgarra cruaidh
'S gum b' fhuathach leinn e thi'nn 'nar car.
Le bhondal du ciar-dhu craicionn
Le lionan[1] breac as dath ruadh air.
Le churrachd mu chiona-mhaoil cheusaidh
Bha geur 's e ro-ghruamach.
'S aon sùil mhullach an clar-aodainn,
'S e sior-dheanadh air Mac Cumhail.
Sin mar labhair Mac Cumhail,
" Na leigibh an duine seachad
Cuiribh air guailleadh ri cheile
'S cumaibh uaibh am fear odhar."
Fios do shloinnidh b' aill leinn uait
O'n tharladh dhuit tighinn 'nar car.

[1] *Lionan.* There are doubts as to the word here meant. Some versions would lead one to think that the mantle of skins which the smith wore in some parts had become stained and rusty.

'S gu'n innseamaid a rìs beachd-sgeula
De tha thu air a shon.
"Una ni Mhulcain b'i mo mhathair
Aona-bhean a b' fhearr (torach) cloinne
'S a Righ! gur niarachd bean a dh' àraich
Mi fhin 's mo dha bhrathair eile
'Se Lunn Mac Liobhunn m' ainm baistidh
'S mi gaisgeach 's fhearr an taobh-sa
'S cuiridh mi sibhse fo gheasan
O'n is luchd tha freasdal arm sibh
Sibh g'am leantuinn buidhean shocrach
Siar gu dorus mo cheardaich."
"Cion an t-aite 'm bheil do cheardach
No 'n fheaird sinne ri faicinn?"
"Bi sibhse nise 'ga faotainn,
'S ma dh' fhaotas mise cha-n fhaigh sibh."
Thug Lunn as mar ghaoth tuath earraich
Mach bhar beannda dubh an t-sleibh
'S cha ghearradh e ach aona-cheum
Thar gach h-aona ghleann ruadh fasaich
Dol seachad siar air an tulaich
Chas am buidheann air a cheile
Bu bhuidheann dhiu sin an gobhainn
'S bu bhuidheann eile dhiu Daorghlas.
'S bha Fionn a nuair sin air roinne
'S beagan do dh' uaislean na Féinne.
"Fosgail gu luath," ors' an gobhainn.
"'S na druid romhain," arsa Daorghlas.
"Na fag mise so am ònrachd
An aite teann 's mi m' aonar."
"Oganaich is àilleadh snuadh
'S earbsach mi a luath's do chas
'S éiribh a sios gu luath
'S leigibh a falbh-bhalach a steach.
'S shaoil leam nach robh riamh aig Fionn
Na nochdadh a ghnùis do 'm thigh
Gum meal thusa t-ainm a Chaoilte
'S cha bhi Daorghlas ort o nuair so."

CONAN, who was an old man apparently, and bald, had the name of being irritable, and of no strength till he got his first disgrace over ; he was then as powerful as any other man. He never appears ridiculous in the sense of foolish or feeble, but he made himself liable to be laughed at from the boldness with which he thrusts himself forward, and asked to be allowed to measure himself with the most redoubtable heroes, and to be made spokesman to the most powerful enemy. In combat or wrestling match, even a woman could over-throw him at first. He was made prisoner, by the binding of his two hands to his belt and behind his back (*ceangal nan trì chaoil*), the tying of the three smalls—*i.e.*, his two wrists and the small of his back (*a chaol-druim*). Sometimes, as in the contest with Conn, Son of the Red, the two feet were also tied together, and the hero was left prostrate, without power to raise himself or to move. " The bald Conan, of a truth, on Conan were placed the five ties under the same binding" (*Chaidh air Conan maol gu deimhin na coig chaoil fo'n aon cheangal*").

He figures in some recitations as a man much esteemed by Fionn, and accompanying him on his excursions. As evidence of his short temper, there is a popular saying, that when Conan was among the devils he said, " If I am ill off they are no better" ("*Beatha Chonain measg nan deamhan. Ma's olc dhomh cha'n fhearr dhoibh*"); or, as it is sometimes said, " ' Blow for blow and scratch for scratch,' as Conan said to the devils" ("*'Buille air son buille, agus sgrioch air son sgrioch,' mar thuirt Conan ris na deamhain*") ; or, as the

saying is used by Sir Walter Scott, "'Claw for claw
and devil take the shortest nails,' as Conan said to the
devil" (see *Waverley*).   He was the master of the
hounds, and is mentioned as one of those who went with
Fionn to the House of the Yellow Field, and as having
accompanied Fionn when he was walking out with four
others of the most prominent men of the Fians, and
were made to go to the House of Talkativeness, where
Fionn found his missing men.   He also figures in other
stories as uncovering the poisonous fang of Bran, the
magic dog that Fionn had, and was of use on many
occasions.   He is also mentioned, it will be recollected,
in the lay or ballad of Conn, Son of the Red, as well
as in other stories.   It is said that on one occasion,
when the Fians were in the Mountain Ash dwelling
(*Bruighin Chaoruinn*), they became transfixed to their
seats, but a drop of royal blood would loosen them.
Conan was left to the last.   By that time the drop of
royal blood had become exhausted, and he said to
Dermid, who was releasing them, "If I were a pretty
woman, you would not have left me to the last"
("*Na'm bu bhean bhoidheach mi cha'n fhàgadh tu mi*").
Dermid then tore him away, leaving Conan's skin to the
seat.   Though Conan was the weakest of the host, yet
there was the combat of a hundred on his hand (*comhrag
ceud air a laimh*).   He never saw a man frown but he
thought it his duty to strike him, nor saw a door open
that he did not enter.   When he struck, the life of a
man was in every blow (*Bha beatha duine air a dhorn
na'm buaileadh e*).

THE CATTLE OF THE FIANS.

IT is said that the strongest and best horse which the Fians had, White Front (*Blar Aghan*), was killed by the *Glas tarruing fhogharaidh*, or the hauling of crops in harvest from wet places to dry ground by means of sledges or *carns*, and these, as may readily be supposed, were on wet ground a severe burden upon even the strongest horse.

The *Glas-ghoileam* (Grey-cheek) was the cow the Féinne had, and the milk of which (there was a mouthful for each), along with shell-fish, kept them alive when game was not to be found, hence the story of the "Rock of the Mouthful", which is as follows :

THE STORY OF THE ROCK OF THE MOUTHFUL (CREAGAN A' BHALGUIM).

It is told that once when the Féinne were in Skye and the chase was lost, Thinman (*Caoilte*), who was the swiftest of the band, was sent to look for the deer, whilst they themselves gathered limpets at Loch Snizort. He found them somewhere to the north of Lynecan. The locality of this place (*Loighneachan*) is not known, and it is possible that the tradition came from some other place, perhaps from Ireland. When he saw the game, he gave a shout which was heard by the rest of the Fians, who were at the time eating shell-fish at Loch Snizort. They heard

> "The shrill, hard cry of swift Thinman,
> To the north of Loineachan."

> "Eigheach caol cruaidh Chaoilte luaith
> Aig taobh tuath Loighneachan."

The one who had a mouthful of shell-fish and of the Grey-cheeked cow's (*Glas-ghoileam*) milk at the time squirted out the unsavoury morsel, and the place where this was done is called the Rock of the Mouthful (*Creagan a' bhalgnim*). The rock at the place is certainly coloured, or rather discoloured, as if it had been done by the mouthful thus thrown out. Immediately the heroes set off to where the chase was to be found.

The bed of the Grey-cheeked Cow (*Glas-ghoileam*) is at the Kid Rock (*Creag nam meann*), behind Kinsburgh (*Ciunebor?*), in Skye. It is said that Hiniosdail, in Skye, was one of her grazing places. The other places where it grazed in Skye were:

> " Eisgeadal is Toisgeadal,
> 'S càrn a' Choin is Bràigh Bhran,
> 'S Uisgescadar 's Suilescadar
> 'S a' Bheinn Mhoràig ceann an loch,
> 'S Acha-choire as Màlagan."

WHAT became of the Féinne, whether they were disbanded, or came to a natural end, is not mentioned in
tales about them. The first misfortune that befell them
of the series which ended in their extinction, was a
fight which occurred between the two hosts of which
they were composed.

When Dermid had fled and was in hiding, he one
day lay concealed in the foliage of a tree. Oscar and
Goll were below playing at *tailcasg*, or chess. (Some
say that Dermid was dropping little berries on the
squares on which Oscar was to play next; others say
this is not implied in the expression.) Goll at last
said:

> "Dermid's faithful teaching
> Has made Oscar's ready play."

> "Teagasg dileas Dhiarmaid
> Rinn iomairt calamh Oscair."

To which Oscar replied, "Though you little esteem
Dermid, we loved him" ("*Ge beag ortsa Diarmad ba
toigh leinne e*"). From less to more a battle was begun
between the two hosts, so fierce that the shouts were
heard a mile off (*chluinnteadh fad mile meallanaich an t-
sluaigh*). On that occasion, however, peace was restored;
but, after the loss sustained by the burning of Brugh
Farala and the death of their most redoubtable heroes,
the Fians seem to have dwindled away, and to have
been no more a power in the land; it was natural
enough that they should be no longer recognised as
of paramount power when their wives and growing
youth were destroyed by the burning of this tem-

porary residence. Fionn himself does not seem ever to have had the same power after the severe wound inflicted upon him at the death of Garry by his own sword, which never left a remnant of its blow (*nach d' fhag riamh fuigheal beum*), till that day. His son Ossian, whose name in modern times has received a recognition and provoked a discussion beyond that of any other bard or poet of the Celtic race, survived his father and all the heroes of his time ; hence, " like Ossian after the Fians," has become a saying universal throughout the whole Highlands, meaning or used when a man is left alone after all his friends have died or disappeared. " I am", said a man who felt himself thus solitary, " Ossian after the Fians" ("*Is mise Ossian an deigh na Féinne*"). " You are", said a person who was listening to him, and did not think much of his character or complaint ("*'S tu, 's tusa muisean an deigh na Féinne*") —" You are the nasty fellow after the Féinne."

The story runs in Skye, and also in the Long Island, that Ossian's mother was a deer, and the song is still to be fallen in with, of which this forms a part :

" If you are my mother, and art a deer."

" Ma's tu mo mhathair-sa gur fiadh thu."

And the first time this became known was when the Féinne were eating venison after Thinman (*Caoilte*), as already told, found the deer at Lynecan (*Loighneachan*), and the Féinne went thither. Ossian, on being offered a bone, said : " When every one eats the shin-bone of his mother, I will eat the thin shin-bone of my own mother" ("*Dar dh' itheas na h-uile fear calpa a mhathair ithe mise calpa caol mo mhathair fhin*"). The version of the song which the writer fell in with is as follows :

Ossian's Mother a Deer. (1)

" If thou art my mother, and art a deer,
   I will say horon o ho
     E ho hyri riivig
  Ho ro, hy horun o ho.

If thou art my mother, and art a deer,
   I will say horun o ho.

You will be afraid of what dogs can do,
If you go to high hills,

You will be afraid of artisans, (2)
Artisans and their dogs.

If Brian would take from me his murmuring,
Before my sweetheart will hear my voice."

" Ma's tu mo mhàthair-sa gur fiadh thu
   Their mi horunn o hò
     E ho haori rithi-bhag
  Hò rò haoi ; horunn o hò.

Ma's tu mo mhàthair-sa gur fiadh thu,
   Their mi horunn o hò.

Bi' t-eagal roimh ghniomh nan con,
Ma theid thu na beannaibh àrda

Bi' t-eagal roimh chlann na cearda
Clann na ceairde 's an cuid chon.

Gu'n caisgeadh Brian dhiom a strannan
Mu'n cluinn mo leannan mo ghuth."

Notes.

(1) " Ossian's mother a deer."—The reciter (Skye) said Ossian's
mother was a deer, and that she only got one touch on his forehead with her tongue. On that spot (*air an oisin sin*) fur like

deer's fur (*cuilg an fhéidh*) grew ; hence his name. A man at
Lochaweside said he heard a deer nursed Ossian, but not that it
was his mother. This account tallies with the belief held that the
deer were a fairy race. To keep this matter from being talked of,
Ossian was sent to the Land of Youth (*Tir na h-Oige*), which the
party from whom the story was heard said he supposed was some
island near Skye : Holm's islet, or Fladda Chuain. When Ossian
came ashore he was making his way along a road near a field where
a party was working at harvest work. He made inquiries, and the
company told him that, by the last accounts they heard of the
Féinne, they were in Ireland. He made his way to Ireland, and
found his daughter, whose name the writer heard tell was Anna,
married to Patrick of the Psalms (*Padruig nan Salm*). Some say
that this Patrick was the same Patrick who blessed Ireland
(*Padruig a bheannaich Eirin*) ; but others maintain that he was
different. The kain that Patrick had over Ireland (*A' chàin bha
aig Padruig air Eirin*) was as much food as was necessary to
maintain Ossian. Ossian's own daughter was very niggardly and
scrimp in the food with which she supplied the aged hero.

Cain is a common Gaelic word for a rent-charge or tax.
It is said of a man of a voracious appetite that he would eat
the kain that Patrick had over Ireland.

(2) " You will be afraid of artisans."
" Bi' t-eagal ort roimh chlann nan ceard."

The word *ceard* denotes an artificer of any kind, and is in
meaning, as well as derivation, the same as the Latin *cerdo*, a
workman. It now denotes usually workmen to whom the name
of tinkers are given. These wandering Bohemians were the sole
skilled artizans among the people of the Highlands ; at all events,
they were most skilled in the making of horn spoons and delicate
work, such as putting teeth in wool-cards, etc. At the present
day the term is one of reproach rather than of commendation.
There is a song which shows that the word, at no remote time,
was one applied to excelling merit. In the song of MacRobert
the Tinker occur these words :

" I gave my affection, why ?
Guess you, who to,
To the son of Robert the Tinker.
Not the tinker who makes the spoon
Or puts teeth in the wool-card :
But the tinker of war weapons,
With whom the hunt prospers.

Black-cock and roebuck.
When you go up the frowning height,
With your gun and dog,
You close the eye
And bend the knee,
The deer son is then without cheer,
Losing its blood on the dew.
I gave my affection—why deny it?—
To the hunter of the red deer hind,
Otter, and thick-lipped seal."

    "Ho rì hùg o
Thug mi' cion, de fàth?
    O haoriri horuinn ho rò hùg ò
Tomhais sibh-se co dha?
Do Mhac Raibeart an ceard
Cha 'n e 'n ceard a ni 'n spàin
No dh' fhiaclaicheas càrd;
Ach ceard a dheanadh nan arm,
Leis an cinneadh an t-sealg
Coileach dubh is boc-earb
Nuair dhìreadh tu 'n stùc,
Le d' ghunna 's le d' chù,
Chaogadh tu 'n t-sùil,
Is lùbadh tu 'n glùn,
Mac an fhéidh bhiodh gun sunnd
Call fal' air an drùchd,
    Thug mi 'n cion, c'uim an ceil mi?
Do shealgair na h-eilid,
An dobhrain duinn 's an ròin mheillich."

OSSIAN AFTER THE FIANS.

THE Fians had disappeared, none of them surviving but Ossian. When he went to Ireland after the Fians, and lived with St. Patrick, who was married to his daughter, it was said the daughter was so niggardly to her father that seven skewers (*seachd deilg*) were put by him in his coat to keep it from hanging too loosely. Patrick was building a temple[1] at this time.

There was a large stone to be put in the temple, so large that the sixteen masons employed in the work could not lift it into its place. Ossian said that if he got the food of the sixteen masons, he would lift the stone himself. The food was prepared, but, from niggardliness, he only got the food of fifteen, and six skewers came out of his coat. He was led out, and he lifted the stone and put it in its place. He then fumbled over it with his fingers, and returned into the house.

Patrick came to him and said that the stone was not exactly in its proper bed, and he was to come out and put it right.

"As it is," said Ossian, "so it will be. If I had got the meat of the sixteen masons I would have put it right."

He then called to his grandson to lead him out, as he had recovered part of his strength. They went on till they came to a loch, when Ossian said to the boy: "Do you see a grassy hillock in the loch? Lead me to it."

---

[1] All the buildings erected by Saint Patrick seem to have been temples, as St. Patrick's Temple (*Teampull Phadruig*) in Kenavara Hill, Island of Tiree, etc.

They went out in the lake, and Ossian plucked up the grassy hillock and took with him a cauldron which was below it, and they went away. They then reached a high, steep rock, with a hole in its face. Ossian asked his grandson to direct his hand into the hole, out of which he took the bone of the Black Elk (*Lon-Dubh*).

"Now," said he to the boy, "put your fingers in your ears as tight as you can for a short time."

The boy did this, and Ossian whistled loudly with the bone of the Black Elk.

"Did that hurt you?" he said to the boy.

"No," said the boy.

"What do you see coming?" asked Ossian.

"I see beasts coming together."

"Put your fingers in your ears again."

He did this. Ossian whistled again.

"What are you seeing now?"

"As many more coming."

He whistled the third time.

"I almost think," said the boy, "that every living creature is coming."

"If I had now the strongest and laziest lad we had among the Fians, with the strongest and laziest dog."

The dog called *Biorach mac Buidheig*, and the lad whom they called *Tòn Ruadh*, then came. The dog went among the beasts and was slaying them, and the servant lad was gathering and piling them above each other. When there were enough, as he thought, he came and sat beside Ossian; but the dog could not be stopped. The boy said the dog was returning.

"What is he like?" Ossian asked.

"Its mouth is open, and I can see the liver and lungs on the floor of his chest" (*An gruan 's an sgamhan air urlar a chleibh*).

"When he comes, see that you direct my hand into his open mouth" (*craos*).

6

He did so, and Ossian took out its liver and lungs, and killed it.

He then told the servant lad to kindle a fire and boil water in the cauldron. This was done, and when the water boiled he told his grandson to go away before he did him any injury. "For", he said, "I am outrageously hungry" ("*Tha confhadh orm gu biadh*"). ·

When he ate the meat, he said to the servant lad : " Now take as much as you want."

The boy then returned where he was, and Ossian said to him : "Three third parts of my hearing and three third parts of my sight are restored to me. Go home, your grandfather leaves you his blessing."

The boy left him and went home, and no one ever saw or heard Ossian after that ('*s cha'n fhacadh 's cha chualadh duine Ossian riamh tuilleadh 'na dheigh*).

In his hours of recreation from religious services, according to a lay in existence, Patrick was in the habit of coming to see Ossian, for well he liked his glorious talk (*O'n sann leis bu bhinn a' gloir*). Ossian used to tell Patrick tales of the (*Fèinne*) Fians, and these were all put into writing by Patrick. When, however, he heard about the bone of the huge deer, in the marrow-hole of which an unusually large bone of the deer then in existence could turn, he thought that the whole stories told by Ossian were mere inventions, and in his indignation he threw the writings into the fire. It was in this way that the history of the Fians was lost, and this was deplored by Patrick himself when the bones of the (*Lou dubh*) Black Elk were brought home by his son, the grandson of Ossian. This breed of deer had a brown stripe along their back (*slat dhonn 'nan druim*), and was called the race of the Two Stick Kine (*Siolachadh Bo Da Bhiorain*).

They used to have warm discussions about religion, in which Ossian always maintained that Fionn and the

Fingalians were quite able to take care of themselves against all comers, especially God, of whom Patrick was everlastingly talking. In a poem called "Ossian after the Fians" ("*Ossian an deigh na Fèinne*"), said by Mac-Nicol to have been composed in modern times by a smith, who was called the second Ossian,[1] the word *chubhal* occurs in the discussion between Ossian and Patrick. Ossian lost temper over the statements of Patrick about hell, and the Fians being confined there. The bard could not understand how, if the Fians were there, they did not make themselves masters of the place, and be free from any control over them. It was then that Patrick said :

"Though little you think of the humming of a fly,
 Or the mote in the sunbeam,
Without the leave of the Almighty King,
 Not one crease would be in the fold of thy shield."

"Ge beag orts' chubhal[2] chrònanach
 'S monran na grèine

---

[1] See Highland Society's Report on Ossian.

[2] The word *cuileag* is now the form of the word *chubhal*, to denote a fly, as *eibhleag* is used instead of *eabhal*, a burning peat, which survives in the saying :

  "A burning peat on the cheek—
   Women fulling and tailors."

  "Eabhal air gruaidh—
   Mnathan luadh 's taillearan."

A red spot on the cheek produced by inability to supply sufficient food to the workers. This is illustrated in the question asked by Fionn (see Stewart's *Collection*, p. 545) :

   "What is hotter than fire?"
   "De 's teotha na 'n teine?"

  "The face of a good man when people come
  And he has not meat for them."

  "Gnuis duine mhaith gus an tigeadh aoidhean
  Gun bhiadh aige dhoibh."

Gun chead do'n Righ mhoralach
Cha deid feicidh dh' fhile do sgcithe."

St. Patrick seems to have been as tenacious and fearless in the expression of his own opinions as Ossian
was of his own. There is a poem preserved, "Ossian's
Prayer" ("*Urnuigh Ossiain*"), in which Ossian is said
finally to have adopted the tenets of St. Patrick, and to
have been sincere in repentance for any evil he may
have done :

" The succour of the twelve Apostles
  I take to myself to-night ;
And if I have done a heavy sin,
  May it be put beneath hillock or in pit.'

" Comrach an da Abstal dheug
  Gabham thugam fein an nochd
'S mo rinn mi peacadh trom
  Gu'n càrar e 'n tom na'n slochd."

There is a curious expression, that the end of the
Fians was the going of Fionn to Rome (*Turus Fhinn
dhol do'n Roimh*).

Tradition still makes mention of Ossian having been
in person remarkably strong and handsome. He could
boast of being able to overtake the hind of the red
deer, and hold it by the ear, at its utmost speed, and
that on the darkest night he could take out a thistle-
thorn. Whatever opinion we may form of the works
published by Macpherson, either as to their merit, or
their authenticity, or their antiquity, there can be no
question of this—in fact, it is outside of any question
that has ever been raised—that there are expressions
and sentiments of the highest merit, as emanations
from a gifted and poetic mind, to be found in the lays
and ballads which tradition ascribes to Ossian. The
popular mind has ascribed to him not only royal parent-
age and the highest poetic merit, but everything con-

nected with him has a fairy and wonderful effulgence of
magic influence.

One of the poems or ballads which have been preserved among the people, and uniformly ascribed to
Ossian, and which every mind is open to form an
opinion about, is the "Lay of the Red Cataract" (*"Eas
Ruadh"*). The poetic idea underlying this ballad
is one especially deserving of examination and close
attention. It solves many questions in regard to unwritten compositions, and their preservation for centuries
from one generation to another, the high opinion pre-
vailing as to the Gaelic bard, the merit ascribed to him,
and the rush which was made when Macpherson's work
appeared.

The ballad in question is outside the region of controversy, and due praise might seem at first to be
exaggeration. The main idea of the ballad is that of a
young and beautiful princess rejecting the advances of
a bold and warlike prince. This idea is worked out by
the poet in a manner that makes the composition particularly noble and attractive. It is founded on the
calm of an early summer day, when nature's face is fair
and breaks into bloom and blossom, the beauty that
covers sea and land disappearing before a storm rising
in the daytime. When the young and haughty beauty
throws herself on the protection of Fionn, and the king
undertakes to defend her against all comers, and the
prince comes after her, and a fierce conflict ensues, we
have more than the elements of a beautiful poem. The
reader will condone the following further explanation of
the subject.

The princess is the daughter of King Under Waves
(*Righ fo Thuinn*), and the prince is a Son of the King
of Light (*Mac Righ na Sorcha*). On a calm day all
nature seems reflected in the water, a person sees not
only himself, but houses, trees, mountains, and all the

beauty of earth so mirrored : this is the Kingdom Under
Waves. When a gale rises and the surface of the water
is ruffled, the beauty disappears and the charm
vanishes. As to the region of *Sorcha* (Light), from
which the prince is represented as coming, it is noticeable in Gaelic that *s* begins words denoting ease and
motion, or gentle flow, while *d*[1] denotes what is hard, stiff,
stubborn, and difficult to move ; thus, *soirbh* means calm,
gentle, quiet, affable, pliant, easily moved, while *doirbh*
means rough, fierce, hard, difficult in manner or temper.
The initial particle *so*, prefixed to adjectives or sub-
stantives, denotes facility, aptness, ease, equality, and
sometimes goodness ; *do* implies, as an initial syllable,
the reverse, sometimes difficulty, sometimes impossi-
bility. For the purpose of comparison between *s* and
d may be quoted also *sona*, happy ; *dona*, evil and
unhappy ; *sùbailt*, supple or easily bent ; *dùbailt*,
double ; *socair*, easy, at rest ; *docair*, difficult and
uneasy ; *sochair*, privilege or adventure ; and *dochair*,
loss or mischief ; *saor*, cheap or free ; *daor*, dear or hard
bound. *Dorcha*, dark, has its opposite, *sorcha*, clear, or
light.

The gale denoted by the prince of *Sorcha* is not one
arising from darkness or cold, but springing up in the
day time and driving away before it the calm and
beauty of the early summer. The increasing heat of
early summer is laden with bliss and beauty, even to
inanimate nature ; the air is then redolent of joy and
youth, and "breathes, as it were, to mankind a second
spring." The simple prose narrative of the incident
which Ossian has worked into the poem is that the
redoubtable heroes of the Fians, with Fionn himself at
their head, were at the seaside, probably somewhere in
the north of Ireland, when a dark object like a mist was

[1] This comparison of *s* and *d* extends to other languages besides
Gaelic.

observed in the offing ; as it came nearer it proved—at
least so the poet tells us—to be a coracle, or small boat,
coming to land. When it came near, it was seen
to contain a solitary woman. It came into the
customary harbour; and when the woman landed, she
was observed to be one of supreme beauty and dignity,
so much so that all the heroes held their peace in her
presence. Fionn himself came to the shore ; she
addressed him in tones of great respect, appealed to him
for succour, and told him who she was herself, and the
cause of her coming ; that she was flying from the
advances of one whom she could not tolerate, and who
was coming after her. The king of the warrior band
gallantly undertook to protect her against anyone that
would come. They had scarcely finished speaking when
the sea came in rising waves, angry and violent, as if agi-
tated by a storm, and another of very warlike appearance
came after her on a horse. A person from whom this tale
was heard, said he could not understand how the prince
could have come on a horse, but it is not difficult to
understand how the rising waves could be represented
as a steed of great speed and strength, "when the
blackening waves are edged with white," and their
onslaught threatens to overpower all who may try
to stand against them. The strongest heroes of the
warrior band stand between the wave and the princess ;
but the wave breaks in violence on the shore, and
threatens to take her away. A battle royal ensues, and
at last the stormy prince is subdued and is buried with
regal honours. The name of the prince was *Baoighre
Borb* (" A Fierce Ruffian"). *Tarbh Baoighre*, in some
places, is the name of the magic water-bull from which,
it is said, all calves that are crop-eared (*corc-chluasach*)
come, and, generally, the word *baoighre* means a wild,
senseless individual. The *g* or *gh* in the middle of the
word, which in English is expressed by *gg*, furnishes a

help towards an explanation of a term very common in abusive language. The princess remained with Fionn and his men for a year and a day, or, in other words, it was calm and prosperous with them for a considerable time.

Some collectors who have fallen in with this lay say that Tiree is the Kingdom Under Waves, and *Sorcha* Ardnamurchan, or some place near. In search of this kind of explanation even Portugal has been brought in as the place from which the fiery prince came. The level character of Tiree, so different from the rest of the islands of Scotland, makes it not surprising that some of the islanders look upon it as a kingdom lower than the sea. They say that from the west a boat will come to it faster than it will go from the island out west to sea, because in the former case it is descending a brae or slope. In many parts the spray is seen right across the island, rising on the opposite shore ; and in the centre of the island, where there is a plain said to be 1,500 acres in extent, in a high tide and stormy weather the sea comes over the beach on one side, and there is nothing to interfere with its flowing into the sea on the opposite shore. It thus divides the island into two, but the water is not so deep as to prevent passage from the east and west side of the island. Ardnamurchan derives its name from the numerous headlands ending in the point so prominent.

The version of the poem with which the writer fell in was heard from one who had learned it perhaps forty years ago from a native of the island of Eigg, who had come as herdsman to the former minister of this parish. This is mentioned as showing what a hold the poems and tales of the Fians had upon the minds even of those who were neither bards nor musicians, and were entirely unaware of all the questions which were roused by Macpherson. There is therefore no question about its

being popular lore, and this is corroborated by the Dean
of Lismore's version, which is also outside of the Macpherson controversy. The poem is as follows :

THE RED CATARACT.

A day we were with but few in number
At the Red Cataract of slow-moving fish, (1)
We saw sailing in the open sea
A large coracle with a woman in it.

We all stood on the hill-side,
Fionn of the Fian host and Goll,
Looking at a coracle which was
Most beautiful in its motion :
A woman with two oars parting the waves.

It made no stay in its coming,
Till it came to a stop in the usual harbour ;
And when it came ashore at the Cataract,
A lovely woman rose out of it.

Her radiance was like that of the sun ;
Mild was her demeanour and appearance,
The maiden who came from afar ;
We of a truth held our peace before her

She came to Fionn's pavilion,
And she sweetly saluted them.
The Son of Cumal returned her salutation
Fittingly and with measured words.

The King of fairest inquiry asked,
" As you are welcome, fair, newly come daughter,
Tell us indeed, I ask,
What tribe you are from ?

" The purpose of your journey from every quarter,
Young maid of loveliest form :

The journey that brought you from afar,
Will you not give us the purport of?"

" I am the daughter of King Under Waves :
I would shortly tell you my delay[1] :
There is not a land over which the sun circles,
Where I have not sought your gallant heroes."

" Maiden, who traversed every way,
Young daughter of fairest charms,
The journey you have taken from afar,
Will you not tell us its object in very truth?"

" My succour I lay upon you, if you are Fionn,
Fionn, father of all fair women :
The meaning of my journey and success
Is that you take upon you my succour quickly and
     early."

" I will undertake to succour you, woman,
Against your pursuer ;
But that you tell us in very truth
Who is in pursuit of you?"

" He is hard chasing me at sea :
A warrior of utmost keenness, close after me :
The Son of the King of Sorcha of Red Shields,
A chief who is called the Fierce Baoire.

" Spells I put in his head
That Fionn would take me over the salt sea,
Although great is his prowess and good fortune."

Oscar answered with ready loftiness,
The hero who could put a stop to every king :
" Though Fionn was not here,
You would not go with him as wife."

---

[1] *I.e.*, the cause of my stopping.

We saw coming on a horse,
A champion, who was greater than others,
Traversing the sea with speed,
The same direction the woman had come.

His helmet was close-fitted to the head
Of the fearless man and strong ;
A ridged target, not to be repelled,
Was from elbow to chest :

A large, heavy sword in his hand,
In the hand of the hero fearless and bold,
Displaying feats above his head,
As he came over the crests of the waves.

The look of a noble man, and the eyelash of a king
In the head of the man of goodly form ;
Good was his complexion and white his teeth ;
Faster was his horse than any stream.

That steed came to land,
And the man who was not smooth towards the Fians ;
Nine [two] heroes of us were there
To meet him—[it is a shame to tell it].

Regarding the champion who came to land
Asked the King of best fame :
" Do you know yourself, woman,
Is that the man of whom you speak?"

" I know, Fionn, son of Cumal,
That he is harmful to your Fians,
And will threaten to take me away with him,
Though great your strength is in the Fian host."

Oscar rose, and Goll rose :
Fierce was their slaughter to the ground in fight,
And they stood in front of the host
Between the big man and the woman.

He showed neither blade nor shield
To any hero or Chief who was there,
But slighted the Fians,
Till he himself reached Fionn.

The hero of comeliest form came,
With fury and strength in his head,
And swept with him the woman,
Though she was under the protection of Fionn's men.

MacMorna gave a sudden strong throw,
And his two hands were hard after it,
And though the shot did not touch the warrior's body,
Of his shield it made two halves.

The Oscar threw with utmost fury
A bloody spear from his left hand,
And killed the man's steed.
(Mighty was the deed that with us grew).

When the steed fell on the plain,
He turned with rage and fury,
And he threatened, though it be a hard matter,
A combat with fifty heroes.

Outside of myself and my father,
Fifty dauntless heroes went to the encounter :
Though great was their strength in the conflict,
He was like to slaughter them all with his hand.
(He would leave us bound
And take the woman with him.)

He gave two blows right merrily,
With perseverance to every one of these ;
We would all be under the sod
If you had been restricted to man-to-man.

We quickly set nine times nine men
Before the hard strife ceased ;

The painful tying of the three smalls
On each warrior of these he put.

The Clanna Morna, hard was their case:
The number that were killed hard was the tale to tell;
And none were there who escaped
But his body was full of wounds.
(They were for a year with Fionn being healed.)

Till Goll, of lively temper, advanced
To strike the man in the narrow path,
Whoever might see them then,
Rough was their prowess and movements.

They had swords on their strong points,
Belabouring bodies and shields;
And the bout of combat the two had
We never saw before.

Were it not for the fifty stout heroes
Who went to meet him at first,
We would be helpless under his control,
If he had got from us his fair demand.

The Son of Morna transfixed by his hand
The Son of the King of Sorcha [a great tale to tell]:
It is a pity of any race from whom the woman came,
Since the Big Man from the ocean was slain.

After the fall of the great man—
The wound from the sea, hard was its step—
The daughter of King Under Waves was
Kept by Fionn for a year among the Fian host.

We buried at the foot of the Cataract
The warrior of strongest onslaught and deed,
And we put on each finger
A gold ring as honour to a King.

Eas Ruadh.

Latha dar dhuinn air bheag sloigh
  Aig Eas Roidh an ciginn mhall (1)
Chunnaic sinn seòladh air lear,
  Curach mòr agus bean ann.

Gu'n sheas sinn uile air an t-sliabh
  Fionn nam Fian agus Goll
Ag amharc a churaich b' àille gniomh,
  Bean da raimh a 'sgoltadh thonn.

Cha d' rinn i tàmh ann 'na teachd,
  Ghabh i cala sa phort ghnà
Air teachd air tìr aig an Eas
  Do dh' éirich as maca mna.

B' ionnan dealra dhi 's do 'n ghréin
  Bu chaoin a méin 's a dealbh
A nighinn thainig an céin
  Do bha sinn fhein roimpe soirbh.

Thainig i gu pubull Fhinn
  'S bheannaich i gu binn doibh,
Fhreagair Mac Cumhaill i rìs
  Gu cubhaidh dhi 's gu foil.

Dh' fhiosraich an righ bu ghlan fios
  "Air d' fhàillte nighean ghlan ùr,
Ach gu 'n innse tu gu beachd
  Co fhreumh as an d' thàine tu.

"Brigh do thuruis as gach ròd
  A nighean òg is aille dealbh,
An turus mu'n d' thainig tu 'n céin
  Nach d' thoir thu dhuinn féin a dhearbh."

"Is nighean mi do Righ fo thuinn
  Dh' innsinn duibh gu cruinn mo dhàil
Cha-n 'eil tìr m' an iadh a' ghrian
  Nach d' iarr mi fein do laoich fhial."

"A ribhinn a shiubhail gach ròd
  A nighean òg is àille dealbh
An turus mu'n d' thainig tu 'n céin
  Nach d' thoir thu dhomh fein gu dearbh."

"Mo chomrach ort, ma's tu Fionn,
  Athair Fhinn a mhaca mna
Brìgh mo thuruis is mo bhuaidh,
  Gabh mo chomrach gu luath trà."

"Gabham mu d' chuimrich a bhean,
  Roimh aon fhear tha air do thì :
Na'n innseadh tu gu beachd,
  Co e am fear th' air do thì."

" Tha e 'gam bheò-ruith air muir,
  Laoch is mòr guin air mo lorg.
Mac Righ na Sorcha nan sgiath dearg
  Triath g'an ainm iad am Baoire Borb.

"Geasa do chur mi 'na cheann,
  Gu'm beireadh Fionn mi thar sàil,
Ge mòr ghnìomh agus àgh."

Labhair Oscar le glòir mhir
  Laoch sin a choisgeadh gach righ,
"Ged nach biodh Fionn aig an Eas,
  Cha rachadh tu leis mar mhnaoi."

Do chunnaic sinn a' teachd air steud,
  Laoch bha mheud thar gach fear ;
Siubhal na fairge gu dian,
  An iul chiadna ghabh a' bhean.

A chlogada teannda mu cheann
  An fhir nach bu tiom, 's bu treun,
Sgiath dhrimneach nach teid air ais
  O uilinn, gu cneas a chléibh.

Bha claidheamh trom toirteil 'na làimh,
  An laimh an laoich nach bu tiom 's bu treun,

'S e cluich nan cleas os a chionn
　　'S e tighinn an drimlinn a 'chuain.

Neul flath agus rosg righ
　　An ceann an fhir bu chaomh cruth.
Bu mhath a shnuadh 's bu gheal a dheud,
　　Bu luaithe steud na gach sruth.

Thainig an steud sin air tir
　　'S am fear nach bu mhin ris an Fhéinn
Caogad laoch a bhitheamaid ann,
　　G'a choinneachadh (ri innseadh gur nàr).

"De 'n t-suinn?" nuair thainig air tìr
　　Dh' fharraid an righ bu mhath cliù,
"An aithnich thu fein, a bhean,
　　An e sud am fear a deir thu?"

"Aithneam, a Mhic Cumhail, 'Fhinn,
　　Gur puthar leam e do d' Fhéinn
'S gu'n geall e mise thoirt leis
　　Ge mor bhur neart anns an Fhéinn."

Dh' éirich Oscar is dh' éirich Goll
　　Bu bhorb an casgairt lom sa chath,
'S sheas iad an gar an t-slòigh
　　Eadar am fear mòr 's a' bhean.

Cha d' fhiach e lann no sgiath
　　Do laoch no triath g'an robh ann
'S gu'n d' rinn e tair air an Fhéinn
　　Gus an d' ràinig e fein Fionn.

Thainig an laoch bu mhath tlachd
　　Le fraoch 's le neart 'na cheann
'S gu'n do sguab e leis a' bhean
　　'S i air guaillibh fhearaibh Fhinn.

Thug Mac-Morn an urchair gheur,
　　As dha laimh gu cruaidh 'na deigh:
'S ged nach do bhean an urchair da chreubh
　　Do a sgiath gu'n d' rinn e da bhloigh.

Thilg an t-Oscar le làn fheirg
  A chraosnach dhearg a laimh chli,
Agus mharbhadh leis steud an fhir,
  Bu mhor an t-euchd a chinnich leinn.

Nuair thuit an steud air an Leirg,
  Is thionndaidh e le fearg is fraoch
'S bhagair e ge cruaidh an càs
  Comhrag air caogad laoch.

Nach bhuam-sa 's bho m' athair fhein.
  Chaidh caogad laoch nach tiom 'na dhàil,
Ge mòr an spionnadh 's an treis,
  Gu'n gheall e 'n casgairt le laimh.
('S dh' fhàgadh e sinne fo shreing
  'S bheireadh e bhean leis.)

Bheireadh da bhuille gu mear
  Gu dian do gach fear dhiu sin
Do bhitheamaid uile fo ùir
  Mar biodh thu ag comhrag fir.

Chuir sinn naoi naoinear gu luath
  San iorghuill chruaidh mu'n do sguir
'S ceangal guineach na tri chaol
  Air gach laoch dhiu sin do chuir.

A chlanna Morna, cruaidh an càs
  Na fhuair bàs bu mhòr an sgeul
'S cha robh aon a thainig as
  Gun a chneas fuidh iomadh ceuchd.
  [Fad bliadhna 'gan leigheas aig Fionn.]

Do dhruid Goll an aigne mhir
  A bhualadh an fhir sa chaol ròd,
Ge be chiteadh iad an sin
  Bu gharbh an goil 's an gleò,

Bha claidheamhna ac' air an sòc
  A leadairt chorp agus sgiath
S an tineal còmhraig a bh' aig an di 's
  Cha-n fhaca sinne roimhe riamh.

Mur bha 'an caogad laoch garbh
    Bha 'n dail nan arm dha an tòs
Bhitheamaid gun chobhair fuidh sprochd
    Na'm faigheadh uainn a cheart chòir.

Thorchuir Mac Morna le a làimh
    Mac righ na Sorcha, sgeula mòr
'S mairg treubh a'n d' thainig a' bhean
    O'n mhilleadh am fear o'n chuan.

An deigh tuiteam an fhir mhòr
    An goin do 'n chuan, cruidh an ceum
Do bha nighean Righ Tir-fo-thuinn
    Bliadhna aig Fionn san Fhéinn.

Thiodhlaic sinn ag cois an eas
    An curaidh bu mhor treis is gniomh
Chuir sinn air a h-uile mear
    Fàinn òir mar onoir do Righ.

NOTE.

(1) The exact locality denoted by the Red Cataract (*Eas Ruadh*) is not clear from any description the writer has fallen in with. It has been identified with the Salmon Leap on the river Bann at Coleraine, in the north of Ireland. To this supposition an objection is, that the Salmon Leap is some distance from the sea, and the coracle with the princess could not well be seen; neither could the steed of the prince who attacked them, nor the breaking waves be such as to cover the land to that extent. At all events, the poem suggests that they were at no distance from the sea-shore.

The word which has been rendered "fish" is itself problematical; many reciters say *an eiginn mall* ("in slow need"), and it is quite possible that the warriors living upon hunting and fishing may have been at the time scarce of food, and want ever makes those who fall under its iron hand less energetic in their movements (*Cha'n 'eil an t-acras faoin :* "Scarcity of food is not a matter to be neglected"). If the chase was hid, and fish had betaken themselves to deep waters, the strongest man might have been rendered slow in action.

In this way the poet Ossian has worked the irreconcilable elements of storm and sunshine into a poem associated with the warrior band of which he himself was a leading and prominent member.

———

The following poem never appeared before in print, and the person from whom it was written down [Allan MacDonald, Mannal, Tiree] thought himself the sole possessor of it.[1] The writer has not fallen in with any one else who knew it, or heard of anyone likely to know it. According to the preamble prefixed to it, Ossian had become old and blind. The poem is evidently, as stated in the preamble, the work of an old blind man ; there is a presumption created that it might be the work of Ossian. The vividness of the description of a cold and stormy night shows the author to have been observant in earlier and better days, and to have had his attention taken up with Nature in her waste and wildest forms, and to have retained a power of description worthy of previous and better days. The poem is here given without alteration, and left to the reader's own judgment.

[1] A very similar incident and a very similar poem are preserved in two Irish 12th century MSS., LL. 208*a*, and Rawl. B. 502. It is told of Finn and his servant Mac Lesc, *i.e.*, Lazy Lad, how, finding themselves one night on Slieve Gullion, Finn orders Mac Lesc to seek for water ; Mac Lesc excuses himself on the ground of the terrible state of the weather, in a poem beginning :—

"Cold till doom !
The storm has spread over all,
A river in every bright furrow,
And a full loch in every ford."

The same poem is also found in connection with the 15th cent. Ossianic tale, *Cath beinne Etair*, and has been printed by Prof. K. Meyer, *Revue Celt.*, xi, 125 *et seq.* –A. N.

OIDHCHE DHOIRBH (STORMY NIGHT).

When Ossian was an old blind man, he had three men-servants and a servant-maid; and every night he sent one of the men to see what kind of night it was, and however wild it might be, he took one of them on his shoulders. and went to the cattle-fold. The men conspired to represent the night as excessively stormy, and if Ossian went as usual, to take a tubful of water and a birch broom, and dash water in his face the whole way. The maid persuaded him to go on his usual round. When he reached the fold, and found the night calm, he sent his servants no more.

First said—

> Outside there is deep murmuring,
> With heavy rain from the tops of trees,
> And I cannot hear the sound of waves (1)
> For the heavy splash of dripping rain. (2)

Second said—

> The trees of the wood are trembling,
> And the birch becoming black-matted masses;
> Snow ever killing birds: (3)
> Such is the tale outside.

Third said—

> The face of the elements is to the east,
> White snow and black deluge:
> What makes the field so cold
> Is the hard-drifting and falling snow.

Servant-maid said—

> Rise now, Ossian,
> To see the white-shouldered, white headed cows,
> As the cold, thawing wind
> Is taking the slender trees of the woods from the
> hillocks.

Is ann amuigh tha 'n torman trom,
  Le uisge trom o bhàrr nan crann
'S cha chluinn mi farum nan tonn (1)
  Le cidhe trom a chimhin chrann. (2)

Tha croinn na coille air chrith
  'S am beithe fàs 'na charra dubh,
Sneachda sior-mharbhadh nan eun, (3)
  'S ionnan 's an sgéul tha muigh.

Tha aghaidh na siona ris an ear,
  Sneachda geal is dile dhubh,
'Se dh' fhag an fhaiche co fuar,
  An cathadh cruaidh is an cur.

Eirich thusa Oisiain,
  Choimhead a 'chruidh ghuaill fhinn, cheann-fhionn
'S tha gaoth fhuar an aiteimh
  Toirt slatan coill a cnocan.

NOTES.

(1) It is said that the sound of the waves is not to be heard when snow or rain is falling heavily; it stops the conveyance of sound.

(2) This obsolete expression, "*Le cithe trom a chimhin chrann,*" is illustrated in the version given by Mr. Campbell of Islay (p. 120, *Leabhar na Féinne*) of the contest of Conn, Sutherland version, and is explained in a foot-note. *Cithe* denotes the heavy splash of blood which the heroes showered in their contest.

(3) A night of violent east wind, killing even the birds of the wood, must have been wildly cold. Such severity of weather is hardly ever known to occur.

We do not know who Ossian's wife was, but there is a tradition that her father lived in a place called the (*Grianan Corr*) Extra Sunny Place. The description of this place is given in a brief extract which has been fallen in with. His own daughter having on one occa-

sion asked the poet, " Who was the handsomest man
among the Fians ? " he said :

> " My good daughter, I could once
> Catch the hind of the red deer
> At its utmost speed,
> And I could take a thistle-spike
> From its wound
> In the blinding, dark night,
> Although I am to-night
> A decrepit old man
> Who cannot take
> Himself from the well,
> Nor from the house."

* * * * * *

> We reached the Extra Sunny Spot,
> Which was thatched with the down of birds ;
> It had door-posts of gold,
> And doors of fluted grass.
> " For whom is the wife asked ? "
> " She is asked for Ossian, son of Fionn."
> " Though I had twelve daughters,
> He would get his choice of them,
> For his exceeding good name
> Among the Fians."

> " Mo dheagh nighean bha mi uair
> A ghlacainn eilid air luathas a ceum
> 'S bheirinn bior foghnain mach
> San oidhche dhorcha dhall
> Ged tha mi nochd
> Ann am dhiblidh sean laoch
> 'S nach d' thoir mi mi-fhein as an tobair
> No 'n aitreabh."

. . . . . .

> Rainig sinn an Grianan Corr
> Bh' air a thutha le cloimhteach eun
> Bha ursainnean ris do 'n òr,

'S còmhlan do'n Iondrain. (1)
" Co dha dh' iarrar a mhnaoi ? "
" Iarrar i do dh' Oissiain Mac Fhinn."
" Ged bhi 'agam da nighean dheug
Gheibheadh e raoghain diu
Air son a ro-chliù
Anns an Fhéinn."

NOTE.

(1) *Ionndrain*, rendered " fluted grass", is long, hard, white grass like sea-bent, and is to be found in marshy ground throughout Mull and in that direction. It is used for thatching houses, and thatch made of it is said to last seven years.

OSSIANIC BALLADS.

The following ballads are also given, to make this work as complete as possible, so far as the writer's opportunities enable him. They exhaust all the materials connected with the Fians that have been fallen in with by him, and if in some parts fragmentary, they are at least free from the obscurity and uncertainty that clog and detract from the merits of all compositions to which the word "doctoring" or "cooking", *i.e.*, interpolating, can be attached. These ballads and poems were sung or recited in a melodious tone peculiar to themselves which was called *Cronan na Féinne* (the melody or purling of the Fians). It might originally have been accompanied by the music of a harp, but, as the writer heard it, it was entirely vocal. It would depend very much on the character of the reciter whether the " O tha" repeated three times after each stanza was the remains of an older melody, or only an attempt at mimicry.

The verse of the purling (*cronan*) which the writer heard is:

CRONAN NA FEINNE.

" Is lionar cutral, 's lionar sgiath,
 Is lionar lùireach is lann gharbh,
 Is lionar Tòiseach 's mac righ ò
 'S cha robh aon diu sin gun airm
 O thà, o thà, o thà."

———

MANUS.

" Cleric! who chantest the psalms,
  I am convinced your judgment is not sound,
Why should you not listen for a short time to a
      tale
  About the Fians—you never heard before?"

" For your authority, son of Fionn,
  And though you highly esteem the Fians,
The voice of the psalms throughout my mouth,
  That is music enough for me."

" Do you compare your psalms
  To Fionn-recitations about bared weapons?
Cleric! I would not reckon it a disgrace
  To separate your head from your body?"

" I take thy protection, great one,
  The words of thy mouth are sweet to me,
And the tale heard of Fionn:
  Joyful to me is the mention of the Fians."

A day that we were hunting on a sea side slope,
  We did not fall in with the chase,
There were seen very many ships,
  Sailing high from the east.

" Who is it that I will get
  To go for news from the people?

(Mac-Cumhail spoke fast)
    He will get praise, and due meed."

Conan came near.
    "O King! Whom would you like to send,
But truly wise Fergus your son,
    Since he is wont to be ambassador?"

" Ill betide you, bald Conan,"
    Said Fergus of fairest mien ;
" I will go to get word from them,
    For the Fians, but not at your request."

Young white-handed Fergus rose
    To the road from the shore to meet the men,
And of them asked in civil tones,
    Who the people were that came from the
        east ?

" Manus is our leader,
    The honourable Chief of the Red Shield,
He will take the wife from Fionn,
    And Bran over the waves, in spite of him."

" Though you are so boastful of yourself,
    And that you think so highly of your people,
As many as have come from the far-off sea,
    They will not take the wife from Fionn.

" Fionn will hold stout contest,
    With yourself before you get the wife,
And the Fians will fight hard
    With your people, before you can get Bran."

Fergus, my own son, came,
    The counterpart of the sun in likeness,
To tell us of the people,
    King! clear and loud was his voice.

We spent that night till day,
   It was not music to us to be silent.
Wine and secrecy, flesh, and waxen lights,
   That used to be our music.

They unfurled *Maol nan Dorn* (Fisticuffs?),
   The banner of young Ronald, son of Morlum.
They unfurled Geur-Iomlan,
   The banner of young Dermid O Dwino.

We unfurled the Terrible Sheaf,
   The banner of young Oscar my brother,
Though there stood not on earth or land
   A banner that could war against it.

We raised the Sunbeam on high,
   The banner of Fionn, great was its prowess,
Weighted with gems of gold,
   And truly it was highly esteemed.

There were nine chains in it
   Of pure gold extending to the ground,
And nine times nine warriors about every chain,
   Urging it in front of the lofty Hero.

Bounteous Manus was overthrown,
   In presence of the rest, on the sward,
And on him, though it was no kingly honour,
   Was put the tie of the three smalls.

Conan came down to us,
   The son of Morlum, who was ever doing mischief.
" Let me at Manus of the Swords
   That I may cut off his head from his body."

" Ill betide you, bald Conan,
   Friendship nor love I have not for you.
Since it happens that I am at Fionn's mercy
   I love it more, than to be at your beck."

" Since you happen to be at my mercy,
   I will not contemn a worthy man;
I will set you free,
   Hand of might, to wage a battle.

" You will get your choice now,
   Leave to go home to your own land,
Friendship and fellowship and love,
   Or else to take what you can from the Fians."

" As long as I live,
   Or the breath is in my body,
One blow against thee, Fionn,
   I regret what I have done against thee."

" You did it not against me,
   It was to yourself you did the hurt.
As many people as you brought from your own
      land
   Will not again return thither."

———

   " A chléirich a chanas na sailm
      Is deimhin leam nach maith do chiall
   C'uim nach eisd thu tamull sgeul
      Air an Fheinn nach cual' thu riamh ?"

   " Air a chumha-sa, mhic Fhinn,
      'S air an Fhéinn ge mor do gheall,
   Guth nan salm air feadh mo bheoil
      Gur h-e sin is ceòl domh fhéin."

   " Am bheil thusa coimeas do shalm,
      Ri Fionn-ghabhail nan arm nochd ?
   A chléirich cha tamailteach leam,
      Ged sgarainn do cheann o d' chorp.

   " Gabham mu d' chomraich fhir mhòir
      Cainnt do bheoil is binn leam fhéin
   'S an sgeul chualas air Fionn
      'S ait leam bhi tigh'nn air an Fhéinn."

Latha dhuinn aig fiadhach na leirg,
　　Cha do thàrl' an t-sealg 'nar car,
Chunnacas na iomada bàrc
　　Seòladh gu h-àrd, àrd o'n ear.

"No co an t-aon a gheibhinn fhéin
　　A rachadh a ghabhail sgeul de 'n t-slògh
(Labhair Mac-Cumhaill gu grad),
　　"Gheibheadh e blogh, agus duais."

Thainig an Conan a nìos.
　　"A righ, co 's aill leat a chur ann?
Ach Fearghus fìor-ghlic do mhac,
　　O'n 's e chleachd bhi dol 'nan ceann."

"Mollachd dhuit-sa, Chonain mhaoil,"
　　Arsa Fearghus, bu chaoine cruth ;
"Theid mise ghabhail an sgeul
　　Do 'n Fhéinn 's cha-n ann air do ghuths'."

Dh' imich Fearghus dòrn gheal òg
　　Do'n ròd an coinneamh nam fear,
'S dh' fhiosraich e dhiu, le gùth fòil,
　　"C' iad na slòigh thainig o 'n ear?"

"Manus a th' òirnn mar thriath
　　Macan mi-aghach na sgiath deirg
'S gu'n d' thugadh e bhean o Fhionn
　　Agus Bran far tuinn, ge b' oil leis."

"Asad fein ge mor do bhosd
　　'S air do shlòigh ge mor do bheachd
A mhiad 's a thainig bho 'n lear
　　Cha toir iad a bhean o Fhionn.

"Chumadh Fionn còmhrag treun
　　Riut fhéin mu 'm faigheadh tu bhean,
'S chumadh an Fhéinn comhrag cruaidh,
　　Ri d' shluagh mu 'm faigheadh tu Bran

Thainig Fearghus mo mhac fhein,
　Mac-samhuil do 'n ghrein a chruth,
Dh' innse sgeul dhuinn air an t-slogh,
　A righ, b' oscara mòr a ghuth.

Thug sinn an oidhche sin gu lò
　Cha bu cheòl dhuinn bhi 'nar tosd
Fion, is folachd, feoil is ceir
　Sin an rud bu cheol duinn fhéin.

Thog iad mach Maol-nan-Dòrn
　Bratach Raonuill òig 'ic Morlum,
Thog iad amach a Gheur-Iomlan
　Bratach Dhiarmaid òig o Duibhne.

Thug sinn amach a Sguab Ghàbhaidh,
　Bratach Oscair òig mo bhrathair,
Ca' na sheas air talamh, no air fonn,
　Bratach gam bu chòir a còmhrag?

Thog sinn a' Ghil-ghréine ri crann
　Bratach Fhinn bu mhòr a goil,
Lomlan de chlachan an òir
　'S deimhin gum bu mhòr a meas.

Bha naoi slabhruidhean innte sios,
　De 'n òr fhior a dh' ionnsuidh an làir,
'S naoi caogad curaidh fuidh gach slabhruidh,
　'Ga iomain an uchd a mhòr laoich.

Gu'n leagadh Manus an àigh
　Am fianuis chaich air an raon
Is dhàsan, ge nach b' onoir righ,
　Chuireadh ceangal nan tri chàol.

Thainig an Conan a nìos,
　Mac Mòrlum bha riamh ri olc,
"Leig mi gu Manus nan lann,
　'S gu'n sgarainn a cheann o chorp."

" Mollachd dhuitse, Chonain mhaoil,
  Càirdeas no gaol cha' n' eil agam duit,
O'n thàrladh dhomh bhi fo ghrasan Fhinn
  Is ionmhuinn leam na bhi fo d' bhreth-se."

" O'n thàrladh dhuit a bhi fo 'm ghràs,
  Cha dean mise tàir air flath,
Leigidh mi thusa ma réir
  A lamh threun gu cuir a chath.

Gheibh thu do roghainn a nis,
  Cead dol dachaigh gu d' thìr fein,
Càirdeas is comunn is gràdh
  Air neo do làn thoirt o' n Fhéinn."

" Cho fad 's a bhios mise beò
  No bhios an deò so ann am chorp
Aon bhuille t' aghaidh, Fhinn,
  'S aithreach leam na rinn mi ort."

" Cha-n ann orm-sa rinn thu e,
  'S ann dhuit fhéin a rinn thu lot.
Na thug thu shluagh as do thìr
  Cha till iad rìs a sin."

NOTE.

This verse, which might be introduced after the sixteenth line,
was heard from a different person :

" If you were worthless Cleric
  With us at the beach to the south,
At the Cataract of the river of peaceful streams,
  You would think highly of the Fians."

"Na'm bi' tusa chléirich chàich
  Againn air an tràigh mu dheas
Ann eas amhuinn nan sruth seimh
  Air an Fhéinn bu mhòr do mheas."

(*Caogad.*) The interpretation that *Caogad* means fifty is given
by Lhuyd, no mean authority; but the explanation that it means

nine is confirmed by a current rhyme as to the duration of the
pregnancy of animals :

> " Three months for a dog.
> Five *caogad* for cat,
> The wife is the same as the cow,
> The big year for a mare."

> " Tri miosan cù
> Coig caogad càt
> 'S ionnan bean 's bò
> 'S bliadhna mhor na làr."

In a table given in some agricultural almanacs the time for
a cat was stated to be forty-five days, and sometimes forty-seven,
and it has been known but very rarely to extend even to forty-
nine. This agrees with the popular observation expressed in the
rhyme of five times nine being forty-five. When the Fians were
attacked by the Osterling, or Eastern Sea, nine *caogad* put their
backs to the door to keep her out (see tale of *Muireartach,
Osterling Sea*), and nine times nine of the Fians put their backs
to the door and nine iron chains binding each other. The old
wife whom the Osterling Sea denotes, gave a kick to the door, the
door flew open, and the warriors were thrown on their backs on
the floor. Even nine is an extravagance as to the number who
were overthrown, but fifty, or nine times fifty, is out of all bounds.

The ballad was learned about forty-five years ago from a very
old man in Balemeanach, Tiree, 1869, by Malcolm McDonald,
Scarinish, from whose recitation it was taken down, 1869.

ALVIN (AILBHINN).

A day that Patrick was in his dwelling (1)
Heedless of psalms, but drinking, (?)
He went to the house of Ossian, son of Fionn,
Since well he liked his lofty talk.

" Are we welcome, generous old man?
To you on a visit we have come,
Hero, soldier-like, and finest of form,
That never refused anything to any one.

I would like to hear from you,
Son of Cumal, of stately and warlike stride,

8

Of the greatest strait in which the Fians ever were
Since first their track was found."

It is I who can tell you that,
Patrick, of the sweet-sounding psalms;
The straitest place in which the men were
From the day on which the Fians of Fionn were set on
    foot.

Fionn neglected to invite to a feast,
Alvin among the first heroes,
And some of the Fians of purest redness,
And their wrath and indignation were roused.

Alvin, son of the cool Fian man,
By whom the edge of the sword was soon made red;
Even so, and Thinman, pure and fresh,
Absented themselves for a year from the dwelling of
    Fionn.

They took (fearsome was their journey)
The ships that were long before our time.
From the small summer residence of the Fians
To Lochlinn's King of slippery shields.

A year and day's term of service to the King
Was engaged to be made by the two of modest form.
The wife of Lochlinn's King of brown shields,
Fell in love heavily and not lightly.

The wife of Lochlinn's King of brown shields,
Fell in love heavily and not lightly
With lovable Alvin of sharp-edged weapons,
And they did deceitfully conceal it.

The wife left the King's bed—
That was the act for which blood was spilt,
To the small summer dwellings of the Fians
They took their journey over sea.

The King of Lochlinn gathered his men,
A large fleet he took with him ;
And what he had at the time
Was nine Kings, and their people with them.

Seven detachments, north and south,
Of men as good as ever were seen ;
Four detachments were we to meet them,
Of goodly Fians of worthy deeds.

But Lochlinners, a fierce company,
Could neither be enraged nor overawed ;
They would take nothing under the sun,
But the total overthrow of the Fian host.

The first message that came from the King,
That was sad news that tried us hard :
As many as there was of us of the Fians of Fionn,
During our time to be taken from us.

Alvin stood the heavy onslaught,
Since he was wont to be in the front ;
The head of Alvin and the son of Leirr
Were won at the second blow.

Thirty leaders of our host,
And the head of Alvin foremost,
These fell by the hand of Ergan
Before the people closed.

Fionn, the noble leader, asked his people,
As many as were there at the time,
Who would strive with Erragon in the conflict,
Before our disgrace was reaped by him.

" That would suit Goll well,
A champion who always backs us !"
" Leave the conflict between Erragon and myself,
And let it be left between us in close quarters."

S 2

" The son of Lovic, and Oscar the champion,
Brown-haired Dermid, and the son of Lego,
Take these on each side of your shield
To protect you from the stroke of the hero."

(" Put Oscar and brown Dermid,
Bent Farquhar and the son of Geil,
To protect him from the blows of the hero,
One on each side of his shield.")

They were not long attacking each other;
They did not do half of it that day ;
The head of Big Erragon of the ships fell,
And Goll was victorious at the ninth hour.

Praised be the soul of my King,
That these two were to escape,
When one man and half of the Fians
Fell on the hillside to the south.

Unless one who was disabled,
Or went over to Greek land,
No one returned to his own land
Of all that the King of Lochlinn brought over.

Latha do Phàdruig 'n a mhùr
   Gun sailm air ùigh ach ag òl (?)
Chaidh e thigh Oisiain 'ic Fhinn
   O 'n 's ann leis bu bhinn a ghlòir.

" An e ar beatha, sheanair shuaire,
   Thugad air chuairt thainig sinn,
A laoich mhileanta 's fhearr dreach,
   Nach d' thug eurabh a neach mu ni.

" Fios a b' fhearr leam fhaighinn uait
   Mhic Cumhail nan cruaidh cheum colg,
An t-aite is teinne 'n robh an Fhiann,
   O 'n bhà-tar riamh air an lorg."

" 'S mise dh 'fheudadh sin duit innse
   Phàdruig nan salm binn
An t-aite 's temne 'n robh na fir
   O 'n latha ghinte Fianntaidh Fhinn.

Dearmad fleagh gu 'n d' rinn Fionn
   Air Ailbhinn an tùs nan laoch,
'S air cuid de 'n Fheinn bu ghlan déirg
   'S gu 'n d' éirich am fearg 's am fraoch.

Ailbhinn mac an Fhianntaidh fhuair,
   Leis an deargta gu luath roinn,
Mar sud is Caoilte glan ùr
   Dh' eitich bliadhna roi mhùr Fhinn.

Thugadar (gum b' ogluidh 'n triall),
   Na luingeis bha cian roi 'r linn,
O àiridh-Lugha nam Fiann
   Gu righ Lochlainn nan sgiath sliom.

B' e fasda la 's bliadhn' aig an righ
   Rinn an dìthis bu chaoine dreach,
Ghabh bean Righ Lochlainn nan sgiath donn
   Trom cheist mhòr 's cha robh e beag,

Ghabh bean Righ Lochlainn nan sgiath donn
   Trom cheist mhòr 's cha robh e beag,
Air Ailbhinn ghreadhnach nan arm geur
   'S rinneadh le ceilg roi chleith.

Ghluais a 'bhean a leab' an Righ
   ('Se sud an gniomh mu 'n doirteadh fuil)
Gu àiridh-Lugha nam Fiann,
   Thugadar an triall thar muir.

Chruinnich Righ Lochlainn a shluagh,
   Cabhlach cruaidh gu 'n d' thug e leis
'Se sin a bh' aig' air an uair
   Naoi righrean 's an sluagh leis.

Seachd cathanna, deas agus tuath,
   De 'n sluagh a b' fhearr gam facas riamh,

Ceithir cathan sinne 'nan dàil
De Fhianntaidh àillidh bu ghlan gniomh.

Ach Lochlainneach, a 'bhuidhean bhorb,
Aig feabhas an colg chum gniomh
Cha ghabhadh iad ni fuidh 'n ghrèin
'S an Fhéinn uile bhi 'gan dith.

Chiad teachdaireachd thàinig o 'n rìgh
('S sgeul tiom' sud chuir dhinn gu luath).
Na bha againn de Fhianntaidh Fhinn
Bhi ri 'r linn ga thoirt uainn.

Fhreasdal Ailbhinn an còmhrag cruaidh
O 'n 's ann da nach bu dual a bhi air for.
Ceann, Ailbhinn, agus Mhic Leirr
Bhuidhneadh air an darna beum.

Deich ceannarda fichead d' ar slòigh
'S ceann Ailbhinn fein air tùs
Bha sud air làimh Iorghuill mhòir,
Mu 'n deachaidh na slòigh an dlùths.

Dh' fhiosraich Fionn flath 'ga shluagh,
Na bha 'n uair sin dhiu ann,
Co bhuineadh ri Iorghuill san treis
Mu 'm buineadear leis ar tàir.

" Bu mhath fhreagradh sud air Goll,
Sonn a tha air ar cùl ! "
" Leagar eadar mi 's Iorghuill san treis
'S leagar eadar sinn an cleas dlù."

" Mac Luthaich is Oscar an sonn
Is Diarmad donn is Mac-a-Léigh
Thoir sid air gach taobh do d' sgéith
G' ad dhideineadh o bheum an laoch."

(" Cui ribh Oscar 's Diarmad donn
Fearchar crom 's Mac-a-Ghéill
G'a dhion o bhuillean an laoich
Fear dhiù air gach taobh mu sgéith.")

Ge b' fhada thug iad greis
   Cha d' rinn iad a leth 'san là,
Thuit ceann Iorghuill mhòr nan long,
   'S bhuidhinn Goll air a naoidheamh trà.

Buidheachas do anam mo righ
   Gu 'n robh an dithis sin ri tigh 'nn as
Fear is darna leth nam Fiann
   Thuiteam air an t-sliabh mu dheas.

Mur robh fear a chaidh o fheum
   No chaidh air a' Ghréig a null,
Cha deachaidh fear gu' thir féin
   De na thug Righ Lochlainn a nall."

NOTES.

Mùr, a dwelling, is connected etymologically with the Latin *murus*, a wall. The cells or places of shelter in which the early Christians seem to have contented themselves, were probably merely huts or places that would protect them from the elements and rain, while they pondered over the manuscript in which the Gospel tale was told.

The Book of Psalms seems also to have attracted much attention, and the repetition or intonation of psalms to have been a favourite occupation.

The writer has heard it put forward that the word *òl*, rendered drinking, may be a corruption from the word *oil*.

This Iorghuill, or Erragon, seems to have been a kind of bully or champion kept by the North King, a strong man and ready swordsman.

Greece is apparently a vague name for some remote or unknown place on the continent of Europe. In the unpublished tale (*sgeulachd*) of "The Soldier of Misfortune", there is an account of a feast at which five kings sat. The King of Little Greece, and the King of Big Greece, the King of Blue Greece, and the King of Red Greece, and the King of Branched Greece (*Righ na Gréige bige, 's Righ na Gréige mòra, Righ na Gréige Gùirme, 's Righ na Gréige Deirge, 's Righ na Gréige Meanganaich*).

CONN, SON OF THE RED.

A TALE of Conn, Son of the Red,
Full of heavy wrath,
Coming to avenge his father's death
On the worthies and high dignitaries
Within the big bounds of Ireland.
A tale of Conn, the best, the manly,
The stout, the stalwart, the gentle, the comely.

Which was the biggest, the Conn or the Red?
Said Ossian, in the sweet-sounding words of his mouth,
Or were his shape and form the same
As the Red, the big, the active, the lightly moving;
The same as the Red One, the lightly moving.
Much bigger was Conn, much more, very much,
Coming towards our people.
Drawing his boat in
From the environments of ocean and strait;
In ocean and in straits.

He sat on the knoll near us,
The very heroic and most valorous man;
As if you were to see a whirlpool,
Or the ebb of the sea against strong waves;
Or as the sound of billow in boiling waves
In the utmost strength of the billows.
In the utmost fury of the great man,
In search of avenging his father's death.
He rose to the folds of the clouds,
Above us, in his next exploits,
Westward in the bulking of the clouds.

He could work ready plays,
In the face of the clouds.
He sat on outside knolls,
The mighty, strong, big man,
And he placed his sword on a hero's account
Without fear of the strife.

The like of him we never saw
For his strength and mightiness of deed,
And many a warrior was unweariedly
Giving him obedience and great tribute.

    Then when came cheerful, exceeding handsome
      Fergus,
At his father's instance (as I would wish),
To ask news from the tall man :
" What the cause may be of your journey to Ireland.
Great, victorious, eager Conn,
Pleasant, joyful, merry.
I am come to learn from you,
What the cause is of your coming to the land ?"

" Why should I not tell that to you, Fergus,
And carry you it with you ?
My father's ransom I would have
From you, and from the nobles of the men of Ireland.
The head of Goll and his two big sons,
The head of Conan and his two valued sons,
The head of Finn, supreme Head of the host,
Finn and Fasdal,
And the heads of the Clanna Morna altogether,
Or all that are alive in Ireland,
In Ireland from sea to sea,
As a ransom for one man,
To yield to my yoke,
Or combat of five hundred
To-morrow morning.

Five hundred big men,
To set them to combat with my worst man
Out to-morrow.
And that I separate their heads from the bodies,
Of Finn, Conan, and Cormac."

" Let me at him," said Coreven,
" That I may take off his head."
" Don't you speak, Coreven," said Fionn,
" And utter not such a foolish proposition ;
He will not be subdued without guile,
By two-thirds of those that are in Ireland."

" Let me at him," said Conan,
" That I myself may take off his head."
" Evil betide you, hold you your peace, bald Conan
    (said Fionn),
Will you not stop your forwardness ever ?"

Then it was that Conan
Weakly, ill, faint, without sense,
Entirely against the will of the Fian King,
Like a turn to the left hand, to his hurt.
And when the well-formed hero saw
Conan putting on his armour,
He caught a door-bar,
As he fled wildly :
Many were those caused by it,
Of knob, and big lump,
Outcry and loud shouting from Conan's head,
No less loud
Than the sound of waves against a beach,
And the whole host of the Fians
All hearing him.

On bald Conan of a truth
Were put the five ties under one binding.

Then were sent out six-score big men
Of the best of families and people,
And he took a manly rush through them,
Like a hawk through a flock of little birds,
As quick as a strong mill-wheel.
Many a shape changed appearances,
And forms their shape, with hardness of sword-blades.
Many a head and half limb,
And many a skull lay here and there,
Five hundred more though they were there
Would fall in one mass.
Conn, still sounding a challenge-note on his shield,
Asking combat—and an evil asking it was,
And the Féinne uttered a hard cry of distress,
At the slaughter of their numerous people,
Till there were felled by him the ten-score big men,
Of the best of families and people.
To tell you a history,
The Fians never were
So frightened for one man.

Then spoke Fionn :
" Goll, son of Morna of great deeds,
Why should you not rise Goll?
Man whose wont was ever to succour us,
The desire of every town,
And strong hero in time of need.
It is too bold in me to threaten with Conn (you),
And the whole race of Morna.
But why should you not take off his head manfully,
As you did to his father heretofore ?"

" I would do that for you, Fionn,
Man of warm, sweetly-sounding words,
Though it was by you Clanna Morna fell, changed,
But that hatred and secret thoughts be laid aside,
And we all be of one mind,

Though the whole Fians were killed
To the loss of one man,
I myself, and my strong men would be with you,
King of the Fians, to succour you."

   Then went
Five hundred of us to meet him,
And Goll was prepared to meet them.
Like a hawk on a covey of birds, though of a size.
Numerous were then to be found there
One with one eye, and one with one hand,
And though as many more were there,
They would be found dead around him.

   Then when Goll
Was going to the contest,
Goll moved in his hard attire
In presence of the multitude.
   In that hour,
White and red was the face of the man of strife
As he went into the strife,
Flowing hair, yew-like, on rough hill-side,
Crimson cheeks like dried yew,
Sheltered under eyebrows bent and narrow,
Sinking in steep inclines,
Remembering the greater mystery.

He put his shield buckled,
Crooked, narrow-topped,
On his left hand,
And took his heavy-wielding, dashing,
Hard sword
In his right hand.

   Then when began the two warriors
Of best form,
The earth was made
To shake tremulously,

Splitting the knives of shields,
And shields of phantoms.
Shedding much blood,
From the ever-moving hands of each.
Three flashes they would emit,
A flash of fire from their armour,
A flash of sound from their bucklers
A flash of flesh and blood,
From their frames and their whole bodies.

Then it was,
Till the tide fell back,
And the clouds bent down,
And the elves of the hills
Came out to be amused and amazed.

Eleven days and a time,
Sorrowful were men and women,
Till there fell by Goll of blows
The big, valiant man, with great difficulty.
A joyous shout the Fians gave,
Such as they never gave before,
On seeing powerful Goll victorious,
Over the great, the boastful, the arrogant Conn.

CONN MAC AN DEIRG.

Sgeulachd air Chonn Mac an Deirg
Air a lionadh le trom fheirg,
Dol a dhioladh éiric athar gun fheall,
Air mhaithibh 's air mhòr uaisle
Air chriochaidh mòra na h-Eirinn.
Sgeulachd air Chonn fear fearail
An sonn calma caoin ceanail.

" Co dhiu bu mhotha 'n Conn no 'n Dearg?"
Ars Oisian nam briathran binne beòil !

" No 'm b' ionnan dealbh dha is dreach,
'S do 'n Dearg mhòr, mhear, mheamnach
Dha fhein 's do 'n Deargan mheamnach?"

Bu mhotha 'n Conn gu mòr mòr
Tighinn an caramh ar slòigh,
Tarruing a luingeis a steach
A crioslaichibh cuain agus caolais,
An cuan agus ann an caolas.

Shuidh e air an tulaich 'gar còir
Am fiui curanta ro-mhor
Mar fhaiceadh sibh coire chrnim
Mar thraghadh mara ri treun thuinn
No mar fhuaim tuinne ri teth tuinn
Aig ro mhiad falachd an tuinn
Aig ro-mhiad feirg an fhir mhoir
'S e an tòir air éiric athar a dhìoladh
Dh' eiricheadh e ann am frilleinibh na nial
Os air cionn anns an ath-mhiad
Siar ann am baileibh na h iarmailt.

'S dh' iomaradh e air cleasan coireach,
Ann an aodann nam fireiltean
Shuidh e air tulachan corr,
Am fiùi curanta, ro-mòr,
'S chuir e chlaidheamh air sgàth laoich,
'S gun eagal aimhreit air.
A mhac samhuilt cha 'n fhacas riamh
Air ghaisge 's air meud a ghnìomh
'S gur ioma laoch bha gun sgios
Toirt da geill agus mòr chìs.

　　Sin 'nuair thainig Fearghus mìrlum aluinn
Air chòmhairle, athar mar a b' àill leam,
Ghabhail sgeul do 'n fhear mhòr,
" De fath do choiseachd do dh' Eirinn?
A Chuinn mhoir, bhuaghaich, bhrais,
Shùgach, ait, àibhinn.

Dh' fhiosrachadh thainig mi dhiot
Ciod e fath do thuruis do 'n tir ?"

"C' uim nach innsinn sin duit-sa, Fhearghuis,
Agus buin leat e
Eiric m' athar a b' àill leam,
Bhuaitse 's bho uaislean uile fir Eirinn,
Ceann Ghuill 's a dha mhic mhòir
Ceann Chonain 's dha mhic muill
Ceann Fhinn flath an t-slòigh
Fhinn agus Fhaisdeil,
'S cinn chlanna Morna gu h-uile,
Na na bheil beo an Eirinn
Na Eirinn, o thuinn gu tuinn,
Ann an éiric aon duine.
A gheilleachduinn do 'm aon chuinn,
No comhrag coig ciad,
Air maduinn am màireach.
Coig fichead fear mòr
Chuir an comhrag ri m' fhear diubhalach
Amach am màireach
'S gu 'n sgarainn an ceann o 'n coluinn
Dh' Fhinn, agus Chonan, agus Chormaic."

"Leigibh mis' thuige," arsa Coiribhin,
"'S gum buininn, an ceann deth."
"Na labhair thusa, Choirìbhin," arsa Fionn,
"'S na tig air còmhra co cli sin :
Cha chiosnaichear e gun fhoill,
Da thrian 's na bheil an Eirinn."

"Leigear mise g' a ionnsaidh," arsa Conan,
"'S gam buininn fhin an ceann deth."
"Marbhasg ort, uisd thusa a Chonain mhaoil," arsa
        Fionn,
"'S nach sguir thu d' lonan gu brath."

Ach sin 'nuair chaidh Conan
Lag, dona, meata, mi-cheillidh,
An an-toil do uile righ na Féinne

Mar char tuaitheal g' a aimh-leasadh ;
'S 'nuair chunnaic an laoch bu dealbhaich,
Conan dol an glaic armachd,
Rug e air a druill,
'S e teicheadh gu h-albhaidh.
Bu lionar sin a gheibht' ann,
Plùc agus garbh-mheall,
Glaodh agus iolach àrd an ceann Chonain :
'S na bu lugha e
Na fuaim tuinne ri tràigh
'S feachd na Feinn'
Uile 'ga eisdeachd.

Chaidh air Conan maol gu deimhin
Na Coig chaoil fuidh 'n aon cheangal.

Sin mar chaidh sia fichead fear mòr,
De mhaithibh teaghlaich is slòigh ;
'S thug e ruathar fir foruinn,
Mar sheabhag roi 'ealt mhin ean.
Cho luath ri garbh roth muilinn
'S ioma cruth a chaochail greann
'S cuirp ath-chuimte le cruas lann,
'S ioma ceann 's leth chas
'S ioma claigionn thall 's a bhos
Coig ciad eile ged bhiodh ann,
Gu 'n tuiteadh sid air aon bhall,
'S Conn a' calcadh a sgiath
'G iarraidh comhraig 's gum b' an-iarr
'S gu 'n do leig an Fhéinn gàir chruaidh
Ri diochaidh a' mhòr shluaigh.
Gus na thuit leis na deich fichead fear mòr
De mhaithibh teaghlaich is sloigh ;

Dh' innse dhuibhse eachdraidh,
Nach do ghabh an Fheinn riamh,
Leithid do dh' eagal roi aon-fhear.

Sin nuair labhair Fionn,
" Ghuill-ic-Morna nam mòr ghnìomh
C' uim nach éireadh tusa, Ghuill,

Fhir a chleachd ar cobhair riamh,
A mhiann sùla gach baile
'S a laoich làidir na teug bhail
'S dàna leam Conn a bhagradh ort
'S air Clanna Morna gu h-uile
'S nach tugadh tu 'n ceann deth gu fearail,
Mar rinn thu g' a athar roimhe."

" Dheanainn-sa sin duitse Fhinn
Fhir nam briathra blatha binn
S gur h-ann leat fhein a thuit
Clanna Mòrlum mùghta ;
Ach fuath agus falachd chuir air chùl
'S bitheamaid uile de dh' aon rùn,
Ged mhairbhte 'n Fheinn uile
Gu diochadh aon duine
Bhithinn fhin 's mo thréin leat,
A righ na Féinne, g' ad chobhair."

Sin nuair chaidh
Còig ciad againne 'na dhàil
'S a bha Goll rompa ann an gràs
Mar shealbhag air ealt air a meud,
Bu lionar sin a gheibht' ann,
Fear air leth-shùil 's air a làimh ;
S urrad eile ged bhiodh ann,
Gum faighteadh marbh mu thiomchioll-san iad.

Sin 'nuair bha Goll,
Dol a chur a' chòmhraig
Ghluais Goll 'na chulaidh chruaidh
Ann am fianuis a' mhòir shluaigh
Anns an uair sin,
Bu gheal 's bu dearg gnùis an fhir Iorghuill,
Dol an tùs na h-iorghuill
Fhalt chleachdach iubhar gharbh-shléibheach,
Gruaidh chorcur mar iubhar caoine,
Fuidh fhasga na mala chama-chaoile,
Sioladh ann an caolartaibh corrach,
Cuimhneachadh na mòr fholachd ;

9

'S chuir e sgiath bhucaideach,
Bhacaideach, bharra-chumhann,
Air a làimh chlì ;
'S a shlacanta curanta,
Cruaidh chlaidheamh,
'Na làimh dheis.

Sin nuair thoisich an dà laoch,
Bu dealbhaiche,
Chuireadh an talamh
Air bhalla-chrith ;
'Sgoltadh nan sgeana sgiath
'Sgoltadh nan sgiathan sgleò,
A' dòrtadh na fala mòire,
O laimh imeachdaich a chèile.
Tri dithean gu 'n cuireadh iad dhiu,
Dith teine da 'n armailbh
'S dith cailce da 'n sgiathaibh,
'S dith fal' agus feòla
Da 'n cneas agus da 'n cìth-cholainn.

Gum b' e sin doibh-san,
Gus an thuit an tràigh
'S an do chrom na neòil,
'S an d' thainig siochairean na beinne,
Ghabhail aighear agus ioghnaidh.

Aon latha diag agus trà
Gum bu tursach mic is mnài
Gus na thuit le Goll nam beuman
An sonn mòr air cheart èiginn.
Gàir eibhinn gu 'n d' rinn an Fhiann
Nach d' rinneadh leo roimhe riamh
Ri faicinn Ghuill chrodha an uachdar
Air Conn mòr mear uaibhreach

NOTE.

Choig chaoil, rendered five ties, are really the tying of the two
wrists (*caol nan duirn*), the small of the back (*caol-druim*), and the
two feet at the ankles (*caol na coise*), which would leave the person
so tied without the power of defence, or even running away.

THE MUILEARTACH.[1]

THE story of the Osterling, or Eastern, Sea was published in the *Celtic Review*, No. 2, 1881. It is here
given from its having always been looked upon as
closely connected with the history of the Fian band, and
also from its own merits. The name of the principal
character in this tale is pronounced indifferently, and by
the same reciters, *Muireartach* and *Muileartach*, and is
construed by them sometimes as a masculine, but most
commonly as a feminine, noun. There is no difficulty
in deriving it from Muircartach, the Eastern Sea.

This tale has been selected as a fair specimen of tales
at one time common in the Western Islands and Highlands of Scotland, and still to be occasionally fallen in
with. It relates, as almost all the popular tales of the
Scottish Celts do, to Ireland. Copies in print of the

---

[1] The writer was under the impression, at first, that the word
Muileartach, the Osterling Sea, which the Fians encountered,
denoted the Western Sea, but further reflection upon the meaning
of the word satisfies him that, like the English word Osterling, it
rather denotes the Eastern Sea. The invasions of the Norsemen,
both to Ireland and the Western Isles, were from the east, and it is
the Eastern Sea that is said to bring them. The points of the
compass are not very strictly looked to either at sea or on land,
the rising of the sun in the east and its setting in the west being
sufficient for ordinary purposes, and it was sufficiently known that
the Lochlin invaders had come from some place lying to the east,
also that Argyle, or Erra-ghaidheal, is the eastern part of the Celtic
world, lying as it does to the east of Ireland. The exact geo-
graphy of the Lochlin invaders is not known, but they came from
some place to the east of Scotland, whether north-east or due east
was not strictly inquired into.

tale, or parts of it, are to be found in Campbell's *West Highland Tales*, iii, 122 ; several versions in *Leabhar na Féinne*, by the same excellent collector ; and one in Gillies' Collection. Of the version here given, Part I has never appeared in print. It was written many years ago from the dictation of Duncan M'Fadyen, Caolas, Tiree, and has been compared with other oral versions ; and Part II from Duncan Cameron, constable, Tiree, in 1871.

In the translation, " Fin-Mac-Coul" is adopted as a better rendering of *Fion Mac Cumhail* than the more familiar and euphonious Fingal, a name which had its origin with Macpherson. Similarly, " Fians" is adopted for *Féinne*, a collective noun, and *Fiantan*, a plural noun, instead of Fingalians or Fenians, names which have other ideas now associated with them. " Fin-Mac-Coul" has more of the ludicrous idea attached to it than belongs to the Gaelic name. It is as old as Barbour, who uses it in the poem of " The Bruce" (*circa* 1380).

Historically, this tale is worthless, as it cannot be accepted as a *memento* of, or in any way relating to, a sea-fight between Norsemen and Celts. It is, however, of considerable interest to the student of history, as showing personification at work, and the manner in which the creations of fancy harden into acceptance as historical facts. The tale is a myth, in the true sense of that word. Of the reciters, some believed it to record a real, some a possible event—thus agreeing with Mr. Campbell, who says (*West Highland Tales*, iii, 144), " I suspect the poem was composed in remembrance of some real invasion of Ireland by the sea-rovers of Lochlann in which they got the worst of the fight, and that it has been preserved traditionally in the Hebrides ever since." The *Muileartach* (Eastern Sea), here personified, is appropriately represented in the tale as the nurse or foster-mother of Manus, King of Lochlin, who falls to

be identified with Magnus Barefoot, King of Norway.
That potentate is said in history to have made, towards
the end of the eleventh century, extensive conquests
along the north and west coasts of Scotland, and also in
Ireland. He was killed near Dublin, in 1103. The
epithets applied to the *Muilcartach* leave no doubt as to
the personification. The sea-rover is her foster-child.
She is ill-streaming (*mì-shruth*), abounding in seas (*muir-
-each*), bald-red (*maol-ruadh*), white-maned (*muing-
fhionn*). She has long streaming hair, and is finally
subdued by being let down into the ground to the waist,
the mode in which water is best subdued. She is also
represented as terrific (*uamhannach*), as having a roaring
wide open mouth (*bha gàir 'n a craos*), etc. Any one,
who has seen the sea in a storm, will understand the
appropriateness of the description. It is also to be
observed that, uniformly in popular lore, she is slain by
Fin-Mac-Coul himself, and not by the band of men of
whom he was leader. Fin was not the strongest of the
Féinne or Fian-band, but the solver of questions (*fear-
fuasgladh ceisd*) and adviser. The blades of the Fians
passed as harmlessly through the body of the *Muilcartach*
as the knife through flame. Fin, who represents brain,
intellect, subdued her by letting her down into the
ground. Manus, who was acquainted with northern
seas, imagines, as the only way in which she could be
killed, (1) her being swallowed by a hole in the ground,
or (2) her being frozen over.

It is said that this was the first day on which the Fian
fair-play (*cothrom na Féinne*) was broken. Previously it
was a law of the band to oppose only one to one ; but
this day, Fin told them to attack the *Muilcartach* before
and behind (*air a cùlthaobh 's air a beulthaobh*).

Another tale of popular lore relating to the Fian-band,
in which personification is unquestionably at work, is
that of *Ciuthach mac an Doill*, whose name is but a slight

alteration from *Ceathach*, and means, " Mist, son of the
Blind Man." He came in from the sea to the cave in
which Diarmid and Graine had taken refuge, in a night
so stormy that Diarmid, the third best hero of the Fians,
would not on any account venture out of the cave.

In the whole of the Fian-lore there is much that
seems purely imaginative. And it is upon this supposition of personification that the localisation in so many
places of the Fian traditions, and their strange extrava-
gances, are best explained. The classical reader will
remember how Hercules, also a personification of bodily
strength, was found by the Romans in every place they
visited.

Upon this view—the supposition that the incident is
entirely the work of imagination—the ballad is interesting and poetical. The Eastern Sea, in one of the
gloomier aspects which it frequently presents among
the Islands of Scotland, a bank of mist, a darkening
shower, a high tide, or a fierce gale, is converted by the
poet's fancy into an old woman who is the foster-mother
of the Pirate-King who infests the coast. A solitary
star twinkling through the darkening clouds, becomes
an eye glimmering in her gloomy forehead ; the agita-
tion of the sea, waves swept into spindrift or breaking
wildly on the rocks, the roaring of the waves, and the
Skerries covered with tangle, are readily converted into
her rocking motion, streaming hair, gloomy looks, projecting red teeth, and loud laughter. Following up the
idea, the superiority of the Norsemen at sea is represented by the old woman taking away the Cup of Victory. Betrayed into over-confidence, the Norse king
engages in battle on land and is defeated. This is
represented by the poet as an inroad of the Personified
Sea.

The explanation of the *Muileartach* is further
strengthened by the representation of an enclosure

having been made for the great fight, denoting the confining of water within manageable limits, by the *Muilcartach* being called *sglèò*, a spectre, a film, a vapour, or an indistinct appearance, and by her combating the heroes like a flame.

At the same time, while there is much in the stories of the Fians that can be explained as personifications and poetical fancies; there is much, such as the death of Oscar, that appears as like real history and tradition as anything to be found in authentic records.

For archæological or other scientific purposes, it is essential that ballads of this kind, and indeed everything got from oral sources, should be presented to the reader "uncooked", that is, without suppression or addition, or alteration, which is not pointed out.

PART I.

THE Fians were for keeping the kingdom from the Lochlinners (1). Fin was their king. There was a battle between them and Manus at Dun Kincorry in Ireland. When Manus went home, his foster-mother (nurse), the *Muilcartach*, said that she would go to fight Fin, and to take from him the "Cup of Victory" (2)—a vessel of clay, of which it was said that it was by drinking from it, the Fians were always victorious. Manus said he would send men with her, but she refused. She would take with her only her husband, the Ocean Smith, and a loop of iron, called the Little Ridged Crutch. She went at full speed to Dun Kincorry. The Fians saw something big and monstrous coming; and Fin said, "If he has traversed the universe, and gone round the world, it is Manus's foster-mother, and she wants something particular." The Fians went into the house and nine times nine of them put their

backs to the door, and put behind it nine chains inter-
lacing each other. (She pulled a tree, and swept off the
branches, and had it for a stick. The Ocean Smith
stayed at the boat. They put nine wooden bars behind
the door, and nine feet in stone and lime, and nine times
nine (3) put their backs to the door.)

Fin was looking out, and she came and spoke in a
low voice :—

She.

I am a poor, poor old woman,
That have come hotly pursued ;
I have travelled the five-fifths (4) of Ireland,
And found not a house to let me in.

Fin.

If you have travelled all that,
It is the mark of a bad man ;
And though your claw grow green beneath you,
You will not get an opening from me.

She.

That is an evil custom for a king's son,
Who ought to show heroism and great deeds ;
That you should be called a king's son,
And not give a night's lodgings to an old woman.

Fin.

If it be manners, or meat, or hospitality
You want, old woman !
I will send the meat of a hundred men,
And take away from me your talk, old woman !

She.

I am not in need of your wretched meat,
Neither do I care for your great sadness ;
I would prefer the warmth of your great fire,
And partake with your dogs.

Fin.

Will you not kindle a fire for youself,
Where you can blow it with your breath ;
And put a load of fuel to your stout body,
[*Var.*—Break down small branches against your hump]
And wisely warm yourself at it?

She.

The six best heroes among the Fians,
Put you them out on the sward ;
And when the snow reaches their waist,
They cannot kindle a fire.

[*Var.*—The nine nines who are within,
Between thatch and wattled-wall—
The snow would reach their waist-bands,
And they could not kindle a fire.]

The old woman of hardest conflict,
Gave a kick towards the door ;
And before she turned back the sole of her foot,
She broke the nine chains of iron from their inter-
    lacings.

[And she threw the heroes on the breadth of their
backs on the floor.]

Fin avoided her ; and she went to the chest of jewels,
and took with her the "Cup of Victory".

The men arose—
Thinman (7) rose, and the rest rose,
And rose the plier of the oars, (8)

to go after the old woman.

They could not overtake her. Oscar, the strongest of
the Fians, went after her. He caught her by the foot at
the brow of the hill of Howth. Her grey hair was
hanging behind her, and Oscar caught it. He sprang,

and put three plies of the grey wreathed hair of the old
woman about his fist.   Before he in any way checked
her (lit., put a wrinkle in her), they sank to their waists
in snow.   " Ho, ho," she said, " young man, you have
hurt me !   If it be food or drink you want, you will get
it when I reach the boat."   [Var., reach the Ocean Smith
and you will get it. (9)]   " It is not that I want, but to take
your grey hair to my grandfather."   " Ho, ho, are you
one of that sort ?"   She drew over her wreathed grey
hair below her left arm, and she laid her hand gently
upon him ; and he himself heard the noise of every bone
breaking in his body.   " If you have strength to go
home, tell Fin that I have got the ' Cup of Victory'."

He returned, and she went to Lochlin.   Manus re-
solved to fight Fin.   He gathered his men, and went to
Dun Kincorry to fight Fin.

They met, and commenced at each other.   All the
Lochlinners were killed, and the "Cup of Victory"
was recovered.   Manus was bound, and put under oaths.
It was then that Conan said :

> " Let me to Manus of the swords,
>   That I may separate his head from his body."

Manus then said :

> " A little blow against thee, Fin,
>   I repent me of what I have done to you."

VARIANT.

[Then when the old woman of great fury
Gave a kick to the door,
She broke the nine fastenings
Before her full speed was checked ;
And she entered the dwelling of Fin
And caught Fin's Cup in her crooked claw.
She leapt upon the red rushing water of the oars,
With Fin's Cup in her right hand.
Fin leapt quick, quick,

After the feet of the old woman,
And caught the Cup,
Since to him belonged its Virtue and Power.
Thinman, son of Roin, caught
His big sword and his two spears ;
And the active, youthful Oscar caught
The embroidered skirt that was round her body.
They took the apple from the wretch ;
And if they did it was not without a struggle :
And if her head was not put on another body,
Her soul never obtained mercy.
High was her place, and high her growth,
High were her sails for age (?), (10)
An iron crowbar under her,
And two teeth westward from her open mouth ;
Such a darksome old woman
Was not seen since the days of Cu-chullain.[1]] (11)

PART II.

He (Manus) went home bare and empty handed. His fostermother asked for his men ; and he said they were lost. " King !" she said, " that ever I gave the juice of my side to you when you could not kill Fin, seeing he is only a halfman" (*i.e.*, one of the twins). (12) " I shall go now ; and as many men as you have lost I shall take from the Fians in twenty-four hours." "I shall raise", said Manus, " my ships and go with you." She would not hear of this, but that the Smith should go with her. He was good at telling stories, and would tell everything to Manus, when they came home. The Smith was not willing to go, though he had only heard of Fin ; but she caught him, and threw him into the boat. They took their sea journey. A little gentle breeze came after them from the lower part of the hills and from the

---

[1] See p. 137, stanza 9.

heights of the trees, that would take foliage from a hill, and willows from a tree, and little young rushes from their base and roots. They began to throw the sea aside, flashing, flapping, foaming, against the blackness of the old stone, and the pitch-blackness of the boulder-stones, the biggest beast eating the smallest beast, and the smallest beast doing as best it could ; the little sea-birds betaking themselves to rest and shelter in the wisp of the main-mast. She (the boat) would cut the hard slender stalks of oats with her very stem, for the great excellency of her steersman. (13) " Look up," she said to the Ocean Smith, "and try and see land." When he looked all round about him, he saw land and said, " If it be land it is small, and if it be a crow it is large." " That is true, my good fellow," she said ; " we have not the boat at its proper speed." They put out the small broad-bladed, ridged oars, and every time they stretched their backs they took in water over the gunwale of the boat. For all the evils and tossings they got, they reached land and drew up the boat above the beach (lit., " in the top of the shore"), where the boys of the town could not make sport or laughing-stock of it. She bade the Ocean Smith go behind a hillock at the back of the wind and in front of the sun, where he could see everybody and nobody could see him. (14) He did this, and she went on. Unfortunately, the Fians were sleep-ing on their arms, and twenty-four of them were on their breasts. She began to kill them with the iron loop.

> " She killed twenty-four of the Fians,
>   Alvinn himself foremost
>   Fell by the hand of the great Conflict,
>   Before the warriors came to close quarters."

Then commenced the Fians and the Carlin wife, and were thrashing and slashing and working away at one

another. She was intercepting them like a flame down
and up. She was tall. Oscar asked to be sent himself
against her, and she was heavily buffeting him, and
driving him backwards, and Fin's courage fell. He told
them to take spades and cut below her, and drive her
backwards to get a chance of engaging and striking her.
They made a hole and drove her back, until she fell in.
She was still intercepting them like a flame ; but for all
the evils and tossings they got, they killed the old
woman before they stopped. It was then they raised
a battle-shout for joy ; and then twenty-four of the
Fians, who were in Corry Glen, when they heard it,
knew that some trouble had come on the Fians. They
rushed over, and one of them said to a companion,
" King ! wilt thou not thyself tell me how she was when
she was on her legs ?"

" I am not able to tell that to any but to one who saw
her."

LAY OF THE " MUILEARTACH".

A day we were on Eastern hillock,
Looking on Erin all around,
There came upon us over a slimy heavy sea,
A spectre (15) heavy and not grey ;
Two teeth projecting westward from her gaping
    mouth,
And four fathoms from around her lower part.
Twenty-four of the Fians,
And Alvin himself foremost,
Fell by the hand of the great Brawler
Before the people closed. (16)
Then spoke Goll,
The hero who was never behind :
" Let me towards her for a while,
That I may show her a feat of strength."

The old woman was tearing at him and driving him backwards ; and Fin lost courage at that time. It was then that he ordered them to cut the earth below her sole, and to let her to the place of her girdle into the ground. She was intercepting us down and up like a flame ; but for all the evils and tossings we got, it was then we killed the old woman and raised the battle-shout.

When the Ocean Smith, who was behind the wind and in front of the sun, heard that the *Muileartach* had been slain, he put out to sea [here repeat the rhymes descriptive of sea journeys] and reached Lochlin alone. Manus met him, and asked where he had left the old woman. "She has been killed," said the Ocean Smith.

"Wretch, she has not been killed ; but when you saw the doughty deeds she was doing, you fled."

"Oh, she has been killed!"

"Hole of the earth has not swallowed her, nor has she been drowned on brown slippery sea, and there were not people in the universe who could kill my *Muileartach.*"

"No one slew her but the Fians, the people who were never overcome ; and never one has escaped from the people of the yellow wreathed hair."

Thus the Old Woman finished her journey.

VARIANT OF PART II.

A day the Fians were on an Eastern knoll (17)
Gazing at Erin all around,
There was seen coming over the waves
A hideous apparition—a heavily rocking
    object. (18)
The name of the dauntless spectre
Was the bald-red, white-maned *Muileartach.*
Her face was dark grey, of the hue of coals,

The teeth of her jaw were slanting red,
There was one flabby eye in her head,
That quicker moved than lure-pursuing mackerel.
Her head bristled dark and grey,
Like scrubwood before hoar frost.
When she saw the Fians of highest prowess,
The wretch coveted being in their midst.
At the outset of fury and slaughter,
She performed an over-keen, thankless deed ;
She slew in her frolic a hundred heroes,
While loud laughter was in her rough mouth.

*   *   *   *   *

You will lose the forelock of your scrubby head,
In lieu of having asked for Oisian's goodly son.

*   *   *   *   *

They offered her compensation, if she would turn back
the way she came. She would not take all the valuable
jewels in Ireland till she would get—

The heads of Oscar, Oisian, and Fin,
Goll, and Corral.

*   *   *   *   *

They made an enclosure for the great fight,
Lest the apparition on the field should change.
The four best heroes among the Fians,
She would combat them altogether,
And attend them each by turns,
Like the shimmering beam of a flame.
Mac-Coul of good fortune met
The wretch, hand to hand.
Her flank was exposed to the violence of the blows,
And there were drops of his blood on the heath tops.
The *Muileartach* fell by Fin,
If she did, it was not without strife ;
A trial like this he did not get
Since the day of Lon MacLioven's smithy,

They lifted the Old Woman on the point of their
　　spears,
And tore her asunder in pieces.

　　　　The tale ran northwards
To the borders of Lochlin of many people ;
And the Smith went with its purport
To the palace of the High King.
" A mischief has been done," said the Ocean Smith,
" The red *Muileartach* (19) has been killed."
" If the porous earth has not swallowed her,
Or the broad bare sea drowned her,
Where were the people in the universe
Who could slay the white-maned *Muileartach* ?"
　　" The *Muileartach* fell by the Fians,
The company that never was touched with fear ;
Nor hatred or change comes
On the comely people of yellow wreathed hair."
　　" I will give words again,
If the smooth *Muileartach* has been killed,
That I will not leave in Fair Erin
Hillock, place of shelter, or island,
That I will not lift in the cross-trees of my ships,
Erin fairly-balanced, full weight ;
If it does not take to kicking at sea
When it is being lifted from its sea-walls,
I shall put crooked hooks into the land,
To draw it from its fastenings."
" Numerous are the shipmen, O Manus !
That could lift the fifth-part of Erin ;
And there are not as many ships on salt water
As would lift a fifth-part of Erin."
Eight and eight-score ships,
Were raised of forces, and they were numerous,
To raise the ransom of the *Muileartach*.
　　　*　　　　*　　　　*　　　　*　　　　*

They went ashore at the harbour of the Hill of Howth. The well-beloved Fergus, the son of Morna, went on a message to them ; he offered them satisfactory indemnity (20) if they would return the way they came.

> He offered them eight hundred banners
> Beautifully coloured, and war-dresses ;
> Eight hundred dogs on leashes (?) ; (21)
> Eight hundred close searchers (?) ;
> Eight hundred short-haired, red-cheeked men ;
> Eight hundred helmets full of red gold,
> Although they got that, they would not return till
>   they got
> The head of Oscar, Oisian, and Fin,
> Goll, and Çorrall.

> *   *   *   *   *

> "You will betake yourselves smartly across the sea,
> Or remain to your hurt.
> The biggest ships you have taken across the sea,
> With winds hard blowing,
> If there be as much blood in your bodies,
> It will swim on your backs."

Then fought they the great day, and very great day— the day of the battle of the Hill of Howth,

> Where many a head was lowered,
> And neck was rendered bare.
> Not a single man escaped
> But half a hundred men,
> That went like the current of a stream seaward,
> With the battle-shout driving them.

A' Mhuileartach (A' Cheud Earann.)

Bha na Fiantan air son an rioghachd a chumail bho na Lochlainnich (1). Bha Fionn 'na righ orra. Bha blàr eatorra' fhéin agus Mànus aig Dùn-Chinn-a'-choire ann an Eirinn. Dar a chaidh Mànus dhachaidh, thuirt a mhuime, "A' Mhuileartach", gu'n rachadh i thoirt blàir do Fhionn agus gu'n tugadh i uaithe an Corn-Buadhach (2), soitheach creadha, air an robh e air 'fhàgail, gur ann le deoch òl as a bha an Fhéinn' daonnan a' faotainn buaidh. Thuirt Mànus gu'n cuireadh e daoine leatha, ach dhiult i. Cha tugadh i leatha ach an duine aice, Gobhainn nan Cuan, agus lùb-iarruinn, ris an abradh iad, an Trosdan beag, druimneach. Ghabh iad gu astar gu Dùn-Chinn-a' choire. Chunnaic an Fhéinn' rud mòr duaitheil a tighinn, agus thuirt Fionn, " Ma shiubhail e 'n domhan, agus ma chuairtich e 'n saoghal, is i muime Mhànuis a th'ann, is tha rud sònruichte a dhith oirre." Chaidh an Fhéinn' a stigh do'n tigh ; agus chuir naoi naoinear an druim ris an dorus, agus chuir iad naoi slàbhraidhean iarruinn an glacaibh a chéile.

Spìon i craobh agus sgrios i dhi na meanglain, agus bha i aice 'na bata. Dh'fhuirich Gobhainn-nan-Cuan aig a' bhàta. Chuir iad naoi druill air an dorus, is naoi troidhean an cloich 's an aol, is chaidh naoi caogad (3) le an dromannaibh ris an dorus.

Bha Fionn a' scalltuinn a mach, agus thàinig ise, agus thuirt i an guth iosal—

Ise.

Is mise cailleach thruagh, thruagh,
'Thàinig air a dian-ruaig ;
Shiubhail mi còig-chóigeamh (4) na h-Eirinn,
'S cha d' fhuair mi tigh a leigeadh a stigh mi.

Fionn.

Ma shiubhail thusa sin gu h-uilidh (5)
'S comharra sin air droch dhuine ;
'S ged uainicheadh do spuir fodhad,
Uam-sa cha'n fhaigheadh tu fosgladh.

Ise.

'S olc an cleachdadh sin do mhac rìgh,
Do'm bu dual gaisg' agus mòr-ghniomh;
Mac rìgh 'ga ràdhainn riut,
'S nach tugadh tu cuid oidhche do chaillich.

Fionn.

Ma 'se modh, no biatachd, no fialachd,
'Tha dhìth ort, a chailleach !
Cuiridh mise thugad biadh cheud fear,
'S tog dhìom do sheanchas, a chailleach !

Ise.

Cha'n'eil mise 'm feum do bhidh bhochd,
'S cha mhò a's àill leam do mhòr sprochd ;
B'fheàrr leam a bhith am blath's do theine mhòir,
'S a bhith an comith ri do chonaibh.

Fionn.

Nach fhadaidh thusa teine dhuit féin,
Far an séid thu e le t' anail ?
'S cuir cual chonnaidh ri d' gharbh-chneas,
[*Var.*—Pronn geugan beaga ri do chruit]
'S dean gu crionna ris do gharadh.

Ise.

An t-seisear laoch a 's fheàrr 'san Fhéinn'
Faic thusa air an raon a mach iad ;
'S 'nuair ruigeas an sneachd an crios doibh,
Cha 'n urrainn iad teine fhadadh.

[*Var.*—An naoi naoinear 'ga bheil a stigh
Eadar an tugha 's an fhraigh ;
Ruigeadh an sneachd dhoibh an crios,
'S cha rachadh leo teine fhadadh.]

Thug a' chailleach, 'bu chruaidh còmhrag,
Breab a dh'ionnsaidh na còmhla ;

10 ²

'S mu'n d'thill i bun-dubh (6) a coise,
Bhrist i na naoi slàbhraidhean iarruinn á glacaibh a
chéile [agus thilg i na laoich air an druim-direach
air an ùrlar].

Sheachainn Fionn an rathad oirre ; is ghabh ise gu cisde nan
scud, agus thug i leatha an Corn-Buadhach.

Dh'éirich na daoine,
Dh'éirich Caoilt' (7) is dh'éirich càch ;
'S dh'éirich fear-iomairt nan ràmh, (8)
A dh'fhalbh an déigh na caillich.

Cha b' urrainn doibh breth oirre.   Chaidh Oscar, am fear
'bu làidire do'n Fhéinn' as a déigh.   Rug e oirre air chois aig
uchd Beinn-Eadainn.[1]   Bha 'falt liath a' slaodadh rithe, agus
rug Oscar air.   Thug e dùi'-leum, agus chuir e tri duail do
fhalt cas, liath na caillich m'a dhorn.   Mu'n tug e sreamadh
aisde, chaidh iad fodha gu 'm meadhon an sneachda.   "Ud !
ud ! a laochain !" ars' ise, "ghortaich thu mi.   Ma 's e biadh
no deoch a tha dhìth ort, gheibh thu e 'nuair a ruigeas mise
an iùbhrach."   [Ruig Gobhainn-nan-Cuan 's gheibh thu e. (9)]
"Cha'n e sin a tha dhìth orm, ach t'fhalt liath a thoirt a
dh'ionnsaidh mo sheanair."   "Ho ! ho ! an ann diubh sin thu ?"
Tharruing i nall a falt cas, liath, o 'gàirdean toisgeil, agus
leag i a làmh gu h-cutrom air, agus chual e fhéin fuaim a
h-uile cnàimh.

" Ma tha spionnadh agad a dhol dachaidh, innis do Fhionn
gu bheil an Corn-Buadhach agam-sa."

Thill e, agus chaidh ise do Lochlainn.   Chuir Mànus roimhe
blàr a thoirt do Fhionn.   Chruinnich e a dhaoine, agus chaidh
e gu Dùn-Chinn-a'-choire a thoirt blàir do Fhionn.

Choinnich iad, agus thoisich iad air a chéile.   Bha na Lochlainnich uile air am marbhadh, agus bha an Corn-Buadhach
air 'fhaotainn air 'ais.   Chaidh Mànus a cheangal, agus chaidh
mionnan a chur air.   'S ann an sin a thuirt Conan—

" A leigeil gu Mànus nan lann
'S gu'n sgaradh e 'cheann o 'chorp."

---

[1] Beinn-Eadair (The Hill of Howth, near Dublin).

Thuirt Mànus an sin—

"Buille bheag a' t' aghaidh, Fhinn,
'S aithreach leam na rinn mi ort."

[Sin dar a thug a' Chailleach bu mhòr fearg
Breab o dh'ionnsuidh na còmhla,
'S bhrist i na naoi ceanglaichean a sìos
Mu'n deachaidh stad air a teann-ruith ;
'S chaidh i stigh do mhùr Fhinn,
'S rug i air cuach Fhinn 'na croma chròig.
Leum i air eas ruadh nan ràmh,
'S cuach Fhinn 'na deas làimh.
Leum Fionn gu cas, cas,
An déigh chas na Caillich
'S rug e air a' chuaich
O'n 's ann leis 'bha 'buaidh 's a brigh.
Rug Caoilte Mac Ròin
Air a chlaidheamh mòr 's a dhà shleagh ;
'S rug an t-Oscar meamnach òg
Air an léine shròil a bha mu cneas.
Thug iad an t-ubhal o'n bhéist ;
'S ma thug cha b' ann gun streup ;
'S mar deachaidh an ceann air coluinn eile,
Cha d'fhuair a h-anam riamh tròcair,
B' àrd a h-ionad, 's b' àrd a fàs,
B' àrd a cuid siùil ri h-aois, (10)
Gearmhlàg iaruinn fo 'màs,
'S da fhiacail siar o 'craos ;
Leithid na ciaraig chaillich,
Cha'n fhacas o linn Chuchullin]. (11)

Chaidh e (Mànus) dhachaidh lom, falamh. Dh'fhoighneachd a
mhuime air son a dhaoine, agus thuirt e gu'n robh iad air an call.
"A righ !" ars' ise "gu'n tug mi riamh sùgh mo thaoibh
dhuit, is nach rachadh agad fhéin air Fionn a mharbhadh, 's
gun ann ach leth-dhuine. (12) Bithidh mise nis' a' falbh,
agus uiread 's a chaill thusa bheir mise as an Fhéinn' an
ceithir uairibh fichead."

"Togaidh mise," arsa Mànus, "mo chuid loingeis, agus théid mi leat." Cha chluinneadh i so, ach an Gobhainn a dhol leatha. Bha esan math gu naigheachdan innseadh, agus dh'innseadh e do Mhànus a h-uile ni dar a thigeadh iad air an ais. Cha robh an Gobhainn toileach falbh, ged nach d'rinn e ach cluintinn mu Fhionn; ach rug ise air, agus thilg i e anns a' bhàta. Ghabh iad an turus-cuain. Thàinig soirbheas beag ciùin as an déigh o isle nam beann, is o àirde nan craobh, a bheireadh duilleach á beinn is seileach á craoibh, agus luachair bheag, òg, as a bun agus as a freumhach. Thòisich iad air tilgeadh na fàirge fiolcanaich, falcanaich, fualcanaich, air dubha a sean-chloich, 's air piceadh a sonna chloich, a' bhéisd 'bu mhò 'g itheadh na béisd 'bu lugha, 's a bhéisd 'bu lugha a' deanamh mar a dh'fhaodadh i. Càllaga beaga a' chuain a' gabhail fàil agus fasgaidh ann an sop a' chroinn-mhòir aice. Ghearradh i 'n coinnlein caol, cruaidh, coirce, roimh a dubh-thoiseach, aig ro fheabhas a stiùramaiche. (13) 'Seall suas," ars' ise, ri Gobhainn-nan-Cuan, "is feuch am faic thu am fearann." 'Nuair a sheall esan thuige is uaithe, chunnaic e fearann is thuirt e, "Ma's fearann e, is beag e, agus ma's feannag e, 's mòr e." "Is fior sin, a laochain," ars' ise, "cha'n'eil an iùbhrach aig astar ceart leinn."

Chuir iad a mach na ràimh bheaga, bhaisgeanta, dhruimneach; 's cha robh sineadh a bheireadh iad air an druim, nach tugadh iad uisge stigh air beul-mòr a bhàta. H-uile uile no urbhaidhe 'gan d'fhuair iad, ràinig iad tir; is tharruing iad an iùbhrach am bràighe a' chladaich, far nach deanadh macan a' bhaile-mhòir bùird no magadh oirre.

Dh'òrduich ise do Ghobhainn-nan-Cuan dol air cnocan, air cùl gaoithe 's air aodann gréine, far am faiceadh e a h-uile duine, 's nach faiceadh duine idir e. (14) Rinn e sin, is chaidh ise air a h-aghaidh. Gu mi-fhortanach, bha na Fiantan 'nan codal air an cuid àrm, agus bha ceithir-ar-fhichead dhiubh air an uchd. Thòisich i air am marbhadh leis an lùb iarruinn. Mharbh i—

"Ceithir-ar-fhichead de'n Fhéinn',
'S Ailbhinn féin air thùs,

Thuit air làimh na h-Iorghuil mhòir,
Mu'n deachaidh na seòid 'nan dlùth's."

An sin thòisich na Fiantan is a' chailleach, 's bha iad 'a
sliocartaich, 's a' slacartaich, 's a' gabhail d'a chéile. Bha i
'gan ceapadh mar lasair shìos is shuas. Bha i àrd. An sin
dh'iarr Oscar e bhith air a chur 'na h-aghaidh, e féin; 's bha i
'ga throm-liabadh, 's 'ga iomain an comhair a chùil; agus
ghabh Fionn lag-mhisneach. Dh'iarr e orra spaidean a
ghabhail is iad a ghearradh foidhpe 's a cur air a h-ais, gus am
faigheadh iad cothrom iomain no bualaidh oirre. Rinn iad
toll, agus dh'iomain iad air a h-ais i gus an deachaidh i ann.
Bha i fhathast 'gan ceapadh mar lasair, ach na h-uile h-uile no
h-urbhaidhe 'gan d'fhuair iad, mharbh iad a' chailleach mu'n
do stad iad. Thog iad an sin gaoir-chatha le toilinntinn;
agus an sin ceithir-ar-fhichead do na Fiantan a bha an Coire-
Ghlinne, 'nuair a chual iad e, bha fhios aca gu'n robh fargradh
air teachd air an Fhéinn'. Ruith iad a null, is thuirt fear
dhiubh ri 'chompanach:—"A righ fhéin! nach innseadh tu
dhomh ciamar a bha i 'nuair a bha i air a casan?" "Cha'n'eil
mise an urrainn sin innseadh ach do neach a bha 'ga faicinn."

['S e so an t-àite ceart air son Duan na Muileartaich aithris.]

Latha dhuinn air tulaich shoir, (17)
   'Sealltainn Eirinn mu'n cuairt;
Thàinig oirnn bharr muir sleamhain trom,
   Atharnach (15) trom, neò-ghlas.
Dà fhiacail seachad siar air a craos,
   'S ceithir aimhlean 'na màs:
Ceithir-ar-fhichead de'n Fhéinn',
   'S Ailbhinn féin air thùs,
'Thuit air làimh na h-Iorghuil mhòir,
   Mu'n deachaidh na slòigh an dlùth's. (16)
Sin 'nuair a labhair Goll,
   An sonn nach robh riamh 'sa chùil:
" Leigibh mi 'ga h-ionnsuidh greis,
   'S gu feuchainn ri cleas lùgh's."

Bha a' chailleach 'ga riabadh, 's 'ga iomain an coinneamh a

chùil. Agus ghabh Fionn lag-mhisneach an uair sin. Sin an
uair a dh'òrduich e an talamh a ghearradh o 'bonn, 's a
leigeadh gu ionad a crios 'san làr.   Bha i 'gar ceapadh shìos is
shuas mar lasair ; 's na h-uile h-uile no h-urbhaidhe 'gan
d'fhuair sinn, sin dar a mharbh sinn a' chailleach, 's thug sinn
an gaoir-chatha asainn.

Dar a chual Gobhainn-nan-Cuan, a bha air cùl gaoithe 's ri
aodunn grèine gu'n do mharbhadh a' Mhuileartach, ghabh e
mach gu cuan. [Rann mu thurus-cuain.] Ràinig e Lochlainn
leis fhéin : choinnich Mànus e, agus dh'fhoighneachd e dheth,
c'àit' an d'fhàg e a' chailleach. "Mharbhadh i," thuirt Gobhainn-nan-Cuan.

"O bhéisd ! cha do mharbhadh ; ach dar a chunnaic thusa
eaghnadh a bha i deanamh, theich thu."

"O ! mharbhadh i."

"Cha do shluig an talamh-toll i, 's cha do bhàthadh i air
muir sleamhuin lom, 's cha robh do shluagh air an domhan na
mharbhadh mo Mhuileartach."

> "Cha do mharbh i ach an Fhéinn',
>   An dream air nach do thàrladh buaidh ;
>   'S aon riamh cha deach' as
> Air an dream fhalt-bhuidhe chas."

Mar sin chriochnaich a' chailleach a turus.

AN DARA EARRANN.

Latha do'n Fhéinn air tulaich shoir (17)
Ag amharc Eirinn m'a timchioll,
Chunncas a' teachd bhàrr thonn,
Arrachd éitidh, creadhall, trom.
'S gu'm b'e b'ainm do'n fhuath nach robh tiom, (18)
A' Mhuileartach mhaol, ruadh, mhuing-fhionn.
Bha 'h-aodann dubh-ghlas air dhreach guail,
Bha deud a carbaid claon-ruadh,
Bha aon shùil ghlogach 'na ceann,
'S gu'm bu luaith' i na rionnach madhair ;
Bha greann glas-dhubh air a ceann,
Mar choille chrionaich roimh chrith-reotha ;

Ri faicinn na Féinne bu mhòr goil,
Shanntaich a' bhéist a bhith 'nan innis,
An toiseach mire agus àir,
Rinneadh leatha gion gun chomain ;
Mharbh i le 'h-àbhachd ceud laoch,
'S a gàire 'na garbh chraos.

    o   *   o   *   o

Caillidh tu dosan do chinn chrionaich
Air son deagh mhac Oisein iarraidh.

    *   *   o   o   *

Thairg iad dhi cumha, 's i thilleadh an taobh a thàinig i. Cha
ghabhadh i sid na bha sheudaibh buadhach an Eirinn gus am
faigheadh i—

Ceann Oscair, Oiscin, is Fhinn,
Ghoill, agus Choirill.

    o   *   o   o

    Rinn iad crò air son a' chatha mhòir
Mu'n atharraichte air faiche na sgleò,
A' cheathrar laoch a b'fheàrr 'san Fhéinn
Gu'n còmhraigeadh i iad gu léir ;
'S fhrithealadh i iad mu seach,
Mar ghath rionna na lasrach.
Thachair Mac-Cumhail an àigh
Is a' bhéist làimh ri làimh ;
Bha 'taobh-cholluinn ri guin bualaidh,
'S bha braon d'a fhuil air na fraochaibh.
Thuit a' Mhuileartach le Fionn ;
Ma thuit cha b'ann gun strith ;
Deuchainn cha d' fhuair e mar sin,
O latha ceardaich Lon-'ic-Liobhainn.
Thog iad a' chailleach air bharraibh an sleagh,
'S thug iad 'na mireannaibh as a chéil' i.

Ruith an naigheachd ud mu thuath,
Gu crìoch Lochlainn nam mòr-shluagh ;
'S chaidh an Gobhainn leis a' bhrigh,
Gu teach aobhair an Ard-Righ.
" Rinneadh beud", deir Gobhainn-nan-Cuan

" Mharbhadh a' Mhuileartach ruadh ?"
" Mur do shluig an talamh-toll i,
No mur do bhàth muir leathan lom i,
C'àit' an robh do dhaoin' air domhan,
Na mharbhadh a' Mhuileartach mhuing-fhionn?"
" Thuit a' Mhuileartach leis an Fhiann,
A' bhuidheann leis nach gabh-te fiamh.
Cha tig fuath no atharrach as,
Air an t-sluagh àluinn, fhalt-bhuidhe, chas."
" Bheiream-sa briathra a rìs,
Ma mharbhadh a' Mhuileartach mhin,
Nach fàg mi'n Eirinn àigh
Tom, innis, no eilean,
Nach tog mi ann an crannagaibh mo long,
Eirinn coranta, cothromach ;
Mar deanadh i breabanaich air muir,
'Ga togail as a tonna-bhalla,
Cròcain chroma ri tìr,
'Ga tarruing as a tàdhaibh."
" Is mòr an luchd loingeis, a Mhànuis,
'Thogadh còigeamh a dh'Eirinn,
'S cha'n'eil do loingeis air sàile,
Na thogadh còigeamh a dh'Eirinn."
    Ochd agus ochd fichead long
'Thogadar a dh'fheachd 's bu trom,
Thoirt a mach éirig a' Mhuileartaich. (19)

*   &   &   c   u

Chaidh iad air tìr an cala Beinn-Eadainn.[1]   Chaidh Fearghus mùirneach mac Mòirne air theachdaireachd 'gan ionnsuidh ; thairg e dhoibh cumha gun fheall, 's iad a thilleadh an
taobh a thàinig iad.

Thairg e dhoibh ochd ciad bratach, (20)
Caoin-daithte, agus lùireach ;

---

[1] Beinn-Eadair.

Ochd ciad conair mheangain ; (21)
Ochd ciad mion do ionndrainn ;
Ochd ciad gearr-fhaltach, gruaidh-dhearg ;
Ochd ciad làn clogaid d'en òr dhearg ;

Ged gheibheadh iad sin, cha tilleadh iad gus am faigheadh iad—

Ceann Oscair, Oisein, 's Fhinn,
Ghoil, agus Choirill.

" Gearraidh sibh 'ur teann-leum thar muir,
Ar neò fanaidh sibh ri'r n-aimhleas ;
An long a 's mò a thug sibh thar muir,
Le goincaladh,
Ma tha a dh'fhuil 'n'ur collainnibh,
Snàmhaidh i air 'ur dromannaibh."

Sin 'nuair a thug iad an latha mòr agus ro-mhòr—

Latha catha Beinn-Eadainn,
Far am bu lionar ceann 'ga chromadh,
Agus muineal 'ga mhaoladh.
Cha deachaidh aon riamh as,
Ach leth-chiad fear,
'Chaidh mar thriall srutha gu sàil',
'S gaoir-chatha 'gan iomain.

NOTES.

(1) Reciters are not agreed as to this being the purpose for which the Fians were. Some (and this is the most rational of the realistic explanations) say they were a body of hunters that followed the chase both in Ireland and Scotland. As to their having a separate kingdom, tradition makes no mention.

(2) More correctly " Cup of Virtues", or precious cup.

(3) *Caogad* is explained in dictionaries as meaning fifty. It was explained by the person from whom this portion within brackets was heard, that the number who put their backs to the door was nine times nine ; and there are other confirmations of an explana-

tion heard from an old man, that *caogad* was used to signify nine days or times.

(4) In the twelfth century, Ireland was divided into five king-doms—Ulster (*Còige-ulainn*), Leinster (*Còige-Laighinn*), Meath (*Mith*), Connaught (*Conach*), and Munster (*Còige-Mumha*). The rulers of these divisions were styled kings ; and over all was the one called the " High King of Ireland", *Ard rìgh Eirinn.* Cairbre who slew Oscar, was one of these ; and Fin's own genealogy is traced up to the same royal line.

(5) The common form is *uile*, but the various reciters said *uilidh.* This may have been merely the attraction of the emphasis. At all events, not much weight is to be placed upon the peculiarity.

(6) The usual phrase is *bonn-dubh*, "the black sole," which is explained to be the heel.

(7) *Caoille* (Thinman) was called *Daorghlas* (Thorough-grey) till the day when the swords of the Fian chiefs were made in the magic smithy of Lon MacLiovun, of which there is an account in a separate ballad.

(8) This expression is noticeable, as a reference to its being a sea-fight. There does not seem to have been any one in particular of the Fian band to whom this post was assigned.

(9) This sentence, and the others within brackets, are from other oral versions.

(10) The meaning of the word age (*aois*) is not evident.

(11) In tradition, Cuchulin is not mentioned in connection with the Fians. The lays about himself or his chariot are different from anything to be found in Macpherson.

(12) Fin's mother was the daughter of the Ulster smith (*An gobhainn Ullach*), and the ugliest woman in all Ireland. His twin sister was Diarmid's mother.

(13) *Stiùramaiche*, in the Hebrides, denotes the steersman of a particular boat, *stiùradair* a steersman generally.

(14) Rhymes or "runs" (*ruitheannan*), such as this and those preceding, in the description of the sea-journey, are common in Gaelic tales, and are made use of by the reciter on every suitable occasion. They are more or less full, according to the skill of the reciter.

(15) This word and *Arracht*, which is used by other reciters, is most probably from *athar* (the air), and merely denotes an aerial phenomenon.

(16) This is a piece taken unconsciously by the reciter from another Fian ballad, called Ailvinn or Ierghuin.

(17) In various printed versions of the tale, this hillock is called *tulaich oirill*, which may be correct.

(18) The meaning of this line is not very clear ; and it is a mere matter of inference from the sound and collocation of the letters, that they denote some monstrous, lumbering, heavy-moving object, rocking from side to side.

(19) This word, like some others, is conventionally used both in a masculine and feminine form.

(20) Other versions, such as that given by Mr. Campbell in his *West Highland Tales*, vol. iii, 135, make the indemnity ten hundred instead of eight hundred of each article. They all agree in making fine-coloured flags, and dogs, and gold, part of the ransom.

(21) *Conair mheangain* is most probably *coin air mheangain* (dogs on branches), *i.e.*, on withes, or leashes, a most valuable ransom in the days of the Irish wolf-hounds and stag-hounds. In the Long Island, among the Roman Catholic population, a rosary is called *Conair Mhoire*, the beads of S. Mary. *Meangain* is the designation of a certain kind of heather (*fraoch meangain*), and universally in the Highlands *meangan* means a branch, so that the expression may denote some kind of bead. In early times, before the days of coinage, and to the present day among savage tribes, beads were and are valuable as a circulating medium, and as personal ornaments.

In regard to "close" searchers, the existence of *fiondruine* as a name of a metal renders it highly probable that a tribute of it was here meant. The reciter did not know the meaning of the words, though, as in other instances of popular recitation, the sound of the correct words is retained.

In the Island of Tiree, pins or small skewers—of some composite metal resembling bronze—about three inches in length, are occasionally found. They are called by the natives, *Prìne fionn-drainn*.

The "close" searchers may be the smaller dogs.

The short-haired men are doubtlessly slaves or bondsmen, long hair being much affected by Chiefs.

With our explanation, in our introductory remarks, of this tale as a myth, descriptive of a contest between the Sea violently invading the Land, and Human Might, may be compared an anecdote frequently met with, also further illustrative of the popular view of the Fians as the representatives of bodily strength. One of the Fians (*aon dé'n Fhéinn*), looking at the sea breaking in foam, was told that it was laughing at him. He was for rushing out to chastise it.

The idea of personification is, however, entirely lost sight of by reciters, and it belongs to the poet's skill that, while his words are singularly descriptive of the angry Sea, such should be the case. The lines enclosed within brackets (pp. 138-39), written down in 1870, from the dictation of James Cameron, a native of Morven resident in Coll, are illustrative of this, and of the manner in which modern ideas become involved with old tradition.

THE LAY OF THE SMITHY.

(DUAN NA CEARDACH.)

THE following version of the Lay of the Smithy was taken down at Portree, Skye, from Angus MacVurrich, or MacPherson, in October 1871, and is here given as of value to the antiquary in tracing the story of the Cyclops and Polyphemus. It would show that the story may be as old as the dispersion of the human race. The Celts, in taking the story to the extreme west of Europe, and its being found in Greece and Rome, would indicate its early origin. The Cyclops, who framed the thunderbolts of Jupiter, and the one-eyed Polyphemus in his cave, may be but variants of the same story. Allusion to the one-eyed giant, whose dwelling was in a cave, and whose eye was pierced by the roasting-iron, is to be found in many other Gaelic stories ; and when the incident of a story is said to be remote in time, or place, no question as to its truth is thought of. The smith having only one leg, and having a smithy, would lead to his identification with Vulcan, the god of smiths, who was lamed in his fall from heaven. At all events, the story seems older than Rome, or Athens, or even Troy.

A day that we were at Luachair Leathan,
  Like five grouped, was our company ;
Myself, Oscar, and Derglas,
  Lon MacLevan, and MacCumal himself.

There was seen coming from the hill
  A long, dark man, upon one leg,

In a mantle of dark grey skin,
  And an apron of the same clothing.

Fionn spoke, as he stood,
  To the fellow who was passing :
"Where, smith, is your dwelling,
  Or, man with the skin covering?"

"If your supposition is correct,
  Lon MacLevan was my baptismal name ;
I was a while at smith work
  With the King of Lochlin in Gilvin."

"Where, smith, is your smithy,
  Or will we be the better of seeing it?'
"If I can you will not be the better,
  But if you will be the better, see it.

"I lay you under spells,
  Since you are *ambitious of seeing* (?) my smithy,
To be in a dark, dark grey, sickly glen,
  To-night westward from the doors of my smithy."

They then began to hasten,
  Until they formed five companies :
One company of these was the smith,
  And another company was Derglas.
Another company was Derg, son of Druin
(Red the Druid's son ?),
  Fionn was after them, alone.

The smith would take only one step
  Over every dark grey, desert glen,
And they could not see, but with difficulty,
  A piece of his raiment over his haunches.

"Open, open," said the smith.
  "Force it before you," said Derglas.
"I would not leave you in the door of my smithy,
  In a dangerous place alone."

They found then bellows to blow,
  And they found there, hardly a smithy,
Four hands on every smith.
  Hammers striking, and smithy tongs,
And the fairy hammers that answered them,
  Truly better would Derglas answer.

Derglas, the cleaner of the smithy,
  Since he was wont to be standing,
And redder than the ember of the oak
  Was his appearance from his labour.

Then one of the smiths spoke,
  Grimly and gruffly,
"Whence came the thinman, unintimidated,
  Who has spoiled for us our steel anvil?"

Latha dhuinn air Luachair Leathan,
  Mar choigear chrodh-fhionn de bhuidhean
Mi fhin, is Oscar, is Daor-ghlas
  Lon Mac Liobhunn 's bha Mac Cumhail.

Chunncas a 'tighinn o 'n mhonadh,
  Fear fada du 's e air aona chois
Le a mhuntal ciar, dhu craicinn
  Aparan de 'n cididh chiadn' air.

Labhair Fionn, 's e 'na sheasamh,
  Ris an urra bha dol seachad
"C' àit a ghobha bheil do thuineadh
  No fhir ad a chochaill chraicinn?"

"Ma tha agaibh orm beachd sgeula
  Lon Mac Liobhunn b' e m' ainm baist' e,
Bha mi treis ri uallach gobhain
  Aig righ Lochlin anns a 'Gheilbhinn."

"C' àit, a ghobha, bheil do cheardach?
  No 'n fhearrda sinn dhol g' a faicinn?"
"Ma, dh' fheudas mise cha 'n fhearrd' sibh,
  'S ma 's fhearrd sibhse faicibh.

"Tha mise 'g 'ur cuir fo gheasailh
    O' n a 's sibh luchd leasgairt mo cheardach,
Bhi 'n gleannan du ciar du, dochard
    Nochd siar o dhorsaibh mo cheardach."

Thòisich iad an sin ri siubhal
    Gus an deach iad 'nan còig buidheann,
    Bu bhuidheann dhiubh sin an Gobhain,
Bu bhuidheann eile dhiu Daor-ghlas,
'S bu bhuidheann eile dhiu Dearg Mac Druidhean
    Bha Fionn 'nan deigh 's e 'na aonar.

'S cha ghearra an gobha ach aona cheum
    Air gach gleannan ciar dhu fàsaich,
'S cha 'n fhaiceadh iad ach air eiginn
    Sgòd dheth eididh air a mhàsun.

"Fosgail, fosgail," ars' an gobhain,
    "Bruid romhad e," ars' Daor-ghlas.
"Cha 'n fhàgainn thu 'n dorus mo cheardach
    'N aite gabhaidh 's tu 'nad aonar."

Fhuair iad an sin builg ri sheideadh,
    'S gu 'n d' fhuair iad ann eiginn ceardach
Ceithir lamhan air gach gobhain
    Uird a 'lughadh is teanchaire
'S na h-uird shìth bha 'ga freagairt
    'S beachd fearr a fhreagradh Daor-ghlas.

Daor-ghlas fear glanadh na ceardach,
    O b' abhaist da bhi 'na sheasamh
'S bu deirg e na gual an daraich
    A shnuadh o thoradh na h-oibreach.

Sin labhair fear dheth na goibhnean
    Gu grimeach 's gu gruamach
"Co as thainig Caoilte gun tioma
    Mhill oirn an t-innean cruadhach."

Sorrowful am I after Thinman (*Caoilte*),
Since my contemporaries are not alive.

I am filled with sadness, agony, and pain
At parting with my foster-brother,
Thinman (*Caoilte*), my true foster-brother[1]
With whom I could win victory and banner ;
Thinman (*Caoilte*), my perfect fellow-warrior,
And a relief to the Fians in time of need.
He was not Chief of us all,
But the merciful High King.
Have you heard of Fionn's journey
From the side of the big city that was in Ireland ?
The great Cairbre,
Greedy, loud-speaking,
Seized Ireland
Under one rule.

They sent word for us
To Tara,
From Imradack to the battle of Gavra.
They did a deed worse than that,
To be wanting the lordship over us.
We answered the grim champion,
As many of us of all ages as were there.
There were not of the Fians altogether
As many as would satisfy them.
Fifteen hundred and good horsemen
We were, on the white customary way.
We got honour and respect.

———

Is muladach mi 'n deigh Chaoilte,
Nach mairionn luchd mo chon-traonaidh,
Lion mulad mi, cràdh, is goirteas,
'N àm sgarachduinn dhomh ri m' cho-dhalta
Caoilt mo cho-dhalta ceart
Leis an iomarainn buaidh is brat.

---

[1] True foster-brother, *i.e.*, born at the same time, and brought up under the same tuition.

Caoilte mo léir chuir-chatha,
'S am furtach do 'n Fhéinn sa latha
Cha b' e bu cheannard oirnn uile
Ach Ard Righ na tròcaireach.
An cuala sibhse turus Fhinn,
Mach a slios a 'bhaile mhoir bha 'n Eirinn
An Cairbreach mòr
Lonach, labhrach
Ghlacadh leis Eirinn
Fuidh 'n aon smachd
Chuir iad fios òirnne
Gu Teambraidh
O Iomradach gu cath Chabhruinn.
Rinn iad gniomh bu duilleadh na sin
A bhi 'n ti air ar tighearnas.
Fhreagair sinn an cuireadh dòbhaidh
Gach linn uile mar a bha sinn.
Cha robh ann do 'n Fhéinn uile
Na dh' fhàgadh iadsan co buidheach.
Coig ceud deug agus deagh mharcaiche
Bha sinn air an rathad gle-gheal cleachdach.
Fhuair sinn onoir is miadh.

The foregoing fragmentary pieces are given as they
were taken down from a very estimable man in 1871.
The first ten lines are probably part of a lament for
Thinman (*Caoilte*), a contemporary of the poet, and the
rest is of value to those interested in the question of the
real existence of the Fians, as showing that there was
more than one poem or lay in circulation about the death
of Oscar and the battle of Gavra (*Cath Gabhra*); also as
showing, if not explaining, some of the obscurities in the
lay or poem given of the battle of Gavra. It confirms
the statement that Cairbre was a strong, big man, per-
sonally greedy, and ambitious in mind; that Tara's
Hall was the residence of the High King of Ireland;
and that the residence of the leader of the Fians was in
a different place.

WHEN the Fians were for some time without any word
of the chase, and the women still kept their good looks,
while the men were becoming meagre and ill-looking,
on going in pursuit of the chase the Fians left big Garry,
the son of Morna, behind them, to endeavour to find out
what secret means of nourishment the women had. He
found that they lived on the leaves of trees, the roots of
heather, and tops of hazel (*duillich nan craobh, bun an
fhraoich ;* some say *bun na rainich,* the roots of brackens,
ferns ; *'s barr na calltuinn*). While waiting and watching, Garry fell asleep beside an old log of wood, or the
seven sticks of wood, which, like tether-pins, the women
drove into the ground, and the women having observed
him, tied seven plies of his hair (*seachd duail a chinn*) to
the log or sticks, which they drove into the ground.
They then raised the war-cry of the Fians. Every
member of the band was bound to answer this cry
whenever and wherever he heard it. When raised, it
was heard over five-fifths of Ireland, and Garry, on
hearing it, started to his feet, leaving the seven plies of
his hair sticking to the log or pins which had been driven
into the ground. Annoyed by the deceit practised upon
him, he went to the neighbouring wood, and finding a
burden of suitable material, he took it on his shoulders,
and placing it against the dwelling, set it on fire. It was
then that the attention of the Fians was drawn to the
low-lying, coloured smoke, and before long they saw
that their dwelling and home was in a blaze—

"There was seen a low-lying, discoloured smoke,
    The dwelling of Farala blazing high."

"Chunnacas ceo talmhaidh daite,
    Brugh Farala 'na lasair àrd."

They leapt across the sound that separates Skye from the mainland, as already told.

Brugh Farala is sometimes called Brugh Farabheinn, and from the readiness with which the Fians observed it and made their way to it, it is possible it may have been somewhere in Ardnamurchan, or the districts leading to it. The word "Brugh" implies that it was thickly peopled. It is the word applied to dwellings of the Elfin race, and is probably the same word as the English word Burgh or Borough. The description in the Lay would imply that the whole body of the Fian women were there; Garry drove them into the Brugh and set it on fire. He was willing to allow Fionn's wife to escape, and she would get along with her nine (*caogad*) women opposite every finger she had. She thought that number too few, and would not come out unless she got nine nines (*naoi caogad*) for every one of her fingers. The women were burnt, and Garry fled to a cave. In case his place of refuge should be detected by his footprints, it is said that he jumped and made his way backwards into the cave. The appearance then of the footprints was as of those of a person leaving the cave, more than of a person entering it. Some say there was a slight fall of snow at the time, so that the footprints were more distinctly visible. When Fionn came and found the edifice consumed by fire, and no trace of Garry to be found, he put his finger under his knowledge-tooth, and told his men to be quick and catch Garry in the cave. Garry was brought to justice, and was allowed, according to the law of the Fian band, to choose the manner of his own death.

The version of the Lay or Poem of Brugh Farala, with which the writer has fallen in, is as follows:

BRUGH FARALA.

One day that Fionn went with his men
To the grass-covered straths of the Highlands, (1)
They let slip the dogs among the steep-shelving
    ground
Throughout the glens nearest to them.
A plan of little sense then uprose
In the minds of the women of close curling heads ;
And they tied, with well-made pins,
The hero's hair in the folds of wood.
The hero started from sleep,
From the dream which was followed by no good.

Big Garry Mac Molum went
To the wood without any ready step,
And he found everything as we have heard ;
A small tree on his shoulder with him,
And he placed it against the house.

One day that he was splitting wood,
He kindled an unusual fire,
And put it to the side of the dwelling ;
Then to its highest point the burden of wood took fire.
Fionn's wife asked permission to escape
To *caogad* women for every finger she had.
 . . . . A hundred women were there at embroidery
    work,
And a hundred maidens who were betrothed,
And a hundred women nursing children,
Were to be found by us in the long dwelling.
 . . . . Then was seen an earthy dark smoke :
The dwelling of Farala was in lofty flames.
Every one leapt on his spear-point-head,
And MacReithin fell in the Sound.
But before MacCumal came,

The heat had subsided.
He put his back to the dwelling,
And wept for Garry as the first.
Fionn then put his finger under his tooth,
And accepted the knowledge that he got.
" Follow quickly the man who has concealed himself
      from you,
And overtake Garry in the cave."

"Come out," said MacCumal,
"Good son of Morlum, of wretched plans,"
But delay for your life do not ask,
Since you happen to be among our Fians."

"If I got," he said, "my particular request,
Without asking the sparing of my life."
"You will get your special request
Without your life being spared."

"My petition is, that to take my life
Mac-a-Lun be given to Oscar ; (2)
That is my own request,
And to shorten my neck
On the side of Fionn's white thigh."

They put seven grey hides, and seven bundles of
twisted twigs, and seven feet of marshy soil on Fionn's
thigh. Garry's head was placed on that, and Oscar got
Mac-a-Lun—

And quicker than dew upon a daisy
Were heads of arteries cut in Fionn's knee.
Fionn died, and the whole Fian race suffered loss.

————

Latha sin dh' fhalbh Fionn le Fhianntaibh,
Gu sraithibh gorm Innse Gall. (1)
Leig iad na coin ris na leacainn,
Feadh nan gleann a b' fhaigse dhoibh.
Chinn comhairle air bheagan cèill

Aig bannal nan camag dlù,
Cheangail iad le deilge gasda
Falt an laoich ann an ghlac nan crann.
Dhùisg an laoch as a chadal
Le aisling nach math 'na deigh.

*   *   *   *   *

Dh' imich Gara Mòr mac Molum
Chaidh e 'n chòille gun cheum deas
'S fhuair e gach ni mar a chualas
Craobh chrion air a ghualainn leis
'S chur e sid ri taobh an tallai.

Latha dha ri sgolta bhòrdan
Rinn e teine nach bu dual
Chuir e sin ri taobh an tallai
'S gus a dhruim gu 'n ghahh a 'chual.

Dh' iarr bean Fhinn tighinn amach,
'S Caogad bean air son na h-uile miar.
Ciad bean a bh' ann ri òradh,
'S ciad rìbhinn gu cordadh leinn
'S ciad bean 'nam muime fo mhacan,
Gheibht' ann am brugh fada leinn.

Var. (see Notes).

Chunnaic iad ceò talmhaidh daite :
   Tigh Farala 'na lasair àrd,
'S leum gach fear thar bharr chrann sleagha
   'S dh' fhàg iad Mac-an-Reithinn sa chaol.
'S mu 'n d' thainig MacCumhail oirnn
   Bha 'n teògais air dol gu cùl.
Chuir Fionn a dhruim ris an talla
   'S chaoineadh leis Garai air thùs.
Chuir Fionn an sin a mhiar fo dheud fios
   'S ghabh e mu 'n fhios a fhuair.
" Leanabh gu luath fear air folach
   'S beiribh air Garai 'san uaimh."
"Thig amach," arsa MacCumhail,
   " Dheagh mhic Mòlum nan cleas truagh

'S dàl do t' anam na dean iarraidh
O 'n tharladh 'nar Fianntan thu."
" N' am faighinns'," ars' esan, " m' achanaich àraid
As eugmhais m' anam bhi bhuam."
" Gheibh thu t' achanaich àraid
As t' ionnuis t' anam thoirt saor."
" Se m' achanaich fhein bhuin ri m' anam
Mac-a-Luinne thoirt do Oscar : (2)
'Se sin m' achanaich fhéin
A chur mo bhràghad an giorrad
Air taobh sleisde gile Fhinn."

Chuir iad seachd seicheannan glasa 's seachd ceapan caoil,
agus seachd troidhean de thalamh réisg air muin sliasaid
Fhinn ; chuirte ceann Charai air a sin, 's fhuair Oscar Mac-
a-Luin—

Bu liubha na drùchd air feòinean
Ceann cuisle geartt' an glùn Fhinn.
Chaidh crioch air Fionn, agus thainig dith air an
Fhéinn uile.

NOTES.

(1) *Innse Gall* means literally, The Stranger's Place of Refuge.
Some understand by it the Isle of Skye, as in the case of a native
of that island who was in the south. She is stated to have said :

"If I were in *Innse Gall*
I would suit the place well,
Where I could give something away,
And get something."

" Na 'n robh mise an Innse Gall
'S math fhreagairinn ann,
Far an d' ugain rud bhuam,
'S am faigheadh rud."

This supposition that the Fians were hunting in Skye is
strengthened by the Sound which separates Skye from the mainland being called to this day Kyle Rea (*Caol Reithinn*). " Innse
Gall" is understood by others to be the whole Highlands, hence
the expression, *Innse Gall na Gaidhealtachd* (The Highlands,
which are the stranger's place of refuge).

(2) Some reciters say *Ailbhinn*, and others *Fraoch*.

Var.— A hundred maidens at embroidery work,
A hundred maidens of deftest fingers,
A hundred young girls who were pledged to us,
A hundred women nursing children,
A hundred dogs with silver collars.

*   *   *   *   *

That was to be found in the house of hundreds,
And many men in their best attire.

Ciad nionag a bh' ann ri òradh, '
'S ciad nionag bu ghrinne meur,
Ciad Li-bhean ri còrdadh leinn,
'S ciad bean 'nam muime fo mhacan,
Ciad cuilean, ann le cholair airgid.

*   *   *   *   *

Gheibhte sid an tigh nan ceudan,
'S lionar fear 'na eidibh ann.

THE DAY OF THE BATTLE OF SHEAVES, IN THE TRUE HOLLOW OF TIREE.

THE Fians were at harvest-work in Kilmoluag (1), in the true hollow of Tiree ; it was oats they were harvesting. The day on which they went to reap they left their weapons of war in the armoury of the Fairy Hill of Caolis (2). When they were at the reaping they saw the Norsemen coming ashore at Besta. The Fians had neither spears nor any weapons of war. They sent away Thinman and Back of the Wind MacRae, son of Ronan, for the weapons. The Norsemen attacked them, but a sheaf of oats was driven to the waist in Norsemen's body that day. Then Fionn said to the man near him :

"Look if you can see any man coming with the armour."

"I see one man."

"What like is he ?"

"He is as if he had bare wood (*i.e.*, wood stripped of leaves) on his shoulder."

"Are you seeing anyone else ?"

"I do not see anyone but him."

In a little while Fionn again said : "What is his appearance now coming ?"

"He is as though he had three heads on."

"My child is at full speed, that is, his feet going as high as the top of his head as he comes. Do you see any other ?"

"I do see another."

"Is he making any speed ?"

"Yes, enough."

Thinman (*Caoilte*) came, and every man took his weapons, and they and the Norsemen commenced to attack each other, and they drove the Norsemen to the shore.

The Gaelic, which is as follows, is given word for word as it was taken down from the teller of the story.

LATHA CATH NAN SGUAB ANN AM FIOR-LAGAN THIRIDHE.

Bha an Fhéinn a 'deanadh bàrr ann an Cill-Moluac, b' e sin fior lagan Thireadh, agus is e coirce bha aca. Latha chaidh iad a dheanadh na buain, agus dh' fhàg iad an cuid arm ann an ciste nan arm an Dùn a 'Chaolais. Dar bha iad aig a 'bhuain, chunnaic iad na Lochlannaich tighinn air tir ann am Bista. Cha robh sleaghan no airm eil' aca. Chuir iad air falbh Caoilte agus Cùl Guith Mac Rath, 'ic Ronain a dh' iarraidh nan arm. Thoisich ian fhein 's na Lochlannaich air a chéile, 's bha sguab coirce dol gu crios ann an cneas Lochlannaich an latha sin. Thuirt Fionn ri fear bha làmh ris :

"Seall am faic thu aon duine tighinn leis na h-airm ?"

"Chi mi aon duine."

"De choltas ?"

"Tha mar gum biodh coille lomain air a ghuallain."

"Am bheil thu faicinn duin' eile ?"

"Cha-n' eil mi faicinn gin ach e."

An ceann tacain thuirt Fionn a rìs :

"De choltas an dràsd' a 'tighinn ?"

"Tha e mar gum biodh tri chinn air."

"Tha mo leanabh aig làn astar, sin agad a chasan dol co ard ri mullach a chinn, a 'tighinn. Am faic thu tuille ?"

"Chì, fear eile."

"Am bheil astar fodha ?"

"Tha gu leòir."

Thainig Caoilte 's rug gach fear air arm, 's thòisich iad fhein 's na Lochlainnich air a cheile 's chuir iad ruaig air na Lochlainnich gu cladach.

NOTES.

(1) Kilmoluag is farm-land on the north-west side of Tiree. It is now densely populated by a crofter population, but bears traces of having been at one time very fertile. It must suffer a great deal from sand blowing. Moluag, the saint from whom the name is derived, has many places called after him. There is a Kilmoluag in Lismore and one in Skye.

(2) The distance from the scene of their labours to *Caolas* would be about five miles. The fort is a hillock, in which there is to be seen a small hollow called the armoury (*ciste nan arm*), and was, within the memory of those still living, considered a place of strength. It was surrounded by a dry stone dyke, but the stones have been removed to build houses with.

———

This story was written as it was told by Donald Cameron, a native of Tiree, in the year 1865. Many other tales (*Sgeulachdan*) and songs (*orain*) were taken down from him at the time, and the writer cannot but express his admiration of Cameron, as the best reciter he has ever fallen in with, as well as his own good fortune in having met him, and in the stories having been at the time written down. Though these tales are not of historical value, they are of great value as specimens of the power of the language, and remains of habits of thought now rapidly passing away. The names of places in Tiree, and other islands near, bear evident traces of Norsemen having been here at one time subsequent to the settlement of the Gaelic-speaking race ; and there are also traces in the names of some race to which no name can be positively given.

FIN MAC COUL IN THE KINGDOM OF THE BIG MEN.

THIS Celtic hero has been unfortunate in the manner in which he has come before the literary world. At one time he was represented as a giant of portentous dimensions :—

> " His mouth was twelve miles broad,
> His teeth were ten miles square ;"

at another time as a powerful ruler in a state of society comparatively civilised. The authenticity of the poems for which this latter view is responsible is questioned, and has led to a heated controversy sufficient (to say the least) to create a prejudice against him.

Fin, their leader, is a particularly attractive character in popular lore—

> " His house was wide and hospitable,
> Its door was never closed."

> " Tigh farsuing fial
> A chòmhla cha do dhruideadh riamh."

Fin's dog Brăn was a Fairy or Elfin dog, commonly said to have had a venomous claw, which was kept covered except when the dog was engaged in fight. One of the most affecting incidents in the popular tales of Fin is that of his having on one occasion struck this favourite hound.

> " Noble Brăn looked at him,
> And wondered at his striking him ;
> The hand with which I struck Bran
> Pity from the shoulder it was not shred."

> " Dh' amhairc air Bran buadhach
> 'S ioghnadh air e bhith 'ga bhualadh ;
> An làmh leis an do bhuail mi Bran
> 'S truagh o'n ghualainn nach do sgar."

The following tale was not written word for word from the dictation of the reciter ; but full notes were taken, and written out immediately after, so that it may be said that the tale is given in the words of the person from whom it was heard, without addition or suppression.

The tale is particularly valuable as showing how the human imagination runs in similar or analogous grooves. Whoever composed the story, in all probability, never heard of Gulliver ; and the "immortal" Swift never heard of Fin-mac-Coul going to the kingdom of Big Men. The two tales are founded on the same fancy, in representing their heroes as visiting men of gigantic size, compared with whom ordinary mortals are mere pigmies ; but the incidents are so different, and cast in such entirely different moulds, that it becomes probable almost to certainty, that they have no connection with each other.

How Fin went to the Kingdom of the Big Men.

Fin and his men were in the Harbour of the Hill of Howth on a hillock, behind the wind and in front of the sun, where they could see every person, and nobody could see them, when they saw a speck coming from the west. They thought at first it was the blackness of a shower ; but when it came nearer, they saw it was a boat. It did not lower sail till it entered the harbour. There were three men in it ; one for guide in the bow, one for steering in the stern, and one for the tackle in the centre. They came ashore, and drew it up seven times its own length in dry grey grass, where the scholars of the city could not make it stock for derision or ridicule.

They then went up to a lovely green spot, and the first lifted a handful of round pebbles or shingle, and commanded them to become a beautiful house, that no better could be found in Ireland; and this was done. The second one lifted a slab of slate, and commanded it to be slate on the top of the house, that there was not better in Ireland; and this was done. The third one caught a bunch of shavings and commanded them to be pine-wood and timber in the house, that there was not in Ireland better; and this was done.

This caused much wonder to Fin, who went down where the men were, and made inquiries of them, and they answered him. He asked whence they were, or whither they were going. They said, "We are three Heroes whom the King of the Big Men has sent to ask combat of the Fians." He then asked, "What was the reason for doing this, or what was the purport (literally, juice) of their coming?" They said they did not know, but they heard that they were strong men, and they came to ask combat of Heroes from them. "Is Fin at home?" "He is not." [Great is a man's leaning towards his own life.] Fin then put them under crosses and under enchantments, that they were not to move from the place where they were till they saw him again.

He went away and made ready his coracle, gave its stern to land and prow to sea, hoisted the spotted towering sails against the long, tough, lance-shaped mast, cleaving the billows in the embrace of the wind in whirls, with a soft gentle breeze from the height of the sea coast, and from the rapid tide of the red (*i.e.*, tangled-covered) rocks, that would take willow from the hill, foliage from the tree, and heather from its stock and roots. Fin was guide in her prow, helm in her stern, and tackle in her middle; and stopping of head or foot he did not make till he reached the Kingdom of the Big Men. He went ashore and drew up his coracle in grey grass. He went up, and a Big Wayfarer met him. Fin asked who he was. " I am," he said, " the Red-haired Coward of the King of the Big Men ; and," said he to Fin, "you are the one I am in quest of. Great is my esteem and respect towards you ; you are the best maiden I have ever seen ; you will yourself make a dwarf for the King, and your dog (this was Brăn) a lapdog. It is long since the King has been in want of a dwarf and a lapdog." He took with him Fin ; but another Big Man came, and was going to take Fin from him. The two fought ; but when they had torn each other's clothes, they left it to Fin to judge. He chose the first one. He took Fin with him to the palace of the King, whose worthies and high nobles assembled to see the little man. The King lifted him upon the palm of his hand, and went three times round the town with Fin upon one palm and Brăn upon the other. He made a sleeping-place for him at the end of his own bed. Fin was waiting, watching, and observing everything that was going on about the house. He observed that the King, as soon as night came, rose and went out, and returned no more till morning. This caused him much wonder, and at last he asked the King why he went away every night and left the Queen by herself. " Why," said the King, "do you ask ?" " For satisfaction to myself," said Fin ; "for it is causing me much wonder." Now the King had a great liking for Fin ; he never saw anything that gave him more pleasure than he did ; and at last he told him. " There is," he said, " a great Monster who wants my daughter in marriage, and to have half my kingdom to himself ; and there is not another man in the kingdom who can meet him but myself ; and I must go every night to hold combat with him." " Is there," said Fin, " no man to combat with him but yourself ?" " There is not," said the King, " one who will war with him for a single night." " It is a pity," said Fin, " that this should be called the Kingdom of the Big Men. Is he bigger than yourself?" "Never you mind," said the King. "I will mind," said Fin: "take your rest and sleep to-night, and I shall go to meet him." "Is it you?" said the King; "you would not keep half a stroke against him."

When night came, and all men went to rest, the King was for going away as usual; but Fin at last prevailed upon him to allow himself to go. "I shall combat him," said he, "or else he knows a trick." "I think much," said the King, "of allowing you to go, seeing he gives myself enough to do." "Sleep you soundly to-night," said Fin, "and let me go; if he comes too violently upon me, I shall hasten home."

Fin went and reached the place where the combat was to be. He saw no one before him, and he began to pace backwards and forwards. At last he saw the sea coming in kilns of fire and as a darting serpent, till it came down below where he was. A Huge Monster came up and looked towards him, and from him. "What little speck do I see there?" he said. "It is I," said Fin. "What are you doing here?" "I am a messenger from the King of the Big Men; he is under much sorrow and distress; the Queen has just died, and I have come to ask if you will be so good as to go home to-night without giving trouble to the kingdom." "I shall do that," said he; and he went away with the rough humming of a song in his mouth.

Fin went home when the time came, and lay down in his own bed, at the foot of the King's bed. When the King awoke, he cried out in great anxiety, "My kingdom is lost, and my dwarf and my lapdog are killed!" "They are not," said Fin; "I am here yet; and you have got your sleep, a thing you were saying it was rare for you to get." "How," said the King, "did you escape, when you are so little, and that he is enough for myself, though I am so big." "Though you," said Fin, "are so big and strong, I am quick and active."

Next night the King was for going : but Fin told him to take his sleep to-night again : " I shall stand myself in your place, or else a better hero than yonder one will come." " He will kill you," said the King. " I shall take my chance," said Fin.

He went, and as happened the night before, he saw no one ; and he began to pace backwards and forwards. He saw the sea coming in fiery kilns and as a darting serpent : and that Huge Man came up. " Are you here to-night again ?" said he. " I am, and this is my errand : when the Queen was being put in the coffin (lit., dead-chest), and the King heard the coffin being nailed, and the joiner's stroke, he broke his heart with pain and grief ; and the *Parliament* has sent me to ask you to go home to-night till they get the King buried." The Monster went this night also, roughly humming a song ; and Fin went home when the time came.

In the morning the King awoke in great anxiety, and called out, " My kingdom is lost, and my dwarf and my lapdog are killed !" and he greatly rejoiced that Fin and Brăn were alive, and that he himself got rest, after being so long without sleep.

Fin went the third night, and things happened as before. There was no one before him, and he took to pacing to and fro. He saw the sea coming till it came down below him : the Big Monster came up ; he saw the little black speck, and asked who was there, and what he wanted. " I have come to combat you," said Fin.

Fin and Brăn began the combat. Fin was going backwards, and the Huge Man was following. Fin called to Brăn, " Are you going to let him kill me ?" Brăn had a venomous shoe ; and he leaped and struck the Huge Man with the venomous shoe on the breast-

bone, and took the heart and lungs out of him. Fin
drew Mac-a-Luin (his sword), cut off his head, put it on
a hempen rope, and went with it to the Palace of the
King. He took it into the *Kitchen*, and put it behind the
door. In the morning the servant could not turn it,
nor open the door. The King went down; he saw the
Huge Mass, caught it by the top of the head, and lifted
it, and knew it was the head of the Man who was for so
long a time asking combat from him, and keeping him
from sleep. "How at all," said he, "has this head come
here? Surely it is not my dwarf that has done it."
"Why," said Finn, "should he not?"

Next night the King wanted to go himself to the
place of combat; "because," said he, "a bigger one than
the former will come to-night, and the kingdom will be
destroyed, and you yourself killed; and that is not the
pleasure I take in having you with me." But Fin went,
and everything happened as formerly till that Big Man
came again, asking vengeance for his son, and to have
the kingdom for himself, or equal combat. He and
Fin began; and Fin was going backwards. He spoke
to Brân, "Are you going to allow him to kill me?" Brân
whined, and went and sat down on the beach. Fin was
ever going back, and he called out again to Brân. Brân
jumped and struck the Big Man with the venomous
shoe, and took the heart and the lungs out of him. Fin
cut the head off, and took it with him, and left it in
front of the house. The King awoke in great terror,
and cried out, "My kingdom is lost, and my dwarf and
my lapdog are killed!" Fin raised himself up and said,
"They are not;" and the King's joy was not small when
he went out and saw the head that was in front of the
house.

The next night a Big Hag came ashore, and the tooth
in the front (literally door) of her mouth would make a
distaff. She sounded a challenge on her shield: "You

killed," she said, "my husband and my son." "I did
kill them," said Fin. They engaged ; and it was worse
for Fin to guard himself from the tooth than from the
hand of the Big Hag. When she had nearly done for
him Brän struck her with the venomous shoe, and killed
her as he had done to the rest. Fin took with him the
head, and left it in front of the house. The King awoke
in great anxiety, and called out, "My kingdom is lost,
and my dwarf and my lapdog are killed!" "They are
not," said Fin, answering him ; and when they went out
and saw the head, the King said, "I and my kingdom
will have peace ever after this. The mother herself of
the brood is killed ; but tell me who you are. It was
foretold for me that it would be Fin-mac-Coul that
would give me relief, and he is only now eighteen years
of age. Who are you, then, or what is your name?"
"There never stood," said Fin, "on hide of cow or
horse, one to whom I would deny my name. I am Fin,
the son of Coul (Cuwal) son of Looach, son of Trein,
son of Fin, son of Art (Arthur), son of the young High
King of Erin ; and it is time for me now to go home.
It has been with much wandering out of my way that I
have come to your kingdom ; and this is the reason why
I have come, that I might find out what injury I have
done to you, or the reason why you sent the three heroes
to ask combat from me, and bring destruction on my
Men." "You never did any injury to me," said the
King ; "and I ask a thousand pardons. I did not send
the heroes to you. It is not the truth they told. They
were three men who were courting three fairy women
(elfin women), and these gave them their shirts ; and
when they have on the shirts, the combat of a hundred
men is upon the hand of every one of them. But they
must put off the shirts every night, and put them on the
backs of chairs ; and if the shirts were taken from them
they would be next day as weak as other people."

Fin got every honour, and all that the King could give him ; and when he went away, the King and the Queen and the people went down to the shore to give him their blessing.

Fin now went away in his coracle, and was sailing close to land (lit. by the side of the shore), when he saw a young man running and calling out to him. Fin came in close to land with his coracle, and asked what he wanted. " I am," said the young man, " a good servant wanting a master." " What work can you do ?" said Fin. " I am," said he, " the best soothsayer that there is." " Jump into the boat, then." The soothsayer jumped in, and they went forward."

They did not go far when another youth came running. " I am," he said, " a good servant wanting a master." " What work can you do ?" said Fin. " I am as good a thief as there is." " Jump into the boat, then ;" and Fin took with him this one also. They saw then a third young man running and calling out. They came close to land. " What man are you ?" said Fin. " I am," said he, " the best climber that there is. I will take up a hundred pounds on my back in a place where a fly could not stand on a calm summer day." " Jump in ;" and this one came in also. " I have my pick of servants now," said Fin ; " it cannot be but these will suffice."

They went ; and stop of head or foot they did not make till they reached the Harbour of the Hill of Howth. He asked the soothsayer what the three Big Men were doing. " They are," he said, " after their supper, and making ready for going to bed."

He asked a second time. " They are," he said, " after going to bed ; and their shirts are spread on the back of chairs."

After a while, Fin asked him again, " What are the Big Men doing now ?" " They are," said the soothsayer, "sound asleep." "It would be a good thing if there was now a thief to go and steal the shirts." "I would do that," said the thief, "but the doors are locked, and I cannot get in." "Come," said the climber, "on my back, and I shall put you in." He took him up upon his back to the top of the chimney, and let him down, and he stole the shirts.

Fin went where the Fian band was; and in the morning they came to the house where the three Big Men were. They sounded a challenge upon their shields, and asked them to come out to combat.

They came out. "Many a day," said they, "have we been better for combat than we are to-day," and they confessed to Fin everything as it was. "You were," said Fin, "impertinent"; and he made them swear that they would be faithful to himself ever after, and ready in every enterprise he would place before them.

Mar a chaidh Fionn do Righeachd nam Fear Mora.

Bha Fionn 's a chuid dhaoine ann an cala Beinn Eudainn[1] air cnoc, air chùl gaoith' 's air eudain gréine, far am faiceadh iad a h-uile fear 's nach fhaiceadh duin' idir iad, 'nuair a chunnaic iad dùradan a' tighin o'n àird'-an iar. Shaoil leò an toiseach gur h-e dùbhradh frois a bh'ann ; ach an uair a thàinig i ni 'bu dlùithe, chunnaic iad gur h-e bàta 'bh'ann. Cha do leag i seòl gus an d'thàinig i staigh do'n chala. Bha triùir dhaoine innt', fear ri iùl 'na toiseach, fear ri stiùir 'na deireadh, is fear ri beairt 'na buillsgein. Thàinig iad air tìr, is tharraing

----

[1] The name of this hill is uniformly known in *Tales of the West Highlands* (in which it is frequently mentioned) as *Beinn Eudainn*, but in Irish it is called *Beinn Eadair* (the Hill of Howth, near Dublin).

ad a suas i, a seachd fad fhéin, ann am feur tioram, glas, far nach deanadh sgoilearan a' bhaile mhòir bùrd mhagaidh no fhochaid dhi.

Chaidh iad an sin a suas gu lianaig bhòidhich, agus thog an ceud fhear làn a dhùirn de bhulbhagan no morghan chlach, agus thuirt e riu, iad a bhith 'nan taigh briagha, nach robh an Éirinn ni 'b'fheàrr; agus bha so deanta. Thog an dara fear leacag sgliat, agus thuirt e i a bhith 'na sgliat air mullach an taighe, nach robh an Éirinn ni 'b'fheàrr; agus bha so deanta. Rug an treas fear air bad shliseag, agus thuirt e iad a bhith 'nan giubhas 's 'nam fiodh 'san taigh nach robh an Éirinn ni b'fheàrr; agus bha so deanta.

Chuir so mòr ioghnadh air Fionn; agus chaidh e sìos far an robh na daoine, agus dh'fhoighneachd e iad. agus fhreagair iad e. Dh'fhoighneachd e cia as a bha iad, no ceana 'bha iad a' dol. " Is trì gaisgich sinn, a chuir rìgh nam Fear Mòra a dh'iarraidh còmhraig air an Fhéinn." Dh'fharraid e'n sin 'd e 'n t-aobhar a bha air son so a dheanamh, no ciod am fàth no 'n sùgh a bha aig an teachd. Thuirt iad nach robh fios aca; ach gu'n cual' iad gu'n robh iad 'nan daoine làidir, 's gu'n d'thàinig iad a dh'iarraidh còmhraig laoch orra. "A bheil Fionn aig an taigh?" "Cha 'n' eil." [Is mòr bàigh duine r'a anam.] Chuir Fionn an so iad fo chroisean agus fo gheasan, nach gluaiseadh iad as an àit an robh iad gus am faiceadh iad e-san a ris.

Dh'fhalbh e agus rinn e deas a churachan; agus thug e a dheireadh do thir agus a thoiseach do mhuir; agus thog e na siùil bhreaca, bhaidealach, an aghaidh nan crann fada, fulangach, fiùi, a' gabhail nan sugh an glaic na gaoithe 'na cuireagan, le soirbheas beag, lag, laghach, o mhullach nam beann, 's o àirde na h-eirthire, 's o bhuinne nan ruadh-charraigean, a bheireadh seileach á beinn, 's duilleach á craoibh, 's fraoch òg as a bhun 's as a fhreumhaichean. Dheanadh Fionn iùl 'na toiseach, stiùir 'na deireadh, 's beairt 'na buillsgein; agus stad cinn no coise cha d'rinn e gus an d'ràinig e righeachd nam Fear Mòra. Chaidh e air tir, 's tharraing e suas a churachan ann am feur glas. Ghabh e suas, is thachair an taisdealach mòr ud air. Dh'fharraid Fionn cò e. " Is mise,"

ars' e-san, "an Cladhaire Ruadh aig rìgh nam Fear Mòra ;
agus," ars' e-san ri Fionn, "is tusa a tha 'dhìth orm. Is maith
do mhiadh agus do mhodh orm ; is tu òigh a 's feàrr a chunnaic mi riamh ; ni thu fhéin troich do'n rìgh, agus ni do chù
(b'e so Bran) measan. Is fhada o'n tha troich is measan a
dhìth air an rìgh." Thug e leis Fionn ; ach thàinig Fear Mòr
eile, agus bha e dol g'a thoirt bhuaithe. Leum an dithis air
a chéile ; ach dar a bha iad air falluinnean a chéile shracadh,
dh'fhàg iad aig Fionn breth a thoirt. Ròghnaich e an ciad
fhear. Thog e-san leis Fionn thun *palace* an rìgh, agus
chruinnich a mhaithean agus a mhòr-uaislean a dh'fhaicin an
duine bhig. Thog an rìgh e air a bhois ; agus chaidh e tri
uairean mu'n bhaile, agus Fionn air an darna bois agus Bran
air a' bhois eile. Rinn e àite-cadail dhà aig ceann a leapach
fhéin. Bha Fionn a' feitheamh, agus a' faire, agus a' faicin
nan uile nithe a bha dol air aghaidh mu'n taigh. Mhothaich
e gu'n robh an rìgh, co luath 's a bha an oidhche tighin, ag
éirigh agus a' falbh a mach ; agus cha tigeadh e tuilleadh gu
madainn. Chuir so mòr ioghnadh air ; agus, mu dheireadh,
dh'fheòraich e de 'n rìgh c'ar son a bha e falbh a h-uile oidhche,
agus a' fàgail na ban-rìghinn leatha féin. "C'ar son," ars' an
rìgh, "a ta thu feòraich ?" "Tha," arsa Fionn, "air son
riarachaidh dhomh fhéin, oir tha e cur mòrain iongantais orm."
A nis, bha tlachd mòr aig an rìgh do Fhionn ; cha d'fhuair e
ni riamh a bha toirt tuilleadh toileachaidh dha na e ; agus,
mu dheireadh, dh'innis e. "Tha," ars' e-san, "Athach mòr
ag iarraidh mo nighin r'a pòsadh, agus leth mo rìgheachd uile
bhith aige fhéin ; agus cha 'n 'eil duine eile 'san rìgheachd
a's urrainn a choinneachadh ach mi féin ; agus is éigin dol
gach oidhche a chumail còmhraig ris." "Nach 'eil," arsa
Fionn, "aon fhear a chumas còmhrag ris ach thu fhéin ?"
"Cha 'n 'eil," ars' an rìgh, "na chumas cogadh aon oidhche
tris." "Is mairg," arsa Fionn, "a thugrìgheachd nam Fear
Mòra orra. A bheil e ni's mò na thu féin ?" "Is coma
leatsa," ars' an rìgh. "Cha choma," arsa Fionn ; "gabh thusa
fois agus codal a nochd, agus théid mise g'a choinneachadh."
"'N e thusa ?" thuirt an rìgh, "cha chumadh tu aon bhloigh
buille ris."

'Nuair a thàinig an oidhche 's a ghabh a h-uile duine mu thàmh, bha'n rìgh air son falbh mar a b'àbhaist; ach thug Fionn air, mu dheireadh, e féin a leigeadh ann. "Còmbraigidh mise e," ars' e-san, "air neo tha cleas aige." "Is mòr leam," ars' an rìgh, "do leigeadh ann, 's gur leòir leam féin e." "Coidil thusa gu suaimhneach a nochd," arsa Fionn, "is leig mise ann ; ma thig e cas, greasaidh mi dhachaidh."

Dh'fhalbh Fionn, is ràinig e 'n t-àit 'san robh a' chòmhrag ri bhith. Cha robh e faicin duine roimhe, is thòisich e air spaisd-eireachd air ais is air aghaidh. Mu dheireadh, chunnaic e a' mhuir a' tighin 'na h-àthanna teine 's 'na nathair bheumnaich, gus an d'ràinig i shios fodha. Thàinig Athach mòr a nios, is sheall e thuige 's bhuaithe. "D e," ars' e-san, "an dùradan a chi mi 'n sid ?" "Tha mise," arsa Fionn. "'D e a tha thu deanamh an so?" "Is teachdaire mise o rìgh nam Fear Mòra ; tha mòran mulaid agus cruais air ; tha a' bhan rìghinn an déigh bàs fhaotain, agus thàinig mise dh'fheòraich dhìot am bi thu co math a's dol dachaidh a nochd gun luasgan a chur air an rìgheachd." "Ni mi sin," thuirt e-san, agus dh'fhalbh e, is gnòdhan òrain aige 'na bheul.

Dh'fhalbh Fionn dachaidh dar a thàinig an t-àm, agus chaidh e a laighe 'na leabaidh fhéin aig casan leab' an rìgh. Dar a dhùisg an rìgh, ghlaodh e ann an iomguin mhòir, "Tha mo rìgheachd air a call 's mo throich 's mo mheasan air am marbhadh !" "Cha 'n eil," arsa Fionn ; "tha mi'n so fathast, agus fhuair thusa do chadal, rud a tha thu ag ràdh a b'annas-ach leat fhaotain." "Ciamar," ars' an rìgh, "a chaidh thusa as, is thu co beag, ged is leòir e dhòmh-sa, is mi co mòr?" "Ged tha thusa," arsa Fionn, "mòr làidir, tha mise deas, apaidh."

An ath-oidhche, bha'n rìgh air son falbh ; ach thuirt Fionn ris e ghabhail a chadail a nochd fhathast ; "Seasaidh mi fhìn a'd' àit, air neo thig laoch a's feàrr na sud." "Marbhaidh e thu," thuirt an rìgh. "Gabhaidh mi cuid mo thuiteamais," thuirt Fionn.

Dh'fhalbh e ; is mar a thachair an oidhche roimhe, cha'n fhac' e duine, is thòisich e air spaisdeireachd air ais 's air aghaidh. Chunnaic e'n fhairge tighin 'na h-athanna teine 's

'na nathair bheumnaich; agus thàinig am fear mòr ud a nìos.
"A bheil thus' an so a nochd a ris?" ars' e-san. "Tha mi,
agus is e sud mo thurus : 'nuair a bha a' bhan-righinn 'ga cur
anns a' chiste-mhairbh, agus a chual' an rìgh a' chiste 'ga tarraing-
eachadh agus buille nan saor, bhrist a chridhe le cràdh agus le
mulad ; agus chuir a' *Pharlamaid* mise a dh'iarraidh ort gu'n
rachadh tu dhachaidh air an oidhche so, gus am faigheadh iad
an rìgh a thiodhlacadh." Dh'fhalbh an t-Athach air an oidhche
so cuideachd, agus gnòdhan orain aige 'na bheul ; is chaidh
Fionn dachaidh dar a thàinig an t-àm.

'Sa' mhadainn dhùisg an rìgh ann an iomguin mhòir, agus
ghlaodh e mach, "Mo rìgheachd air a call, agus mo throich
agus mo mheasan air am marbhadh!" Agus rinn e gàirdeachas
gu leòir gu'n robh Fionn is Bran beò, 's gu'n d'fhuair e fhéin
fois an déigh a bhith co fada gun chadal.

Chaidh Fionn an treas oidhche ann, agus thachair mar a
thachair roimhe. Cha robh duine air thoiseach air ; bhuail e
air spaisdeireachd. Chunnaic e'n fhairge tighin gus an d'
ràinig i shìos fodha; thàinig an t-Athach mòr a nìos ; chunnaic
e'n dùradan beag ud, 's dh'fheòraich e cò a bha'n sud, is ciod
a bha 'dhìth air. "Thàinig mi g'ad chòmhrag-sa," arsa Fionn.

Thòisich Fionn is Bran air a' chòmhrag ; ach bha Fionn
a'dol air 'ais an comhair a chùil, is bha 'm fear mòr 'ga leanailt.
Ghlaodh Fionn ri Bran, "A bheil thu dol a leigeil leis mo
mharbhadh?" Bha bròg nimhe air Bran ; agus leum e agus
bhuail e a' bhròg nimhe air an Fhear Mhòr ann an carraig an
uchd, agus thug e 'n cridhe agus an sgamhan as. Tharraing
Fionn Mac-an-Luin agus gheàrr e dheth an ceann, agus chuir
e air *ròpa* cainbe e, agus dh'fhalbh e leis gu *palace* an rìgh.
Thug e staigh do'n *chitsein* e, agus chuir e cùl an doruis e.
'Sa' mhadainn, cha b' urrainn an t-*scarbhant* car a chur deth,
no an dorus fhosgladh. Chaidh an rìgh a sìos ; chunnaic e'n
tùchd mòr ud ; rug e air mullach a chinn agus thog se e, agus
dh'aithnich e gur h-e a bh'ann ceann an fhir, a bha a leithid
a dh'ùine 'g iarraidh còmhraig air, agus 'ga chumail o chadal.
"Ciamar idir," ars' e-san, "a thàinig an ceann so an so? Gu
cinnteach, cha'n e mo throich a rinn e." "C' arson," arsa
Fionn, "nach b' e?"

An ath-oidhche, bha 'n rìgh ag iarraidh dol e féin do'n àit-
chòmhraig, "A chionn," thuirt e, "gu'n tig fear a's mò na'm
fear ud a nochd ; agus bidh an rìgheachd air a sgrios, agus tu
féin air do mharbhadh ; 's nach e sin an tlachd a tha mi
gabhail ann thu bhith agam." Ach dh'fhalbh Fionn, is
thachair gach ni mar a thachair roimhe, gus an d' thàinig am
fear mòr ud a rìs ag iarraidh dìoghaltais air son a mhic, agus
an rìgheachd a bhith aige, no còmhrag céile. Thòisich e
fhéin is Fionn ; is bha Fionn a'dol air 'ais. Labhair e ri Bran,
"A bheil thu dol a leigeadh leis mise a mharbhadh ?" Thug
Bran gnùsd as, agus dh'fhalbh e is rinn e suidhe air an tràigh.
Bha Fionn a' sìor-dhol air 'ais, agus ghlaodh e a rìs ri Bran.
Leum Bran is bhuail e a' bhròg nimhe air an Fhear Mhòr, is
thug e'n cridhe 's an sgamhan as. Gheàrr Fionn an ceann
dheth, agus thug e leis e, agus dh'fhàg e air bialthaobh an
taighe e. Dhùisg an rìgh ann an eagal mòr agus ghlaodh e,
" Mo rìgheachd air a call, agus mo throich agus mo mheasan
air am marbhadh !" Thug Fionn togail air féin, agus thubhairt
e nach robh ; agus cha bu bheag gàirdeachas an rìgh 'nuair a
chaidh e mach, agus a chunnaic e'n ceann a bha air bialthaobh
an taighe.
An ath oidhche, thàinig cailleach mhòr gu tìr, agus dheanadh
an fhiacail a bha 'n dorus a beòil cuigeal. Bhuail i beum-
sgéithe : " Mharbh thu," ars' ise, " m' fhear agus mo mhac."
" Mharbh mi," thuirt Fionn. Thòisich iad air a chéile ; agus
bu mhiosa do Fhionn e fhéin a dhion o'n fhiacail na o' n làimh
aig a' chaillich. Nuair a bha i brath foghnachdainn dà, bhuail
Bran i leis a' bhròig nimhe, is mharbh e i mar a rinn e air
càch. Thug Fionn leis an ceann, is dh' fhàg e air bialthaobh
an taighe e. Dhùisg an rìgh ann an iomguin mhòir agus
ghlaodh e, " Tha mo rìgheachd air a call, agus mo throich agus
mo mheasan air am marbhadh !" " Cha 'n 'eil," thuirt Fionn,
is e 'g a fhreagairt ; agus an uair a chaidh iad a mach, agus a
chunnaic iad an ceann, thuirt an rìgh, " Bidh a nis tuilleadh
sìth agams' agus aig mo rìgheachd. Tha an so màthair na
cuain i fhéin air a marbhadh ; ach innis dhomh cò thu. Bha
e 'san tairgneachd agam-sa gur h-e Fionn MacCumhaill a
bheireadh fuasgladh dhomh, 's cha 'n 'eil e ach ochd bliadhna

deug a dh'aois fhathast : Cò thusa, ma ta, no ciod e t' ainm ?"
"Cha do sheas riamh," arsa Fionn, "air seiche mairt no eich
d' an aicheadhainn m'ainm. Is mise Fionn MacCumhaill,
mhic Luthaich, 'ic Thréin, 'ic Fhinn, 'ic Airt, 'ic àrd òg rìgh Eirinn ;
agus tha 'n t-àm a nis dhomh dol dachaidh. Is glé allabanach a
thàinig mi do 'n righeachd agad-sa ; agus is e sid an t-aobhar air
son an d'thàinig mi, gu'm faighinn fios 'd e a' choire a rinn mi
ort, no 'd e 'n t-aobhar air son gu 'n do chuir thu trì gaisgich a
dh'iarraidh còmhraig orm, agus a thoirt sgrios air mo chuid
dhaoine." "Cha d' rinn thu riamh coire orm sa," thuirt an
rìgh ; "agus tha mi 'g iarraidh mile maitheanas Cha do chuir
mise na gaisgich a d' ionnsaidh. Cha 'n i an fhìrinn a dh' innis
iad. 'S ann a bha 'n sid triùir dhaoine, agus bha iad a' leann-
anachd ri trì mnathan-sìth ; agus thug iad sin doibh an léintean ; agus dar a bhios na léintean umpa, tha còmhrag ceud an
làimh gach fir dhiubh. Ach feumaidh iad na léintean a chur
dhiubh a h-uile oidhche, agus an cur air cùl chlaithrichean ;
agus na'm biodh na léintean air an toirt bhuatha, bhiodh
iadsan an là-ar-n-mhàireach co lag ri daoine eile."

Fhuair Fionn gach urram, 's gach ni a b' urrainn an rìgh a
thoirt dà ; agus an uair a dh'fhalbh e, chaidh an rìgh agus a
bhanrighinn, agus an sluagh sìos gu cladach, a dh'fhàgai'
beannachd aige.

Dh'fhalbh Fionn an so 'na churachan ; agus bha e a' seòladh
a sìos ri taobh a' chladaich, dar a chunnaic e òganach 'na ruith
agus a' glaodhaich ris. Thàinig Fionn a staigh dlùth do thìr
leis a' churachan, agus dh' fhiosraich e ciod a bha 'dhìth air.
"Is mise," ars' an t-òganach, "gille math ag iarraidh maigh-
listir." "Ciod an obair a ni thu ?" arsa Fionn. "Is mise,"
ars' e-san, "am Fiosaiche a' s feàrr a th' ann." "Leum a
staigh do 'n bhàta, ma ta." Leum am Fiosaiche a staigh ;
agus ghabh iad air an aghaidh.

Cha b' fhad a chaidh iad dar a thàinig an t-ath-òganach 'na
ruith. "Is mise," ars' e-san, "gille math ag iarraidh maighistir."
"'D e 'n obair a ni thu ?" arsa Fionn. "Is mise meirleach cho
math 's a th' ann." "Leum a staigh do 'n bhàta, ma ta ;" agus
thug Fionn leis am fear so cuideachd. Chunnaic iad an so an
treas òganach a' ruith 's a' glaodhaich. Thàinig iad dlùth do

thìr. "'D e 'n duine thusa?" thuirt Fionn. "Is mise," ars' e-san, "an streapadair a 's feàrr a th' ann; bheir mi suas ceud pùnd air mo mhuin 'san àit nach seas a' chuileag ri latha ciùin sàmhraidh." "Leum a staigh;" agus thàinig am fear so a staigh cuideachd. "Tha mo rogha ghillean agam a nis," thuirt Fionn; "cha 'n fheud e bhith nach dean iad so feum."

Dh'fhalbh iad; agus stad cinn no coise cha d' rinn iad gus an d'ràinig iad cala Beinn Eudainn. Dh'fhoighneachd e de 'n Fhiosaiche 'd e a bha'n triùir Fhear Mòra a' deanamh. "Tha iad," ars' e-san, "an dèigh an suipeireach, agus a' deanamh deas air son a dhol a laighe."

Dh'fhoighneachd e 'n dara uair. "Tha iad," ars' e-san, "an dèigh a dhol a laighe; agus tha'n lèintean air an sgaoileadh air cùl chaithrichean."

An ceann treis, dh'fhoighneachd Fionn dheth a rìs, "'D e ris an robh na Fir Mhòra a nis?" "Tha iad," ars' am Fios-aiche, "'nan trom shuain." "Bu mhath," arsa Fionn, "am meirleach a nis a rachadh agus a ghoideadh na lèintean." "Dheanainn-sa sin," thuirt am meirleach, "ach gu bheil na dorsan air an glasadh, agus cha 'n fhaigh mi a staigh." Trobhad," ars' an streapadair, "air mo mhuin-sa, agus cuiridh mise a staigh thu." Thog e suas air a mhuin e gu mullach an t-simileir, agus leig e nuas e; agus ghoid e na lèintean.

Chaidh Fionn far an robh an Fhéinn; agus anns a' mhad-ainn thàinig iad thun an taighe anns an robh an triùir Fhear Mòra. Bhuail iad beum-sgéithe, agus dh'iarr iad orra tighin' a mach gu còmhrag.

Thàinig iad a mach. "Is iomadh là," thuirt iadsan, "a bha sinne ni 'b'fheàrr gu còmhrag na 'tha sinn an diu;" agus dh'aidich iad do Fhionn a h-uile ni mar a bha. "Bha sibh," arsa Fionn, "mi-mhodhail;" agus thug e orra mionnachadh gu'm biodh iad dileas dà fhéin am feasda tuilleadh, agus deas anns gach càs a chuireadh e mu'n coinneimh.

(From very full notes taken of the tale as told by Murdoch M'Intyre, Kilkenneth, Tiree, in January 1869. —J. G. C.)

ON one occasion when the hunt (*sealg 's sithionn*) was lost, late in the evening, and in the dusk (*anamoch*), a man met Fionn and his men, and said to them:

"You need be under no anxiety (*'s beag ruigeas sibh leas curam bhi oirbh*), I will give half of you food and board for a year and a day, and my brother the Red from Teamhair (*Fear Dearg a Teamhair*) will give food and shelter to the other half."

There were twelve of Fionn's best men (*maithibh*) amissing. Fionn vowed to find them, and when he set out in search of them, he said to his men, "Let no one who was born or brought up in Ireland follow me" (*Na leanadh duine ruga na thoga an Eirinn mise*). It was a custom with Fionn when setting out on a journey never to look behind him, or turn back, a thing believed by many at the present day to be unlucky. Fergus followed him; Fionn hearing the sounds behind him, and not caring to break his own custom or injunction, called out, "Who is it that is following my footsteps?" (*Co sid propadh mo cheaplaich?*) The words used by him in this question are obsolete, but they are valuable as remains of expression that probably date far back in the history of the language. The answer he got was, "I am here, one of your men and Fergus" (*Tha mise so, fear agus Fearghus*).

"Don't you know that not one born in Ireland may follow me? (*Nach' eil fios agadsa nach fhaod fear rugadh an Eirinn mise leantuinn?*)

"But don't you also know that I was not born in Ireland, but in Jura?" (*Ach nach' eil fhios agadsa nach d' rugadh mise an Eirinn ach ann an Diura?*)

Fionn then went on, and found the missing men playing *Taileasg*, in the middle of a mountain *(meadhon monaidh)*. [The Taileasg seems to have been a game like draughts, if not actually the same, or a game akin to it; it may have been chess.] A long-haired Chief *(Gruagach)* came and offered hospitality *(aoidheachd)* in the Little Hut of Talkativeness *(an Bòthan Beag na Bruidhne)*. [The name *Gruagach* is derived from *gruag*, a wig, and denotes a person wearing plenty of hair. It is in this way that Gruagach denoted a Chief, it being the privilege of freemen to wear long hair, as bondsmen were compelled to have short hair *(gearr fhaltach)*; hence, also, supernatural beings, like the *Gruagach* of the Isle of Skye are represented as having the appearance of a gentleman, even to the extent of wearing a chimney-pot or beaver hat. *Gruagach*, at present, is a common name for a young woman.] Goll said they would wait for their master. When Fionn came, the Chief *(Gruagach)* returned and offered meat and drink *(biadh 's deoch)*. Fionn and his men went with the Chief, and on arriving were put sitting on oaken benches, but no meat was given them. The Chief was out and in, and told Fionn that the Big Son of the King of Seana wanted speech and talk till morning ("*Tha Mac Mòr Righ o Sheanaidh 'g iarraidh cainnt 's cracaireachd gu maduinn*"). Fionn told him to bring him in. "You better bring him in," he said, "as I cannot keep him out."

Then it was told that the middle son *(Mac Meadhonach)* of the King of Seana *(Righ o Sheanaidh)*, with sixteen men, similarly wanted admittance and conversation. They were shown in after the same preliminary talk. Then the younger son, and sixteen more, came in, in the same way. After that the King of Seana's daughter, with sixteen attendant maidens, came in and sat beside Fionn.

Fionn said, "You know well it was I slew your

13

father and grandfather, and there never was a night in which I could remember worse than to-night" ("*Cha robh mi riamh oidhche bu mhios' a chuimhneachadh na 'nochd*").

They said, there never was a night in which he could remember better. Then the *Gruagach* (Chief) went out, and, on returning, said there was a wild boar out (*torc nimhe*), and told them to let one of the Feinne take it in for food. Conan went out, and Goll with him, to bring it in, though seven times its weight of earth (*a sheachd urrad fhein do thalamh*) stuck to it. They brought it in, and Conan was sent to measure it against the mane (*an aghaidh a rannadh*). When the meat was ready, the daughter of the King and Conan were nibbling the head of the boar (*crioma ceann an tuirc*). She then said, " Finn MacCumal, a turn at wrestling I would like to have from you" ("*Fhinn 'ic Cumhail, car gleac a b' àill leam uait*"). Fionn answered, "Will you not take the one that is standing?" ("*Nach gabh thu fear tha na sheasamh?*") Conan tried, but was thrown. He was useless until he got over the first disgrace. At this time Dermid released him. [While the Feinne were eating the boar, it was said that a bird could not take in its bill the bone they had (*nach d' thoireadh ian 'na ghob cnàimh bhiodh aca*). This, probably, was in allusion to its size, and the bareness with which they ate the flesh off it.] The men of the King of Tara were getting nothing, and one of them said :

" Fians, it is long since I heard how nasty your eating a boar's flesh was, but I never saw it till to-night." ("*Gu dearbh, mhuinntir na Féinne, 's fhad o na chuala mi, gur mosach dh' itheas sibh torc 's cha-n fhaca mi gus a nochd e*".)

Conan threw a bone at him, saying : " If you had asked it sooner, you would have got it rougher" ("*Na'n*

d'iarr thu na bu luaith e, fhuair thu na bu mholaich e").
The man was killed by the bone.

The Chief was out and in, and said to Fionn : " Finn
MacCumal, a tall man with a black dog is asking for
a dog-fight from you" (*"Fhinn 'ic Cumhail, tha fear mòr
dubh 'g iarraidh comhrag coin ort"*).

Conan went out, and the twelve other men of the
Fians with him, but their dogs were all killed. Fionn
then went out with Bran. There were millions of
people out before him, called up by some sleight of
hand (*iodromanachd*). He began killing the men who
had killed the dogs. Bran's claws were kept covered ;
it went out, and in the hurry only one shoe was taken
off. Conan crept down and took off the other shoe.

Bran killed the Black Dog, and took the heart and
liver out of it (*thug e 'n cridhe 's an grùan as*). It was
then that the owner of the Black Dog said (see tale of
"How Fin was in the House of the Yellow Field") :

> " Were it not for wily Geola,
> And Bran from the greatness of his strength,
> No dog that a leash could be put on
> Would be left by For west in the fort."

Conan then said: " That's you, Bran, my good fellow ;
avenge you your own contumely and disgrace, and I will
avenge my own leash of dogs" (*"Sin thusa laochain,
Bhrain, dioghail thusa do thàir agus do thailceas fhéin,
agus dioghlaidh mise mo lomhainn chon fhéin"*). They
went on killing the men ; there were sixteen strangers
in the house.

The Chief came in, and said : " Go out, Finn, and
check Bran and the men, for they have done enough of
harm" (*air a mheud cron 's gu'n d' rinn*).

Conan came in and sent more men out.

Then all that were in rose against Fionn, and so

13 ²

many of them fell about his feet, that the place in which he was became too narrow (*aimhleathain*). There was a knife, or *iodhach*, on Fionn's side that uttered a cry (*glaodh*) when he was within an inch of his life, and was heard in the five-fifths of Ireland (*ann an còig chòigibh na h-Eirinn*).

The party with the Red King at Tara (*Righ Dearg a Teamhair*) heard it, and waited till they heard it again. They answered it, and when they came they found Conan and twelve men perseveringly killing (*dha dheug cath mharbhadh*). They stripped the bothy (*Ruisg iad a' bhòthag*) and took out Fionn.

FIONN and nine of his nobles, among whom were Conan and Goll with him, each with his leash of hounds (*lodh-ain chon*), were in the hill hunting. At midday, having found nothing, they rested on a hillock (*cnoc seilge*) where game often passed, but they saw none coming. Upon this, Fionn went a little apart, and put his finger under his knowledge tooth (*deud fios*) to see what kept the game away. When he came back he told them that in a short time a hound with a white ear (*gaodhar a chluas bhàin*) would pass, and that they were not to attack it, otherwise the chase would be hidden from the Feinn for a day and seven years. When it passed, all kept in their dogs; but Bran, Fionn's own dog, broke away, and gave chase to the strange dog. He chased it through the hill, and the mud which the dog with the white ear threw from his hind-paws struck Bran in the mouth; and the mud Bran threw from his fore-paws struck the dog with the white ear in the tail. At last, Fionn said: "Bran will break his heart" ("*Sgàinidh Bran a chridhe*"), "and will not catch White Ear; let us go after him." They went, and found Bran lying on the ground, with his tongue lolling out, but without having caught the stranger. "Well," said Fionn, "my good dog, I am glad to find you, though unsuccessful, and though you have driven the chase from us for a day and seven years. We will now go home."

They went away, and towards dusk they saw a light. They had lost their way, and were wandering through the hill. They made for the light, and when they reached it found the master (*Gruagach*) of the house at the door. He blessed Fionn, and Fionn blessed him.

"We have lost our way," said Fionn, "and we have come to ask room and shelter for the night, if we are welcome."

"You would get room and shelter in my house (*sa blothan*), though there were a hundred men with you."

The Feinn went in, and sat near each other in the bothy. As Fionn looked at them to see if he had all his men safe, he noticed that Goll was missing. He said he would go himself and find him, and not a mother's son born in Ireland was to attempt to follow him. "If I find him, I will bring him; and if I do not find him, I will come back alone."

He had not gone far, when he heard a sound as of some one straggling after him (*lapragas*). He turned, and found it was Fergus who was following. "Little bad Fergus," he said, "why do you follow me, when I said not one born in Ireland was to come after me?"

"Yes," said Fergus, "but I was born in Jura;" which was the case. So Fionn allowed him with him.

They found Goll, and the Red Man from Tara (*am Fear dearg a Teamhair*), playing at chess. This man said to Fionn: "Be not under any anxiety for the Feinn, though the chase is hid from you. You will divide yourselves into two parties, and my brother will take the one party and I will take the other, and we will feed you (*beathaichidh*), and allow you to suffer no want."

Fionn thanked him for his offer, but said he could not accept it; he must go back to his men, and provide for himself and them.

"But, Goll," he said, "were you afraid we could not find food for you, when you went away and left?"

"No," said Goll; "but I was obliged to come and play with this man."

After this they returned to the bothy, and the Feinn sat near each other. By-and-by a noise was heard outside, and the master of the bothy (*Gruagach a' bhothain*)

went out, and came and said that the Son of the King
from Senny (*Mac Righ o Sheanaidh*) was outside with a
hundred attendants (*gillean coimhideachd*), seeking shelter;
would he admit them? Fionn said he might, since he was
not strong enough to keep him out (*o nach bu treise esan
gu'chumail a mach*). Before long, noise was again heard
outside; the master of the house went out, and came in
saying, the second Son of the King of Senny was outside seeking admission. Fionn said he might come in, as
he was not stronger to keep him out; and the King's son
came in with his hundred attendants. Before long the
third son of the King of Senny was in a similar manner
admitted, and there were thus in the house, Fionn Mac-
Cumal and his nine men, with a leash of dogs apiece,
and the King of Senny's three sons, with their three
hundred attendants and six hundred dogs. Each company kept together, and Fionn and his men sat close to
each other. Then the King of Senny's daughter and
her hundred handmaids (*maighdeanan coimheadachd*)
came, and was admitted in the same manner as her
brothers. After sitting down and looking about her,
and seeing her brothers, she said to Fionn that she would
try a bout of wrestling with him ("*cothrom gleachd a
b' aill leam uait*"). He said it was not usual for him to
try feats of strength till his men were first defeated.
Conan was then put on the floor with her, and she threw
him and tied his four "smalls"—that is, his wrists and
ankles—together, and threw him behind the rest in a
corner. He lay there, and was hearing Goll laughing
and making fun among the King's daughter's maidens.
At last he cried out, "Goll, son of Morna, if I were a
maiden you would not allow me to lie here tied." "It
is true," said Goll; and he went and loosened him. It
was said that Conan was not worth in any deed of strength
or daring till after he was once disgraced. When he got

loose he cried fair-play, and this being given, he again wrestled the King's daughter and threw her down.

When they had sat awhile, she asked Fionn to go out and bring in a wild boar that was lying at the door, to make food for the assembled company. He said he had never been without a servant, and it was only when they could not do it that he performed any such menial duty, and she told one of his men to go out and take in the boar. He went, but enchantments (*draoidheachd*) were laid on the boar, so that he could not move it. He sent another, but he also failed; and so with the rest of the nine. Fionn said he would go and take it in himself, though seven times its own weight of earth stuck to it. He went and took it in. Conan dressed it and made it ready. He got as his own share the jaw-bone, and as he was picking it one of the King of Senny's men asked it of him. "If you had asked it earlier you would have got it rougher" (or with more flesh upon it) (*Na 'n iarradh tu na bu tràith' e chuirinn na bu mholaich' e*"), and he threw the bone at him and knocked him down.

Then the King of Senny's eldest son asked for a fight of dogs.

The incident of the dog-fight is well told in a version preserved in Stewart's *Collection*, p. 558. (Only the English need be here given.)

THE DOG-FIGHT BETWEEN BRAN AND THE BLACK DOG.

On a day that we were in the hunting-hill
Seldom were we without dogs,
Listening to the cries of birds,
Roaring of deer and elks.

We did slaughter, doubtless,
With our dogs and death-inflicting weapons;
And came to our dwelling at noon,
Joyful, musical, and with right good will.

That night in Fionn's dwelling,
Dear me! delightful was our condition
As we struck strings,
And ate birds, deer, and elk.

Early rose Fionn next day,
Before sun-rise,
And he saw coming on the plain,
between the hills and the sea,
A man with a red cloak and a black dog.

Like this was his appearance:
His two cheeks were as ripe fruit,
His breast was like mountain-down,
Though his hair happened to be black.

He came to us for increase of enjoyment,
This fine lad, so desirable;
On his appearance no shadow would rest,
Asking from the rest a dog-fight.

We let towards him at the beginning of the fight
The best hounds within our walls.
The Black Dog, rough was his onset:
Killed by him were a *caogad* of dogs.

Then Fionn spoke:
"This is a contest that is not weak."
He turned his back to the people,
And, with a frown, struck Bran.

Victorious Bran looked at him,
Wondering that he should strike him.
"The hand with which I struck Bran,
Pity from the shoulder it was not separated.

Then Bran shook the golden chain,
Among the people loud was its yelp,
His two eyes burned in its head,
And his bristles rose for the fight.

"Take the thong from my dog without delay :
Good was his prowess till to-day ;
And let us see sharp strife
Between Bran and the Black Dog.

"Goodly-shaped was my dog,
Its neck-joint far from its head ;
The middle broad, its side burly,
Its elbow sloping, and its claw crooked.

"Yellow paws Bran had,
Two black sides, and underneath white,
The back green (on which hunting would rest),
Erect ears strongly red."

They placed the dogs nose to nose,
Among the people they shed blood.
That was a strong, rough struggle
Before the Black Dog was left dead by him.

"I thought there was not in the Fian host
(Said Eibhinn Oision from the place of tying dogs)
One dog, for all its prowess,
That could give For a deadly wound.

"Were it not for every twist and trick
That Bran had, and its very great strength,
No dog that could be bound with a thong
Would be left by him west in our fort.

"Many a fair, brown maiden,
Of bluest eye and golden yellow hair,
In the kingdom of the King, Tork's Son,
That would give my dog food to-night."

The true, generous hero buried,
In a narrow clay bed, his dog ;
And the Fians buried
In that west fort (fifty?) dogs.

We went with MacCumhaill of golden cups
To play, and to the fort.
King ! joyful and full was our dwelling,
Though none are to-day within its walls.

THE same kind of incidents as are to be found in the tale of "How Finn went to the Kingdom of Big Men" (see tale) about the employment of strangers, occurs in this tale also; and the whole being the product of the imagination, these tales merely show the grooves in which the human fancy runs. Some of the incidents also may occur in other stories not connected with the Fians.

The chase was lost to the Fians. On that occasion, when Fionn was out one day alone, and unaccompanied by any of his men, a man met him, whom he questioned as to the object of his journey, or where he was going. The stranger answered that he was a good servant in search of employment. Fionn then asked him what he could best do. He replied, that he never slept a wink all his life; and Fionn took him into his service. Another met him, and Fionn asked him where he was going, or what was the object of his journey. He said that he was a good servant in search of a master, and Fionn asked him what he was good at. He said that when he listened, he could hear the very grass coming through the ground; and Fionn engaged this one also. He then met another, and asked the object of his journey, and where he meant to go. He said the same as the others, that he was a good servant in search of work, and Fionn asked him what he was best at. He told that he was good at keeping a hold of what he got. "The grasp I get, I never let go." This one was also engaged by Fionn. Still another met him, and after being questioned, and answering in the same way, he said that he was a good thief, that he could steal its egg from the heron though it was looking on with its eyes wide open; and Fionn engaged him. Yet another met him, and in the same manner Fionn questioned him, and, replying as the others had done, he added that he could climb a wall though it was covered with eel-skin. This one was also engaged. Another then met them, and was asked about the object of his journey. He replied as those before him did, and that every stone cast he flung from him would become a stone and lime wall. This one was also engaged. Another met them. He was asked, as before, about his journey and its object. He answered that he was a good servant in search of employment. Being asked what he could do best, he said that he was a good marksman, and would not miss a hair's-breadth with an arrow. Fionn engaged this man also.

He had now his full complement of men. He himself, and the company of them, began to walk onwards. In the evening they came to the King's palace. Fionn observed that the King was sad, and questioned him about the cause of his sadness. The King told him that he had great reason; that the Queen was in child-bed, this being the third child, and the babes were stolen shortly after their birth. Fionn said to him, " If ever you got them kept, you will get them kept to-night."

When the child was born, Fionn said to the one who never slept to keep close at hand to the babe's mother. Then to the One who could hear the grass coming through the ground when he listened, to sit near the other, and, " You who can take the strong firm hold, be found near them." The musical Harper was heard coming to the house. Every person in the dwelling began to fall asleep. The One who never slept began to keep them awake. Then they saw a Hand coming in through the house towards the child. The One who could take the firm grasp rose and seized the hand, but the Hand pulled him—*i.e.*, the One that was in the house—out half-way. The One inside made another attempt, and took off the arm from the shoulders of the One outside. He himself fell, and before he could rise up, the One that was outside put in a hand and took with him the child. Fionn was troubled, as he had said to the King that he would keep the child.

The King was in great anxiety and deep distress, and the Queen also was deeply grieved. Fionn then said that the sky would make a nest in his head and the earth a hollow in his feet "if I do not find your children for you".

On the morrow he launched the galley that was seven years and seven days being tarred and caulked. He and his men went in her to sail the proud seas. They reached a wild, extensive country; they drew the galley up on the green grass while they betook themselves some distance through the country. They did not go far through it when they met a house with its walls covered with eel-skin. "The man," said Fionn, "who can climb a wall covered with eel-skin, climb up and look what you can see." The One climbed up. When he returned he said, "There is a great warrior (giant) sitting in the house ; he is one-armed. He has a child on the palm of his hand, and two other children are playing on the floor beside him." Fionn then said: "The One who can take its egg from the heron when she is looking at it with both eyes, put your hands round his neck, and he will take you up and get the babes." He went up and caught the two boys who were playing, and at last seized the one on the palm of the giant's hand. He then saw a nest with three puppies in it, which he lifted away with him. They (the whole of Fionn's company) now set off for the shore. On looking behind they saw the mother of the puppies coming after them. Then Fionn

said, " You that can make a wall of stone and lime from
every stone-cast you throw, begin to throw." Notwith-
standing this, the mother of the pups was gaining on
them ; they then loosened one of the pups. It was not
long after, however, before they had to unloose another.
When the mother got that one she returned. On reaching the galley they launched it, taking the three boys
and the pup with them. They were but moving from
the shore when they observed the warrior or giant
coming with all speed and fury. He was making the
sea phosphorescent and like a serpent-bite after them.
Fionn in that hour said : " You that can make good use
of an arrow, come near me."

The giant had only one eye in his forehead. The first
arrow that was launched pierced the giant's eye. In
spite of that, however, he was still coming, but the
marksman did not once miss his aim. They were not
long in leaving him floating dead on the surface of the
current. Fionn returned safely to the King's palace
with the three sons of the King.

" Now," said the King, " whatever you ask, to the half
of my kingdom, will be granted."

" I prefer finding your children to the whole of your
kingdom," said Fionn, " since I said they would be preserved to you."

Then Fionn paid the men whom he had employed
their wages, and gave them their liberty. He returned
himself to his own men, and never parted with the pup.
Since he was successful in his journey, he called the dog
Victorious Bran.

MAR FHUAIR FIONN BRAN.

Bha an t-sealg air a casgadh air an Fheinn. Air do Fhionn,
san àm bhi latha mach gun duine leis ach e fhein, thachair
fear air. Chuir Fionn ceisd air, gu de ceann a thuruis, no c'

àite an robh e dol. Fhreagair e gum b' e gille math bha ag iarraidh maighstir 's dh' fharraid Fionn dheth gu de bha e math air. Thuirt e ris nach d' rinn e lochd cadail riamh agus dh' fhastaidh e e. Thachair an ath fhear air 's chur e cheist air c' aite an robh e dol na 'de ceann a thuruis. Thuirt e gum bu ghille math e ag iarraidh maighstir. Dh' fharraid Fionn a so 'de bha e math air. Thuirt e ris dar dh' éisdeadh e gu 'n cluinneadh e feur tighinn roi' an talamh, 's dh' fhastaidh e 'm fear so mar an ceudna. Thachair an ath-fhear air 's chur e cheist air 'de ceann a thuruis na c' aite an robh e dol. Thuirt e mar thuirt an fheadhainn eile gum bu ghille math e ag iarraidh maighstir 's dh' fharraid Fionn gu de bha e math air. Dh' innis e gu 'n robh e math air an rud a gheibheadh e chumail aige. "An greim a gheibh mi ann am làimh cha do leig mi riamh as e," agus dh' fhastaidh Fionn am fear so cuideachd. Thachair an ath-fhear air 's chuir e cheist air gu de ceann a thuruis na c' aite an robh e dol. Thuirt esan mar thuirt iadsan bha roi' gum bu ghille math e 's dh' fharraid e 'de bha e math air 's thuirt e gu 'n robh e math air goid 's gu'n goideadh e 'n t-ubh bho 'n churra 's da shuil 'ga fheathamh. Dh' fhastaidh e 'm fear sin. Thachair sin fear eile air 's anns a 'cheart doigh chuir Fionn ceisd air, fhreagair e mar rinn cach 's bharrachd thuirt e ris gu 'n streapadh e balla ged bhiodh e air chomhdacha le craicionn feasgan. Dh' fhastaidh e 'm fear sin. Thachair an ath-fhear air chuir e ceist air c' aite an robh e dol na 'de ceann a thuruis ; 's gille math mi, ars esan, ag iarraidh maighstir, 's mar thuirt an fheadhainn bha roi, agus n' h-uile spitheag a chaitheadh e gu 'n deanamh e balla cloiche 's aol dhi, 's dh' fhastaidh e 'm fear sin. Thachair an ath-fhear air 's chuir Fionn a 'cheart cheisd air c' aite an robh e dol na 'de ceann a thuruis. Thuirt e gum bu ghille math e bha ag iarraidh maighstir 's dh' fharraid e gu de bha e math air. Thuirt e gu 'n robh e math air saighead 's nach mearachdaicheadh e leud na ròineig. Dh' fhastaidh e am fear sin 's bha nis a ghillean aige. Thug e fhein 's iad fhein gu coiseachd 's gu iomachd 's ann an tighinn na h-oidhche thainig iad gu tigh an Righ. Dh' fhairich Fionn gu'n robh an righ fo sprochd 's chuir e ceist air, " Gu de fath sprochd ?" Thuirt an Righ ris gum bu mhòr sud. Gu 'n robh a' bhean aige ri

saothair cloinne 's gur e so an treasa aon chloinne 's gu'n robh
na leanaban 'gan goid mu 'm bitheadh iad ach tacain air an t-
saoghal. Thuirt Fionn ris, "Ma fhuar thu an gleidheadh
riamh gheibh thu an gleidheadh an nochd." Mar thainig
an leanabh, thuirt Fionn ris an thear nach d' rinn cadal riamh
e shuidhe suas laimh ri mathair an leanaibh, agus sin ris an
fhear chluinneadh am feur tighinn roi an talamh. "Suidh dluth
dha," "'s fhir a ni an greim mòr bi thusa lamh riu." Chual' iad
an cruiteara ceol-mhòr tighinn ionnsuidh an tighe. Thoisich
gach duine bha stigh air dol 'nan cadal. Fear nach d' rinn
lochd cadail riamh, thoisich e air an cumail 'nan dùsgadh.
Chunnaic iad sin lamh tighinn stigh roi 'n tigh, deanamh air
an leanabh. Dh' èirich am fear a dheanadh an greim mòr
's rug e air an Laimh. Thug i fear bha stigh mach gu leth 's
thug am fear bha stigh an ath-spìona, 's thug e 'n Lamh bho 'n
t-shlinnean as an fhear bha muigh 's thuit e fhein 's mu 'n d'
èirich e shin am fear bha muigh a lamh a stigh 's thug e leis
an leanabh. Bha Fionn fo thrioblaid bho 'n thuirt e ris an righ
gum faigheadh e 'n leanabh a ghleidheadh. Bha an righ fo
iomaguin 's fo iarguin chruaidh 's cha b' i 'bhan-righ a b'
fhearr, na 'bu lugha bha caoidh na cloinne. Sin thuirt Fionn,
"Ni an t-athar nead 'nam cheann 's an talamh lag 'nam bhonn,
mur faigh mi dhuit do chuid cloinne."

Maireach chuir e mach bhirlinn bha seachd lathan 's seachd
bliadhna 'ga teàrradh 's 'ga calcadh 's dh' fhalbh e fhein 's a
chuid ghillean innte 's thug iad gu siubhal a 'chuain uaibhreach.
Rainig iad duthaich fhad fhiadhaich, tharruing iad Bhirlinn
suas an talamh glas 's chaidh iad fhein ceumannan mach
feadh na tìre. Cha d' imich iad fad air a feadh dar chunnaic
iad tigh 's a bhalla air chomhdach le craicionn feasgan.
"Fhir," orsa Fionn, "a streapadh balla air chomhdachah le
craicionn feasgan streap suas feuch 'de chi thu." Chaidh e suas
's dar thainig e nuas, thuirt e, "Tha ceatharnach mòr 'na
shuidhe ann 's gun air ach an leth lamh is leanabh aige air a
bhois 's da bhalachan ag iomain feadh an urlar lamh ris."
Thuirt Fionn, "Fhir ghoideadh an t-ubh bho 'n churra 's dà
shuil 'ga fheitheamh cuir do dha laimh mo 'amhaich 's bheir e
suas thu 's faigh na leanaban." Chaidh e suas 's ghoid e 'n da

14

bhalachan bha ag iomain agus ghoid e mu dheireadh am fear
bh' air a bhois. Chunnaic e sin nead agus tri chuileannan
ann 's thog e leis iad. Ghabh iad uile sin thun a chladaich.
Chunnaic iad mathair nan cuileanan tighinn as an deigh. An
sin thuirt Fionn, " Fhir dheanadh balladh cloiche 's aoil do 'n
h-uile spitheag chaitheadh tu, toisich air an caitheadh."

'Na dheighinn so bha i teannamh orra 's leig iad as dhi fear
do na cuileanan, 's cha b' fhada gus am b' éigin doibh an ath
fhear a leigeil as 's nar fhuair i am fear sin thill i. Rainig iad
sin a 'bhirlinn 's charaich iad mach i, agus an triuir bhalachan
's an cuilean aca. Cha robh iad ach gluasad bho 'n chladach
nar mhothaich iad am fomhair 'na luathas 's 'na theas a' tighinn.
Bha e cur na fairge mar theine sionnachain 's mar nathair bheumnach as an deigh. Thuirt Fionn san uair ud, " Fhir tha maith
air an t-saighead suidh dlùth dhomh." Cha robh aig an
Fhomhair ach aon suil 'an clàr 'n aoduinn. A 'chiad saighead a chaith am fear chuir e san t-suil i, 's as dheigh sin bha
e tighinn air aghaidh 's cha do mhearachdaich esan saighead do
na thilg e.

Cha b' fhada gus an d' fhag iad marbh air uachdar an t-sruth
e. Sin thainig Fionn sabhailt air ais gu tigh an Righ 's triuir
mhacan an Righ aige.

" Nis," orsa an Righ, "gu leth mo rioghachd tha t-iarrtus
agad ri fhaotuinn."

" 'S fhearr leamsa ors Fionn, gu 'n d' uair mi do chuid
cloinne na do rioghachd air fad, seach 's gu 'n dubhairt mi gum
bitheadh iad air an gleidheadh dhuit."

Sin phaigh Fionn an luchd-tuarasdail 's leig e gu cead
an coise iad, agus phill e air ais a dh' ionnsuidh chuid
dhaoine fhein, ach cha do dhealaich e ris a 'chuilean 's a
chionn 's gu 'n d' éirich gu math dha air a thuruis, thug e Bran
Buadhach mar ainm air.

THE leading incidents in this tale are closely analogous to those of the tale of " How Fin went to the Kingdom of Big Men" (see page 176). The cause of Fionn's going to the region of Big Men is, however, different, and in this version is also noticeable the swearing upon cold iron, and the prominence given to his dog Bran, who had a venomous or death-inflicting claw. Universally in Celtic lore, Finn MacCumal figures as he is here represented, as extremely careful of his honour and dignity, trustworthy as a friend, and resolute in solving any question or problem. To such a man it is no wonder that the popular mind became attached, and ultimately raised him almost to be a model of what a king, or nobleman, or gentleman ought to be.

The swearing upon cold iron or on the dirk is a well-known practice ascribed to former generations of Highlandmen. The dirk, which was a universal accompaniment of Highland dress, was the readiest form which presented itself of cold iron or steel, the power of which against fairies, ghosts, and all supernatural things was universally believed in, and this form of oath was the most solemn and binding that could be thought of, more so and more rational than "bussing the book", as was known and practised in English courts of law.

The prowess of the dog Bran was the subject of winter evening tales as much as the sword which Fionn was alleged to have had, and which left not a remnant of its blow (*nach d' fhag fuigheal beum*), *i.e.*, that never required a second blow, the first cutting its way completely through whatever object it struck. The other wonderful

instrument belonging to Fionn was the *Ord Fhinn*, or
Fian Hammer, which could be heard in the five-fifths,
or over the whole of Ireland (*coig coigeamh na h-Eirinn*).
In some tales a *sgiath* or shield is mentioned, instead of
this hammer, and whoever heard it, of the Fian band, was
bound to hasten to the rescue of those of their number
who might be in danger. Fionn's wonderful knowledge-
tooth (*Deud fios*), which enabled him to solve any question when he put his finger below it, was also a subject
of marvellous incidents. The tale is

FIONN AND BRAN.

Fionn was out one day in front of his house looking
about him, and no one was with him but Bran his dog,
when he saw a coracle coming to the shore. He went
to the edge of the beach to have a look at it. Then it
drew near and grounded ; three big men one by one
jumped out of it. They put their backs to it, and put it
up seven steps seven fathoms and seven times its own
length on the green grass. They put the masts and
sails underneath and turned it over, so that no one
coming or going could move or launch it. The big men
came to meet Fionn.

"Well," said the foremost of them, "what news has
the herd-boy who has the little dog?"

" I have none," said Fionn, "unless I hear one from the
big men who have come from the sea."

"Our news are that we have come to hold war and
combat with Finn MacCumal, and go you up cleverly
and bring him down."

Thus they said, one after another of them, till at last
Fionn was obliged to say he would go ; but " I lay you
under crosses and spells, and the nine fetters of a roam-
ing fairy woman, a hornless or bald-headed calf, worse
than its name, to take your head off without wages, that

you leave not the place that you are in traversing the shore till I return." He left, and putting out a coracle that was above the shore, went away, taking with him Bran. He sailed over the sea with tide and wind till he reached the Kingdom of Big Men. When he reached land he drew up the coracle seven feet seven fathoms and seven steps on the green grass, and put the sails and masts, the baling-dish and oars, underneath it, and turned it over, so that no one coming the way could move or launch it, and went up to take a look at the country. He did not go far when he saw before him a very tall man going round a tree, and he stepped towards him. Fionn said it was a good day, and the big man said it was. "What news has the dwarf with the lap-dog?" said he to Fionn.

"I have little news," said Fionn, "unless I hear such from the big man who is going round the tree."

"The biggest news that I have," he said, "is this, that it is long since the King has wanted a dwarf and small dog, and that I have them now to bring them to him."

"I am surprised that you spend the day going about that tree," said Fionn.

"It is for firewood," the big man said.

He dragged the tree with him, took Fionn and Bran, and the three went away together. They had not gone far dragging the tree when another big man met them.

"It is long since," he said, when he saw Fionn and Bran, "the King wanted a dwarf and small dog, and I have them here now to bring them to him."

"They belong to me," said the other, "and I will take them to the King." They both began to fight. When they had grown tired, the one who met them last said:

"How little sense we are showing in the work we are doing! Had we not better lay the matter before the dwarf himself?"

They did this, and Fionn said if there was a differ-

ence of choice for better or worse he would follow the
first one whom he met, whether it was for good or
ill to him, and he followed him. They now prepared
a place and kindled a fire with the log of wood they
had taken with them, made ready meat, and took their
dinner. When they had finished, the big man lifted
Fionn on the palm of one hand and Bran on the other
and went to the King. The King was greatly delighted,
and put them in his own chambers. They were to
remain with the King for a year and a day, to give him
pleasure. The dwarf slept near where the King was, and
he observed that the King rose every night, went away,
and returned at dawn cold and wet, and he asked him
what he meant by going out in that way.

"What need I tell that to the like of you?" said the
King.

"For all that," said Fionn, "you may tell it."

"Not to-night," said the King; "go you to sleep as
usual."

On the following night Fionn said to him: "I never had
a master who would not tell me something of his mind
but yourself, and if you will not tell me the reason of
your going away like that every night, I will not stay
here any longer."

"What good will it do me to tell it to so small a
being as you are?" said the King.

"A small man may give good advice," said Fionn.
"No one is so wise as not to be the better of sound
advice; and tell me now what it is that is troubling
you?"

"I am seventeen years without sleep or rest," said the
King, "because of a huge monster who is coming
ashore every night to take from me my kingdom."

"Go to rest to-night," said Fionn, "and allow me to
go to meet it."

"You will be destroyed," said the King.

"You may go to sleep for that part, without any care," said Fionn.

"I have need of that," said the King.

Fionn and Bran were not long at the shore when they saw the great monster coming, one blubbery eye in its forehead, the sea, phosphorescent and heavy, rolling before it, and a seething-white and loudly-roaring sea here and there after it : with the speed of its coming, and the greatness of its strength, it sent its head its own length up on the beach.

"Yes," it said, "what news has the little man who has the small dog?"

"I am sorry that I have that to tell," said Fionn ; "the King is dead, and his nobles sent me to-night to ask you to stay away, this one night, until they would get another, instead of him, to hold combat with you."

"May I believe what you say, little man?" said the Beast.

"I am not covetous of telling lies," said Fionn.

When the King awoke, he cried out in great fear : 'My kingdom is taken from me, and my dwarf and lap-dog are lost to me !"

"Your kingdom is preserved to you, and your dwarf and lap-dog are here," said Fionn.

The King was greatly delighted when he heard Fionn speaking. "It is not known," he said, "when I got such rest and sleep."

Next night the King made ready to go, but Fionn said that he had better let himself go this night yet. When he and Bran reached the shore, he was not long there till he saw the sea coming phosphorescent and in great billows, and the Great Beast with one lumpish eye in its forehead, with the ocean in white foam on every side, both before and after, coming towards him ; and with the speed of its coming, and the greatness of its strength, it dried itself on the beach.

"What news has the little man who has the lap-dog to-night?" it said.

"I have none," said Fionn; "but that the nobles of the kingdom sent me to tell you to return to-night yet, for the Queen fell dead when they were putting the King in the coffin."

"May I believe that?" it said.

"I don't covet lies," said Fionn.

"Certainly; that is worse for you," it said.

Fionn returned home, and went to sleep at the King's feet. When the King awoke, he cried out: "My dwarf and lap-dog are amissing, and that is not the worst, but my kingdom is taken from me!"

"I believe that that is what you most lament—the loss of your kingdom; but your dwarf and lap-dog are here, and you have your kingdom yet."

This gave great relief to the King. He asked Fionn what the Beast appeared like this night.

"I was not at all frightened for it," said Fionn.

When the next night came, the King was not for letting him go. "You have done much good to give me such rest, and I will go to encounter it myself to-night."

"It has no evil intention," said Fionn, "and I may get leave to go to-night yet."

"It will not be so bad to you, at any rate," said the King.

Fionn took Bran with him. He had not long to wait this night when he saw it, the sea, coming phosphorescent before it, in great billows and seething foam, here and there, and as a roaring sea after it; and with the speed of its coming, and the greatness of its strength, it laid its head its whole length on the beach.

"What news has the little man who has the dog to-night?" it said.

"That," said Fionn, "it is absurd of such a great

Monster as you are to be night after night listening to
lies from such a small being as I am."

"Is that how it is?" it said. "You may prepare to
take care of yourself, then," and putting on an appearance
of great wrath, it leaped to attack Fionn, and was well-
nigh wearing him out.

Fionn looked at Bran and said : ".Are you not likely
to remember me to-night at all, Bran?" Bran rose,
went round them, and went back where he was before.
The wrestling was becoming worse for Fionn, and he
looked again at Bran. "You are like to forget me
altogether to-night, Bran."

Bran got up, and took a second turn round them, and
sat where he was before. The contest was now going
so much against Fionn, that he was growing faint. He
looked at Bran and said : "Bran, you need not rise any
more, I am gone ; what you have done for me, you will
never do again ; there is no help for me."

Bran got up and went round till it was behind the
Monster ; it uncovered its venomous claw, put it in its
back, and in the twinkling of an eye the heart and liver
were out. Fionn threw off the head with his sword, and
was part of the way carrying it and part of the way
rolling it before him, till he reached the house. He put
it on a pole before the palace, with the big goggle eye
looking towards the King's window, and he went in
softly and stealthily to his place at the feet of the King.
At midnight the King awoke in great fear; he cried out,
" My kingdom is lost to me, and I have neither dwarf
nor lap-dog left !"

"Neither of them are awanting to you," said Fionn ;
"and if you don't believe it, look out, and you will see
for yourself."

The King did so, and when he saw the head and eye
of the Great Monster, he fell on his knees beside the
bed on which Fionn lay. "It is long since," he said,

"it was foretold that Finn MacCumal was to give rest both to me and to my kingdom. You are Finn MacCoul."

"You do not deserve forgiveness from me," said Fionn. "You sent three big men to my kingdom to combat me without any provocation."

"These are three men who are not observant of any law; they are not my friends, and they have fairy women, who have made them shirts, but when these are taken off they will be as other men. I will give you a drink to make them sleep. When you come to the shore, where they are, you will throw the stoups containing the sleeping-draught near them, and when you get them asleep, you will get an opportunity of getting the shirts from them."

Fionn launched the coracle, and Bran and himself returned. When they were close to the shore, Fionn threw out the stoup containing the sleeping-draught. The big men were traversing the shore as he left them. The stoup met one of them; he knocked out its head and drank the contents, and then he fell into a deep sleep. Fionn threw out another and a third, and the three men were lying equally overcome. He then went up, took off the shirts, and shook the men to awaken them.

" You are here," he said.

" We are," they replied.

" And you are as other men, and I have power and chance to take your lives; you will not be released without coming under a bond of law."

They said they would submit to any covenant by which he would bind them, and they swore on the cold sword to stand by him in right or in wrong; and at any time he might be in danger or difficulty he had only to think of them, and they would be with him wherever he might be, but to restore to them their shirts. And when Fionn went home the entertainment was the fourth greatest ever held among the Fians.

FIONN 'S BRAN.

Bha Fionn mach mu choinneamh an taighe aon latha gabhail
seallaidh, 's gun aige ach e fhein 's Bran, dar chunnaic e
curach a' tighinn dh' ionnsuidh tìr. Chaidh e sios gu braigh
chladaich a dh' amharc oirre 's dar bhuail i sron air an traigh
leum aisde triuir fheara mòra fear mu seach 's chuir iad an
dromannan rithe 's thog iad suas i seachd ceumannan seachd
aitheamh 's seachd fada fhein ann am feur glas, 's chuir iad na
croinn 's na siuil fo 'beul 's chuir iad a beul foidhpe, far nach
faigheadh fear thigeadh na dh' fhalbhadh a carachadh na 'cur
mach. Thainig na fir mhòra an codhail Fhinn. "Seadh," ors
a chiad fhear, "de naigheachd a' bhalaich bhuachaille aig am
bheil am measan?"

"Cha 'n 'eil naigheachd sam bith," ors Fionn, "mur faigh mi i
o na fir mhòra thainig thar a' chuain."

"'S e 'n naigheachd sin gu 'n d' thainig sinn chumail cath 's
comhrag ri Fionn Mac Cumhail, 's leum suas gu tapanta 's thoir
a nuas e." Thuirt iad mar so fear an deigh fir dhiu gus am b'
fheudar dha mu dheireadh a radhainn gu 'n rachadh, "Ach tha
mi 'g 'ur cur-sa fo chroiscan 's fo gheasan 's fo naoi buaraichean
na mna sith siubhlach, laogh maol carach na 's miosa na 'ainm,
thoirt a' chinn gun chosnadh dhibh gun sibh dh' fhagail an
aite sa bheil sibh a' siubhal a' chladaich gus an till mise rithist."
Dh' fhalbh e, 's chuir e mach curachan bha am braigh chladaich
's thug e leis Bran. Bha e siubhal a' chuain le sruth 's le soirbheas gus an d' rainig e Rioghachd nam Fear Mòra. Dar rainig
e tìr tharruin e suas an curachan, seachd traidhean, seachd aith
eamhnan, seachd ceumanan ann am feur glas, 's chuir e na siuil,
's na croinn 's na taomain 's na raimh fo 'beul, 's chuir e air a beul
fodha i far nach fhaigheadh am fear thigeadhan rathad a carachadh n' a cur a mach, 's ghabh e suas a ghabhail seallaidh air an
duthaich. Cha deachaidh e ach beagan astair dar chunnaic e roi'
fear mòr a' dol mu 'n cuairt air craoibh 's ghabh e ceum far an
robh e. Mhol Fionn an latha dha 's mhol am fear mòr an latha
dha-san. "De naigheachd an troich aig am bheil am measan?"
ors esan ri Fionn.

"Cha 'n 'eil bheag sam bith do naigheachd agamsa," ors' Fionn, "mur fhaigh mi aig an fhear mhòr tha dol mu 'n cuairt na craoibhe i."

"Se naigheachd 's motha agamsa," thuirt esan, " gur fhada bho 'n tha an Righ ag iarraidh troich 's measan 's gu bheil iad agamsa nis air son an toirt g' a ionnsuidh."

"Tha e cur iongantais orm thu bhi cur seachad an latha dol timchioll na craoibhe sin," ors Fionn. "'S ann air son cuallach connaidh tha i," ors am fear mòr. Dhraigh e leis i, 's Fionn 's Bran 's dh' fhalbh iad comhla 'nan triuir. Cha deachaidh iad fad air an rathad a' draghadh na craoibhe nar thachair fear mòr eile orra. Dar chunnaic e Fionn 's Bran thuirt e, "'S fhada o 'n tha an Righ air son troich 's measan fhaighinn, tha iad so agam nis 's bheir mi fhein g' a ionnsuidh iad."

"Se mo throich 's mo mheasan-sa th' ann," thuirt am fear eile, "'s fagaidh mi fhein aig an Righ iad." Thoisich iad 'nan dithis air tapaid 's dar bha iad sgith, thuirt am fear thachair orra mu dheireadh, "Nach beag ciall tha 'san obair th' againn, b' fhearr dhuinn ceist a chur air an troich! Co fear 's fhearr leis a leantuinn?" Rinn iad so 's thuirt Fionn ma bha diu 'na roghainn ann gu 'n leanadh esan a chiad fhear thachair air, co aca 'sann gu 'ole na gu 'mhaith a bhitheadh e, 's lean e e. Rinn iad nis aite 's chuir iad teine briagh air doigh leis a' chual chonnaidh 's dheasaich iad biadh 's ghabh iad an dinneir. Dar bha iad ullamh, thog am fear mòr Fionn air an darna bois 's Bran air a' bhois eile dh' ionnsuidh an Righ. Thug e toileachadh mòr do 'n Righ, 's chuir e 'san t-seomar aige fhein iad. Bha iad ri bhi aig an Righ gu ceann latha 's bliadhna air son toilinntinn thoirt da. Bha an troich cadal faisg do 'n aite san robh an Righ, 's bha e tighinn fainear dha gu 'n robh an Righ ag éiridh h-uile oidhche 's a' falbh, 's gu 'n tilleadh e 'm beul an latha fuar fliuch, 's chuir e ceisd air, de bu chiall dha bhi falbh mar sud.

"De ni sin domhsa innseadh do d' leithid-sa," ors an Righ. "Coma sin," orsa Fionn, "innis thus' e." "Cha 'n ann an nochd," ors an Righ; "caidil thusa mar tha thu." An ath oidhche thuirt Fionn ris, "Cha robh maighstir agam fhein riamh nach innseadh rud-éiginn da bheachd dhomh ach thu fhein, 's mur innis thu 'de an t-aobhar air son a bheil thu falbh mar sin h-uile oidhche, cha 'n fhan mise so na 's fhaide."

"De 's fhearrd mise innseadh do chreutair co beag riutsa?" ors an Righ.

"Faodaidh duine beag comhairle mhòr bhi aige," orsa Fionn. "Cha 'n eil h-aon 'sam bith co glic 's nach fheaird comhairle na còrach; agus innis dhomh nis gu de tha cur dragh ort?"

"Tha mise nis os cionn seachd bliadhna deug gun chadal gun socair," ors an Righ, "le béisd mhòr a tha tighinn air tìr h-uile oidhche a thoirt uam mo rioghachd." "Gabh thusa gu tamh an nochd 's theid mise 'na chodhail." "Bi 'dh tu air do sgrios," ors an Righ. "Feudaidh tusa cadal gun churam sam bith air son sin," orsa Fionn. "'S mise tha feumach air a sin," ors an Righ.

Cha robh Fionn 's Bran fad aig a' chladach 'nuair chunnaic iad a' bheisd mhòr a' teachd, aon suil ghlogach 'an clar a h-aodainn, an fhairge, 'na teine sionnachan 's 'na mòr bheumnach roimpe 's na caoir gheala 's 'na muir bheucach, thall 's a bhos air a deigh, 's le luathas a teachd 's le meud a neart bhuail i 'ceann a fada fhein suas air an traigh. "Seadh," ors ise. "De naigheachd an fhir bhig aig am bheil am measan?"

"'S duilich dhomhsa gu bheil sin agamsa ri innseadh," orsa Fionn; "tha 'n Righ marbh an nochd, 's chuir a mhòr mhaith-ibh mise far an robh thu dh' iarraidh ort fuireach air t-ais an aon oidhche so, gus am faigheadh iad fear eile a chumail comhrag riut 'na aite."

"Am feud mi do chreidsin, fhir bhig?" ors ise.

"Cha 'n eil sannt bhriag orm," orsa Fionn. Dar dhuisg an Righ, ghlaodh e le cagal mòr. "Tha mo rioghachd air toirt uam 's mo throich 's mo mheasan air chall orm."

"Tha do rioghachd agad fhathast 's do throich 's do mheasan so," ors Fionn. Rinn an Righ mor thoileachadh dar chualaic e Fionn a' bruidhinn. "Cha 'n eil fhios agam," ors' esan, "c' uine fhuair mise leithid do thamh na do chadal."

An ath oidhche rinn an Righ deas air son falbh, ach thuirt Fionn ris gum b' fhearr dha esan a leigeil ann an oidhche so fhathast. Dar rainig e fhein 's Bran, cha robh e fada sin nar chunnaic e 'n fhairge tighinn 'na teine sionnachain 's 'na mòr bheumadh, 's a' bheisd mhòr 's aon suil ghlogach 'na ceann 's an cuan 'na chaora geala air gach taobh 's roimpe 's 'na deighinn tighinn dh' ionnsuidh a' chladaich, 's le luathas a siubhail 's meudachd a neart thiormaich i i fhein anns an traigh. " De naigheachd an fhir bhig aig am bheil am measan an nochd," ors' ise.

" Cha 'n 'eil," orsa Fionn, " ach gu 'n do chuir mòr mhaithibh na rioghachd mise a dh' iarraidh oirbh fuireach air ais an nochd fhathast, gu 'n do thuit a bh' righinn marbh, dar bha iad cur an Righ 'sa chiste." " Am feud mi an naigheachd sin chreidsinn?" ors' ise.

" Cha 'n 'eil sannt bhriag orm," ors' Fionn.

" 'S cinnteach gur e sin 's duilghe dhuit," ors' ise.

Thill Fionn dhachaidh 's chaidh e laidhe aig casan an Righ; nar dhuisg an Righ ghlaodh e, "Tha mo throich 's mo mheasan air chall, ach cha 'n e sin 's miosa dhomh ach gu bheil an rioghachd air toirt 'uam." " Tha mi creidsinn," ors' Fionn, " gur e sin 's mo tha thu caoidh an rioghachd bhi 'uat, ach tha an troich 's am measan an so 's do rioghachd agad fhathast." Thug so faochadh mòr do 'n Righ. Dh' fharraid e do dh' Fhionn, 'de an coltas bh' air a' bheist an nochd.

" Cha do chuir i eagal sam bith ormsa," thuirt Fionn.

Dar thainig an ath-oidhche, cha robh an Righ air son a leigeil air falbh, " 'S mòr do mhath rinn thu dhomhsa leithid do shocair thoirt dhomh 's theid mi fhein 'na còdhail an nochd."

" Cha 'n 'eil olc sam bith' na beachd," orsa Fionn, " 's feudaidh mise cead dol ann fhaighinn an nochd fhathast."

" Cha bhi i co olc riutsa co dhiu," thuirt an Righ.

Thug Fionn leis Bran 's cha robh e fad 'sam bith an oidhche so dar chunnaic e i 's an fhairge tighinn 'na teine sionachain air thoiseach oirre 's 'na mòr bheumach 's 'na caora geala thall 's a bhos 's 'na muir bheucach as a deighinn, 's le luathas a siubhail 's le meud a neart chuir i 'ceann a fad fhein air a' chladach.

" De sin naigheachd an fhir bhig aig am bheil am measan?" ors' ise.

" Tha," orsa Fionn, " gur mi-cheutach do 'd leithid-sa do bheist mhòir bho oidhche gu oidhche bhi 'g éisdeachd bhriagan bho dhuine co beag riumsa."

" 'Nann mar so tha?" ors' ise, "bi thusa deanamh air do shon fhein," 's chuir i *color* searbh oirre 's leum i an carabh Fhinn, 's bha i brath a sharachadh. Sheall Fionn air Bran, 's thuirt e, " A' bheil thu brath mo chuideachadh an nochd idir, a Bhran ?"

Dh' éirich Bran, 's chaidh e mu 'n cuairt orra, 's shuidh e far an robh e. Bha so an gleachd dol na bu mhiosa do dh' Fhionn, 's thug e 'n ath shuil air Bran. " Tha thu brath mo dhi-chuimhn-eachadh an nochd uile, Bhran." Dh' éirich Bran, 's thug e 'n ath chuairt m' an timchioll, 's shuidh e far an robh e roimhe. Bha a' chomrag nis dol an aghaidh Fhinn co mor 's gu 'n robh e fas fann. Sheall e air Bran 's thuirt e, " Bhran, cha ruig thusa leas éiridh tuille, tha mise ullamh, na rinn thu air mo shon, cha dean gu brath a rithist, cha 'n eil mo chobhair ann." Thug Bran éiridh air fhein 's ghabh e cuairt gus an robh e air cùl na beisde 's ruisg e 'spuir nimhe 's chuir e 'na druim i 's am pripa na sùla bha an cridhe s' an gruadhan aisde mach. Thilg Fionn an ceann dith leis a chlaidheamh 's bha e treis 'ga ghiulan 's treis 'ga iomain roimhe gus an d' rainig e 'n tigh. Chuir e air stob e mu choinneamh tigh an Righ 's an t-suil mhòr ghlocach ris an uineag far an robh an Righ, 's ghabh e stigh gu sniomhach, samhach gu casan an Righ. Air mheadhon oidhche dhuisg an Righ le uamhas 's ghlaodh e, " Mo rioghachd air toirt 'uam 's mi air m' fhagail gun troich gun mheasan."

"Cha 'n eil h-aon diu dhith ort," ors' Fionn, " 's mur creid thu sin thoir suil mach 's chi thu air do shon fhein." Rinn an Righ so, 's dar chunnaic e suil 's ceann na beisde mòire, thuit e air a ghlùn aig taobh na leabach aig Fionn, " 'S fhad," ors' esan, " bho 'n tha e san tairgneachd, gur e Fionn Mac Cumhail a bheireadh clos dhomhsa 's do m' rioghachd. 'S tusa Fionn."

"Cha 'n eil toillteanas agad air mathanas bh' uam," ors' Fionn, " chuir thu triuir fhear mhòra do m' rioghachd a chumail comhrag rium gun aobhar."

" 'S ann tha sin triuir fhear nach 'eil tighinn fo lagh sam bith 's aig nach 'eil bunailt dhomhsa 's aig am bheil mnathan sith arinn léintean dhoibh, 's dar bheirear dhiu iad bithidh iad mar dhaoine eile. Bheir mise dhuit-sa deoch cadail, 's dar ruigeas tu an cladach far am bheil iad, tilgidh tu na soithichean anns am bi an deoch cadail far an amais iad orra, 's dar bhios iad 'nan cadal bithidh cothrom agad air na léintean fhaotainn uapa."

Chuir Fionn mach an curachan, 's thill e fhein 's Bran, 's dar bha iad gu bhi aig cladach thilg Fionn mach an stòp 'san robh an deoch cadail. Bha na fir mhòra siubhal a' chladaich mar dh' fhag e iad. Thachair an stòpan air fear dhiu; chuir e an ceann as 's dh'òl e na bh' ann, 's thainig suain cadail air. Thilg Fionn mach an ath-fhear 's an treasa fear, 's bha iad 'nan triuir 'nan sineadh taobh ri taobh. Chaidh Fionn suas 's bhuain e dhiu na leintean, 's thug e crathadh dùsgaidh orra.

"Tha sibh so," ars' esan. "Tha," ors' iadsan. "'S tha sibh mar dhaoine eile, 's comas 's cothrom agamsa air 'ur beatha thoirt uaibh, 's cha 'n fhaigh sibh fuasgladh gun tighinn fo chùmhnanta lagh." Thuirt iad gu 'm bitheadh iad leagta ri cùmhnanta 'sam bith a dh' iarradh e orra, 's mhionnaich iad air a' chlaidheamh fhuar gu 'n seasadh iad e 'n còir 's an eucoir, 's uair 'sam bith a bhitheadh e ann an éiginn na cruadal, e 'chuimhneachadh orra-san 's gu 'm bitheadh iad aige, ach e 'thoirt dhoibh na léintean air an ais. 'S mar chaidh Fionn dhachaidh b' i an ceathramh cuirm bu mhotha 'bh' aca anns an Fheinn riamh.

CEUDACH SON OF THE KING OF THE COLLA MEN.

THERE were before now three sons of Kings, whose names were the Duke of Green, son of the King of France, the Duke of Pure White, son of the King of Gold, and Ceudach, son of the King of the Colla men. They laid their heads together to go in search of a wife for the Duke of Green, son of the King of France. They came to a great city; they were traversing it and walking through it till they saw such a one as they were in search of at the window of her father's house, the King of Vedia. They struck a challenge on a shield for equal combat, on the upper part or promenade of the city, or else the daughter of the King of Vedia to be sent out.

The combat of warriors was given to them, and they fought it till they did not leave one known warrior to the King that they did not kill. The King said that no one would get his daughter but one who could give a clear spring to the place where she was. [What is here translated "a clear spring" seems to have been a standing leap without the aid of running, or any other accessory beyond that of action of the muscles of the body and feet, the hands being placed on the hips.] This was done by Ceudach, son of the King of the Colla men; he caught a firm hold of her without struggle or hurry, and he had her safe.

It was not yet known who was to get her, as they were all complete warriors. The King said the one whom she preferred to follow would get her. "We will go to the barn," said Ceudach, son of the King of the Colla men. When he got them in the barn he said

15

they would make a whirligig, and place her in the middle, until she grew giddy, then the three doors of the barn were to be opened, and any man whom she followed out was the one who would have her. This was done, and she followed Ceudach, who continued to live with her in her father's house. When they were together some time, it caused him much surprise that she was only to be seen sometimes. One day, as they sat at meat, he said, with a heavy sigh :

"There is many a worse warrior in Fionn's house to-night, though I am of little account here."

"You are not at all of little account," she said.

"Yes," he said, "I am without company or inquiry, and I would prefer to be to-day with Fionn and his nobles. I am not wanted here, and I will go away."

"On the contrary, you are much thought of; it was making clothes for you that I was," and she produced clothes made of every kind of fur.

"I will go at any rate," he said, "and you will stay here."

"If you do," she said, "you will put on the clothes, and I will not stay here ; there will be no separation."

"If you accompany me to the end of my journey it will be on condition that you will not mention my name so long as I live," and she agreed with him. When they reached Fionn's house, he struck a challenge note on his shield, "A warrior in search of service." Fionn came out and asked him who he was and what work he could do. "The employment I can do is to procure and make ready the produce of the hunt before your nobles return next day, if you will allow me to take one side of the hill and put them on the other side."

The pride of Fionn's nobles was offended that any one man should presume to think lightly of them ; but when they came home on the morrow they found the produce of the hunt ready before them. "Tell me what wages you are asking, since you have approved yourself an able worker," Fionn said to him.

"My wages will be," he replied, "to have two-thirds of my own will, while you will have but one-third of your own will, and your wife to have the first say among the women of the Féinne, and my wife to have the second say."

They were now living together pleasantly, till one day a large coracle was seen coming towards the shore, in which there were two women out of all size. One of them jumped ashore and asked Fionn to be sent down ; that she had with her a shirt she had been a year and a day making for him ; and many an incline and rise, downs and ups, she encountered before arriving there. They told Fionn what she said, and he knew it was better for him to avoid her than to meet her. The man with the fur clothes said he would go to the shore instead of Fionn. When he reached it she tried on him the shirt, and it fitted him without a flaw. She then placed a row of little knives on the gunwale of the coracle, and she said to him : "If you are Fionn, you will walk on these knives and they will not cut you."

He did this, and the knives were taking the toes and the heels off him.

"It is easy to know that you are not Fionn,"she said ; "take yourself away, before you are without life or strength."

Fionn was again sent for; he came; the shirt fitted him as if it had been worked on himself, and he walked on the knives without a cut or injury. She then said : "Fionn, I put you under bands and spells, that you will go three times of your own accord to the Kingdom of Big Men, and three times against your own wishes," and they went away.

After that the time came for Fionn to go. When they came down, the women of the Féinne met them.

Fionn knelt to the wife of the man with the fur garment. She said to him : " O King, why do you kneel to me ?"

" It is," said the King, " to ask you to allow your husband to go with me to a far-away region."

" I will do so," she said, " on condition that you bring him back to me, whether he be dead or alive."

They went, and when they were returning, the man with the fur skins said to Fionn : " This is our death ; none of us will return alive home with you. Put a mark on my clothes that you may know me from the others. I and my companions were once playing when the ball went in to an old woman who was making pottery, or delf ; the ball smashed the delf. She asked payment ; we had nothing to pay her with, and we took out the ball in spite of her. She placed us under spells: ' Though you are going together so affectionately and friendly at present, the one will kill the other of you,' she said. The time is now come, and do you put a mark on my clothes."

Fionn did this, and no sooner was it done than war broke out in the sky, and the one killed the other. Fionn threw the other two overboard, and took back the man with the fur garments. His wife met Fionn. " Yes," she said, " you have brought him home."

" I have fulfilled my promise," Fionn said.

" He is not alive, I feel," she said.

They went to the shore, and Fionn showed her the body. She lifted its head on her knees, saying :

> " I would know you by your teeth,
>   And your beautiful wavy hair ;
>   It is a truth, and no lie,
> That you are Ceudach, son of the King of the Colla men."

She asked permission of Fionn to remain this evening at the shore, as she then was. She was not long there, when she saw two men of gigantic size coming towards her from the sea, and the one that was coming after throwing the head of the one who was before him, and the head going on him again as before. With the astonishment she felt, she lifted the sword that Ceudach had saying : " Why should I not try the small play ?" and threw off his head, when she found him alive and as well as when she parted from him.

CEUDACH MAC RIGH NAN COLLACH.

Bha ann aon h-uair roi' so triuir mhac righrean b' iad sin Diuc Uaine Mac Righ na Frainge, Diuc Gle-Gheal Mac Righ an h-òir, 's Ceudach Mac Righ nan Collach, 's chuir iad an cinn ri cheile gu 'm falbhadh iad dh' iarraidh bean do Dhiuc Uaine Mac Righ na Frainge. Rainig iad baile mòr 's bha iad 'ga shiubhal 's a' spaidsearachd air 'fheadh gus an d' fhuair iad sealladh air an te bha iad an toir oirre aig uinneag tigh a h-athar, Righ Mhidia. Bhuail iad beum sgéithe céile combrag no nighinn Righ Mhidia a chur a mach. Fhuair iad combrag gaisge 's chaith iad i, gus nach d' fhag iad aon ghaisgeach air sgeul aig an righ nach do mharbh iad. Thuirt an righ nach fhaigheadh a h-aon a nighean, ach am fear a bheireadh leum nan ceithir seang a dh' ionnsuidh 'n aite 'san robh i. Rinn Ceudach Mac Righ nan Collach so, 's rug e oirre le greim diorrasach gun stri gun chabhaig 's bha i sabhailte aige. Cha robh fios an so cò fear dhiu gheibheadh i bho 'n bha iad uile 'nan làn ghaisgich. Thuirt an righ gum faigheadh am fear a b' fhearr leatha fhein a leantuinn. "Theid sinn do 'n t-sabhal," thuirt Ceudach Mac Righ nan Collach. Dar fhuair e san t-sabhal iad, thuirt e riu gu 'n deanadh iad "a bhuaile mhiosdean" 's gu 'n cuireadh iad ise san teas meadhon gus an tigeadh tuaincalach oirre, 's gu 'm fosgladh iad tri dorsan an t-sabhail 's fear 'sam bith a leanadh i mach dhiu gum b 'e sin am fear leis am bitheadh i. Rinn iad so 's lean ise Ceudach 's dh' fhuirich esan leatha an tigh a h-athar. Dar bha iad comhla car ùine bha e 'cur iongantas mòr air san nach robh i ri fhaicinn ach còrr uair. Latha bha sin dar a bha iad 'nan suidhe aig am biadh thuirt esan 's e tarruing osnadh throm :

" 'S ioma gaisgeach 's miosa an tigh Fhinn an nochd ged tha mise a so air bheagan meas."

"Cha 'n 'eil thu gun mheas idir," thuirt ise.

"Tha," thuirt esan, "mi gun choimhead gun fharraid 's b' fhearr leam gu 'n robh mi an diugh le Fionn 's le 'mhaithibh. Cha 'n 'eil iarraidh orm a so, 's bithidh mi falbh."

"An aite sin 's ann tha moran meas ort; 's ann deanamh eudaich dhuit bha mise," 's thug i mach eudach air dheanamh do na h-uile seorsa bian.

"Falbhaidh mi co dhiu," ors' esan, " 's fanaidh tusa an so."

"Ma dh' fhalbhas," thuirt ise, "cuiridh tu ort an t-eudach, 's cha 'n fhuirich mise an so; cha bhi eadar-dhealachadh ann."

"Ma dh' fhalbhas tu leam air ceum mo shiubhal," ors' esan, " 's ann air chumhnanta nach abair thu m' ainm rium fhad 's a bhios mi beo," 's dh' aontaich i leis.

Dar rainig iad tigh Fhinn bhuail e beum-sgeithe, gum bu ghaisgeach esan air son cosnaidh. Thainig Fionn a mach 's dh' fharraid e co e na ciod an cosnadh b' urrainn dha dheanamh.

"Se an cosnadh a ni mi an t-seilg a dheanamh 's a bhruich, mu 'n dig do mhaithibh-sa dhachaidh am maireach, ma leigeas tu mise air an darna taobh do 'n bheinn 's ma chuireas tu iadsan air an taobh eile."

Ghabh maithibh Fhinn uaill agus àrdan gu 'n gabhadh aon neach fos laimh tarcuis a dheanamh orra, ach dar thainig iad dhachaidh an la 'r 'n ath-mhaireach bha an t-seilg deanta bruich rompa.

"Innis 'de an duais a bhitheas tu ag iarraidh, nis, bho 'n leig thu fhaicinn do dheagh sheirbhis," thuirt Fionn ris.

"Se mo thuarasdal," ors' esan, "da thrian do 'm thoil fhein bhi agam, 's aon trian do d' thoil fhein a bhi agadsa 's a chiad fhacal do mhnathan na Féinne a bhi aig do bheansa, 's an darna facal aig mo bheansa."

Bha iad so tighinn beo gu solasach, gus aon latha am faca iad curachan mòr tighinn dh' ionnsuidh a 'chladaich anns an robh da bhoirionnach gun chuimhseadh air meudachd. Leum té dhiu air tìr 's dh' iarr i Fionn chur nuas, gu 'n robh aice-sa sid léine a bha i latha 's bliadhna a 'deanamh dha, 's gur iomadh aomadh 's h-àitibh roi' an d' thainig i mu 'n do bhuanaich i sid.

Dh' innis iad do Fhionn mar thuirt i, 's dh' aithnich e gu 'm b' fhearr dha seachnadh na tachairt rithe. Thuirt gaisgeach nam bian gu 'n rachadh esan thun a' chladaich 'an aite Fhinn. Dar rainig e chuir i air an léine 's fhreagair i dha gun bheum. Chuir i sin sreath do sgeanan beaga air am faobhar air beul a' churachain 's thuirt i ris, "Ma 's tu Fionn coisichidh tu air na sgeanan sin 's cha ghearr iad thu."

Rinn e so, 's bha na sgeanan toirt nam meoir 's nan sàiltean dheth. "'S fhurasd aithneachadh nach tu Fionn," ors' ise, "thoir thu fhéin as mu 'm bi thu gun chail gun chlì."

Chaidh fios an so air Fionn a rithist 's thainig e 's fhreagair an leine dha mar gu 'n rachadh a deanamh uime, 's choisich e air na sgeanan gun ghearradh gun dochann. An sin thuirt ise, "Fhinn, tha mi 'g ad chur fo bhannaibh 's fo gheasaibh gu 'n deid thu tri uairean do rioghachd nam fear mòra le d' thoil 's tri uairean an aghaidh do thoil," 's dh' fhalbh iad. Goirid an deigh sin thainig an t-am aig Fionn bhi falbh. Dar thainig iad nuas thachair mnathan na Feinne orra. Chaidh Fionn air a ghlun do bhean fear nan cochla craicionn, 's thuirt i ris, "C' ar son, O Righ, tha sibh lubadh air glùn dhomhsa." "Tha," ors' an righ, "dh' iarraidh ort cead an duine agad leigeil leam do rioghachd fad dh' astar."

"Ni mi sin," ors' ise, "air chumhnanta gu 'n toir thu air ais g' am ionnsuidh e, c' dhiu 's e 'bheo na 'mharbh a bhitheas ann."

Dh' fhalbh iad, 's dar bha iad a 'tilleadh air an rathad, thuirt fear nan cochla craicionn ri Fionn:

"Se ar bàs tha so, cha ruig h-aon againn leats' dhachaidh 's cuir thusa comharradh air m' eudachsa los gu 'n aithnich thu mi seach cach. Bha mise 's mo dha chompanach aon uair 'g iomain 's chaidh a' chniad a stigh do thigh cailliche a bha deanamh creadha, 's bhrist a' chniad a 'chriadh oirre. Dh' iarr i paigheadh 's cha robh againn na phaigheadh dhi e, 's thug sin a' chniad mach dh' aindeoin 's chuir i fo gheasan sinn, 'Ged tha sibh falbh comhla co mùirneach càirdeil an drasta,' ors' ise, 'marbhaidh an darna h-aon an t-aon eile.' Tha an t-am nis air tighinn 's cuir thusa comharradh 'm eudach."

Rinn Fionn so, 's cha luaithe bha e deanta na dh' éirich an cogadh as an athar 's mharbh an darna fear am fear eile, 's

thilg Fionn an dithis eile thar bord, 's thug e dhachaidh fear
nan cochladh craicionn.   Choinnich a bhean e.   "Seadh," ors'
ise, "thug thu dhachaidh e."

"Choimhlion mi mo ghealladh," ars' Fionn.

"Cha bheo e tha mi 'g aithneachadh," thuirt i.

Dh' imich iad thun a' chladaich, 's leig e fhaicinn an corp
dh' i.   Thog i a cheann air a glùn, 's thuirt i :

> " ' Dh' aithn 'n air a' dheud thu,
>   'S air a' chul cheutach chlannach,
>   'S fìrinn 's cha bhreug e
>   'Gur tu Ceudach Mac Righ nan Collach.' "

Dh' iarr i cead air Fionn fuireach an oidhche so aig a' chladach
mar bha i.   Cha robh i ach ùine ghoirid ann dar chunnaic i
dithis fhear thar tomhas tighinn far an robh i far a' chuain, 's am
fear a bhiodh air dheireadh tilgeil a 'chinn do 'n fhear a bhiodh
air thoiseach, 's an ceann 'dol air mar bhiodh e roimhe.   Leis
an ionghnadh a ghabh i thog i an claidheamh bh' aig Ceudach s
thuirt i, "C' ar son nach deanainn an cleas beag?" 's thilg i
an ceann deth 's fhuair i sin e beo slan mar dhealaich i ris.

HOW FIONN WAS IN THE HOUSE OF THE YELLOW FIELD,

WITHOUT LEAVE TO SIT DOWN OR POWER TO STAND UP.

Fionn went out walking one day. He had only two of his men and two of the dogs with him. One of them, who was the master of the dogs, was called Conan. The blinding darkness of a snow-storm overtook them, and they looked about for a place of shelter to which they could go. A little old man met them, and welcomed Fionn MacCumal.

"I welcome you," said Fionn; "you seem to have a better knowledge of me than I have of you."

"I have that of you," said he, "and more than that, I put it as charms, and spells, and the nine fastenings of the fairy woman on you, that you will be to-night in the House of the Yellow Field."

"Up and down with your spells," said Fionn.

"Neither up nor down with them," said the old man.

Where the old man was highest they were lowest, until they reached the mouth of a cave; they entered the cave, and the old man said to them, "Keep to one side of the cave." "If none stronger than you will come we will do so," said they. "You do not know in the world," said he, "what may occur to you."

It was not long after this when a youth entered with a dog, having a white spot in its forehead. He saluted Fin-Mac-Coul.

"I bid you welcome," said Fionn; "you know me better than I know you." "I do know you better," the youth said. " I have heard that the Fians keep good dogs, and I have come to ask a dog-fight."

" I have not one of my dogs here," said Fionn, " but two." The names of the dogs were Bran and Geola. At first he allowed Bran to fight the yellow white-fronted dog, but Bran showed no great cleverness. Bran had a death-inflicting spur, or claw, which was always kept covered with a shoe until he had to fight. On this occasion the taking off the sheath or shoe was neglected. Bran would look at Geola, and Geola, in turn, would look at Conan. Then Conan remembered that the shoe had not been taken off Bran, and he laid himself down alongside and took off the shoe. It was no sooner taken off than Bran lifted the venomous claw and killed the dog of the white front. It was then the owner of the dog said :

> " Were it not for the wily Geola,
> And Bran, from the greatness of his strength,
> No dog that a leash could be put on,
> Would be left by For, west in the Fort."

It was not long after this when a great dame came in with sixteen attendant maidens. She greeted Fionn MacCumal.

" I greet yourself," he said ; " you are better acquainted with me than I am with you."

" I am," she said. " I heard that you have good wrestlers, and I am come with my maiden attendants to wrestle with them."

" I have not many wrestlers ; I have only two altogether," said Fionn, and he asked Conan to rise and take a turn at wrestling.

Conan and one of the attendant maidens put themselves in wrestling order, and at the first throw she put him on his knee.

" A King's son on bended knee ; is it permissible for him to rise ?" said he.

" It is permissible," said she.

Conan was never known to do a clever action until he was made to be ashamed. He gave her a high, jolly lift, and laid her flat on the ground ; thus from one to one, till he threw down the whole sixteen. The great woman was now for making her escape.

" You must not do that," said Fionn. " You must try wrestling with me, and it would be no cause of complaint to you if it was the beginning and not the end of the wrestling."

At that she and her attendant maidens left ; and soon after Fionn and those with him saw a great number of people coming to the mouth of the cave. Fionn sent one of his men to ascertain who the people were, and when he was not coming back, Fionn sent the other down. Before long the people poured in upon him. They surrounded him on every hand, till he could neither sit down nor stand up. He was combating them with his sword as best he could ; he had a shield on his side called the Storm Shield, and when it called out it could be heard in the Seven-hundredths of Ireland ; and when it called three times, Fionn would be nearly done for. The first cry that it gave was heard in Kincorry, where Fionn's company then was. When they moved, they did not well know what side to turn to ; but they were not long till they heard it again, and they made straight for it. When they were nearly at it, it gave the third cry. By that time they had dug a hole into the cave above him, and they drew Fionn out, and allowed no one to escape from the edge of their weapons, but one person, to tell what had become of the rest. That was the greatest strait in which Fionn ever was, when he was in the House of the Yellow Field, without power to stand up or sit down.

MAR BHA FIONN 'AN TIGH 'BHLAR BHUIDHE GUN CHEAD SUIDHE NA COMAS ÉIRIDH.

Bha Fionn mach latha 'gabhail sraid. Cha robh leis ach dithis do ghillean 's dithis do choin, 's b'e maighstir nan con fear do na gillean a bha leis, ris an abairteadh Conan. 'De thainig orra ach dalladh chur-sneachda, 's bha iad feuch am faigheadh iad aite fasgach a bheireadh iad mach. Thachair bodachan beag orra 's chur e failte air Fionn Mac Cumhail. "Failte ort fhein," orsa Fionn, "tha aithne agad orm nach 'eil agam ort." "Tha sin agam ort," ors' am bodachan, "'s bharrachd air a sin tha mi 'cur," ors' esan, "mar chroisean 's mar gheasan ort 's mar naoi buaraichean na mna sith gum bi thu 'an tigh 'Bhlair Bhuidhe 'n nochd."

"Sios 's suas d' gheasan," ors' Fionn.

"Cha sios 's cha suas do m' gheasan," ors' am bodach.

Far am b' àirde do 'n bhodach 's ann a b' isle dhoibh san ach gus an do rainig iad beul uamha. Chaidh iad stigh do 'n uamha 's thuirt am bodach, "Gleidheadh an darna taobh do 'n uamha." "Mur dig oirnn na 's treasa na thusa ni sinn sin," ors' iadsan. "Cha 'n 'eil fhios agaibh air an t-saoghal," ors' esan, "dé thig oirbh."

Cha b' fhada as deighinn sin dar thainig òganach a stigh 's cù blàr buidhe aige, 's chuir e failte air Fionn Mac Cumhail.

"Failte ort fhein," ors' Fionn, "tha aithne agad orm nach 'eil agam ort." "Tha sin agam ort," ors' esan, "chuala mi gu 'n robh coin mhath agaibh 's an Fhéinn 's thainig mi dh' iarraidh combrag chon."

"Cha 'n 'eil moran agamsa so," ors' Fionn, "do m' chuid chon ach dithis." Agus b' e an ainm Bran agus Geoladh; 's air tùs leig e Bran chomhrag leis a' chu bhlar bhuidhe ach cha robh Bran deanamh tapadh sam bith. Bha spor nimhe air 's daonnan bhiodh bròg air ach gus am biodh e 'combrag. Aig an am so cha do chuimhnich iad a bhròg a thoirt dheth. Shealladh Bran air Geoladh 's shealladh Geoladh air Conan. 'S ann an so chuimhnich Conan nach d' thainig a' bhròg thar Bran, 's leig e e fhein 'na shìneadh fodha 's thug e dheth a' bhròg.

Cha luaithe bha e air toirt dheth na thog esan a spor nimhe 's mharbh e an cù blàr. Sin mar labhair fear a' choin,

" Mar bi Geoladh nan car,
   Agus Bran roi mheud a lùgh 's
   Aon chù mun dùnabh iad
   Chan fhàgadh For siar san Dàn."

Cha b' fhada an deigh sin gus an d' thainig baintighearna mhòr a stigh 's sia maighdeanan deug coimheadach leatha. Chuir i failte air Fionn Mac Cumhail.

" Failte oirbh p' fhein," ors' esan, "tha aithne agaibh orm nach 'eil agam oirbh." " Tha sin agam ort," ors' ise, "chuala mi gu 'n robh gleachdairean math agad 's thainig mi le m' mhaighdeanan coimhead dh' fheuchain gleachd riu."

" Cha 'n 'eil moran do ghleachdairean agams' ann, cha 'n 'eil agam ach dithis air fad," ors' Fionn, 's dh' iarr e air Conan éiridh a dh' fheuchain car gleachd'; 's air a chiad char chuir i air a ghlùn e.

" Mac Righ air a ghlun," ors' esan, " 's cead dha éiridh?"
" 'S cead," ors' ise.

Cha d' rinn Conan tapadh riamh ach gus an gabhadh e nàire. Thug e an togail àrd aighearach ud oirre 's chuir e air stéil a droma i, 's o thé gu té gus an do leag e an t-sia deug. Bha so an té mhòr air son teicheadh air falbh.

" Cha dean thu sin idir," ors' Fionn, " feumaidh tu gleachd fheuchinn riumsa, 's cha bu dad gearan idir dhuit na 'm b' e toiseach 'bhiodh agad ach deireadh na gleachd." Aige sin dh' fhalbh i fhein 's a maighdeanan coimheadach. Cha b' fhada an deigh sin gus am faca iad moran sluaigh tighinn gu beul na uamha'. Chuir Fionn sios fear do 'ghillean feuch 'de na daoine bha sid, 's mar nach robh e tilleadh air ais, chuir e fear eile sios. Cha b' fhada ach gus an do bhrùchd an sluagh a stigh g' a ionnsuidh. Dh' iadh iad uime air gachlaimh gus nach robh e comasach dha suidhe na seasamh. Bha e 'gan comhrag le 'chlaidheamh co math 's a dh' fhaodadh e. Bha sgiath air a thaobh ris an abairteadh Sgiath Ghaillion, 's nar ghlaodhadh e chluinnteadh ann an Seachd Ceudan na h-Érin i; 's 'n uair bheireadh i trì ghlaoidh aisde bhiodh esan sin air bheul thaobh bhi ullamh. 'N uair thug i 'chiad ghlaodh aisde chual' iad ann

an Dùn Chinn-a-Choire i; 's ann sin bha cuideachd Fhinn cruinn.
'N uair ghluais iad, cha robh fhios aca ceart 'de an taobh a
ghabhadh iad ; ach cha b' fhad ach gus an cualaic iad rithist i,
agus rinn iad direach oirre.   Mar bha iad fagasg dha thug i an
treas glaodh aisde.   Aig an am sin bha iad an deigh an uamh
a tholladh os a chionn, agus sin thug iad Fionn mach, 's cha do
leig iad duine a bial airm ach an aon fhear, air son 's gu 'n
innseadh am fear sin gu de a dh' èirich do chàch uile ; agus 's e
sin an càs bu mhotha 's an robh Fionn riamh, dar bha e 'n tigh
'Bhlàir Bhuidhe (gun chead suidhe no gun chomas cìridh), 's
nach fhaigheadh e suidhe na seasamh.

IN the tale here given, the reader's attention is first drawn to the " Little, thick-set, insignificant man" (*Fear beag, iosal, lapanach*). From another source, the writer has heard this description of him :

> " The little, low-set Swaddler,
> His russet coat and sinewy muscles,
> The hair of his breast pointing upwards,
> The hair of his head reaching to his breast,
> His bag of arrows death-inflicting,
> Without wax or feathering."

> " Am Fear beag, iosal, lapanach,
> A chota lachduinn nan geur cang,
> A ghruag uchd an àird,
> 'S a ghruag àrd air 'uchd,
> A bholg saighde le nimhe,
> Gun chéir gun iteach air."

Lapanach does not mean that he was undersized in the same way that children are, but that he was a full-grown individual, undersized and sinewy, or muscular. Perhaps this adjective, *Lapanach*, is the origin of the name Laplander, the people of Lapland being of smaller height and lower stature than the average European. The Laplanders, although undersized in point of height, are strong in muscle, and their appearance generally is only that of people living in a very cold climate and on fat and unctuous food.

There are many traditional tales in the Highlands of much interest, and referring to more modern times, in which little men of dwarfish, and even pigmy, size figure as good bowmen, slaying men of large size and powerful

make by their dexterity in the use of the bow and
arrow. The reader will readily remember "Little
John", of Robin Hood fame, reputed in his time one of
the most skilful archers of Sherwood Forest. Another
indication of Lappish connection worth attention is that
there was at one time in the Highlands of Scotland a
lullaby for young children, in which the words occur,
"On Deer's milk I was reared" ("*Air bainne nam
Fiadh thogadh mi*"). The writer himself has not been
able to get the words of the lullaby; but these lullabies,
like the names of places, are very enduring in their
existence, and perhaps can yet be fallen in with in
other places and among other people. The rescue of
this and other lullabies and Gaelic antiquities in an
available form would be a boon to the philologist and
anthropologist.

The quiet tackling of even the weakly with misfortune
and formidable events, and the perseverance against
impending calamities denoted by these tales, are lessons
from which everyone can draw a moral for himself.

The word *cang* is to the lexicographer worthy of
attention. It is not a word of common use, but it is
well known in some poetic expressions. The boast of
the young Deer was that no animal ever planted foot on
hillside that could catch it.

> "Slippery and yellow is my skin,
>   And never planted foot on hillside
>   Any beast that could catch me."

> "Sleamhuinn 's as buidhe mo bhian,
>   'S cha do chuir e cang air sliabh
>   Beathach riamh a bheireadh orm."

Leum nan ceithir cang (the agile spring of four
bounds), denotes a standing leap, or one as high and
as far as one is capable of.

Gun ghligteadh nan cang (without a spring in the

muscles), is said of a person entirely exhausted, so that he is unable to rattle his bones, or move a sinew or muscle, however strong these may have been. *'S aotrom cang*, is said of a young person with a jaunty air. The little Swaddler, who was despised by the other nobles as dwarfish, was received by Fionn MacCumhail, and his request was acceded to. Though his request at the time appeared trifling, it proved afterwards to be of great moment. Fionn in this matter appears true to his character as "the real old country gentleman, all of the olden times".

It has been said to the writer that *cang* meant a mark in the centre of the archer's bow, with another towards each end, for the guidance of the archer's aim. In this case the *cang* of the bow may mean the whole *twang* of the bow, implying the whole strength of the weapon, both wood and string. The Gaelic word *cang*, and the English word *twang*, being etymologically and by onomatopœia the same word, and the whole derived from the sound or resonance arising when the arrow is launched. The trebly nimble, or agile leap, is one in which the whole powers of the man's body are exercised, and the muscles are brought into play like the string of the bow.

Eirig was a recompense, or the taking the part of any one, or vindicating his character after death ; and, in this case, it seems to denote the avenging or clearing, and the making good the injury done to Fionn. It does not seem to convey the idea of vengeance, or the requital of loss or injury by a retaliation equally severe.

In the dispersion of languages and primeval tribes the names of places and still surviving indications are much to be looked to, and before parting with the subject it may be permissible to point out that the word already mentioned, *cang*, being connected with the English "twang", from the resonance of the weapon, may also have its analogy and relatives in the Kangaroo and Boomerang of the native Australian, the first of these words in name and meaning being very like *canga ruith*, the hopping or agile leaping of the animal taking the place of what in other animals is running, and the other deriving its name from the sound of the weapon when thrown over the head into the air.

The names of places in the rigorous climate of the North are not very easily come-at-able, most of them being made known to us through alien tongues. Kamschatka cannot but arrest attention from the beginning of the word resembling so much the *Camus*, or indentation of the sea into the land, which is so common in names of undoubted Gaelic origin, like Cambuskenneth, *Camusdionbhaig* in Skye, etc., etc. It is also noticeable from the differentiating noun or locality preceding the adjective or other adjunct by which the locality or place-name is denoted, as well as from its common occurrence in the names of places. It is observable that in Gaelic the differentiating noun always precedes and never follows the place-name, as it always does in English. The person acquainted with both languages can in this respect compare Newton and *Baile-nodha*. *Baile* is in Gaelic at the beginning of the place-name, but in English at the end.

In the tale the word Swaddler has been adopted as a fair translation of *Lapanach*, as the idea conveyed is that of a little, insignificant-looking, and at the same time a sturdy, strong, active individual, though in appearance not lithe or athletic ; or, as it has otherwise been explained to the writer, *Moganach làidir*.

FIONN'S RANSOM.

Once upon a time Fionn and his three foster-brothers, the Red Knight, the Knight of the Cairn, and the Knight of the Sword, went to the hunting hill. They

sat down to look around them, on a sunny, rocky emi-
nence, sheltered from the wind, and in the sun's warmth,
where they could see everyone and no one could see
them. When they were seated there some time, the
Knight of the Sword said, "Is it possible for me to think
that anyone has walked the earth or traversed the air
who could despise or look down upon Fionn MacCumhail when his three foster-brothers are near him?" The
words were hardly uttered when they observed the
darkening and heard the sound of the approach and
passing of a shower from the north-west, out of which
came a rider on a black horse. He came straight where
Fionn was, and struck him on the mouth, knocking out
three upper and three lower teeth. Then the Knight of
the Sword stood and said that the earth would make
a hollow in the sole of his foot and the sky a nest in
the crown of his head before his footsteps would return,
"Until I avenge Fionn's injury." The other foster-
brothers said the same. They then went down to the
shore, and began to fit out a ship to go away in. They
were not long engaged in this work when they saw a
little, low-set, insignificant-looking man approaching the
place where they were. They addressed him, and in
reply he asked the Knight of the Sword for permission
to accompany them on the ship. The Knight of the
Sword answered, "No; of what use would a trifling
little man like you be to us for going in a ship?" He
then made a request of the Knight of the Cairn if there
was any way by which he would be allowed to go with
them on their travels, but the Knight of the Cairn
replied that they had no need of such an unlikely
person as he was in a ship. He then in the same way
asked the Red Knight, who said that it was improper
of him to put such a question. "Who could have the
audacity to take an insignificant-looking creature of
mean, russety appearance, such as you are, in a ship to

sea?" He now went where Fionn was, and told him
that the others had all refused him, and asked him if he
would allow him to accompany him.

" I give you permission," said Fionn; "you are of more
value than a stone, anyhow."

They then launched the ship. They turned the prow
seaward and the stern to land, and raised the speckled,
towering sails against the tall, tough, strong masts
with a slight, soft, gentle breeze that would strip leaves
from trees, willow from hill, and young heather from its
rootlets and grasp, lashing the sea wildly into waves and
foam in the seething expanse far and near, while the
little, crooked, swarthy whelk that was seven years at
the bottom of the sea gave a creaking sound on the gunwale and a thump on the bottom of the boat. Their
murmuring music and lasting sound of grumbling were
the chirning of eels, the gnashing of teeth, the biggest
beast devouring the smaller beast, and the little beast
doing as best it could. The ship could cut a grain of
oats with the edge of her prow from the excellence of
her steering, and Fionn Mac Cumhail was guide at the
prow, helm in the stern, and tackle in the centre, and
they directed her course for the Kingdom of Big Men.
When they had been two days sailing, Fionn desired
the Knight of the Sword to look from the mast whether
he could see land. He went a short distance up the
mast, returned, and said that there was no part or portion of land visible. Then Fionn asked the Knight of
the Cairn to try if he could discern land. He went a
short distance up the mast, and came down, and said that
there was no trace or appearance of land in sight. Fionn
now asked the Red Knight to look closely from him
whether he could get a view of land. The Red Knight
only climbed up the mast a short way when he returned,
saying that there was neither land nor earth to be seen,
nothing but sea and sky. Then the little, insignificant

man stood and said to them, " If you could not acquit
yourselves better than that, you might as well have
remained where you were," and he gave a bound and
reached the top of the mast. When he came down
he said to Fionn, " It is too large to be a hooded
crow, and too small to be land ; but keep the course
you are on." Next day they were in harbour in the
Kingdom of Big Men. When they reached the anchor-
ing ground they could not get to land. There were
three Fiery Darts gleaming all round the harbour. Then
the little, low-set, waddling man put a hollow-shaped,
resisting shield on his right hand, and on his left gave
the standing (or magic) leap of three bounds, and reached
land. After that he took Fionn and his three foster
brothers safely on shore with him. The four then
began to walk abroad through the island. On their way
they met a tall woman with a brown, fat, little lap-dog
at her heels, and every time the lap-dog looked at Fionn
his lost teeth were in their place in his mouth as they
should be, but when the lap-dog turned from him the
teeth dropped out.

The foster-brothers now thought they had found
Fionn's ransom, and they carried off with them the
tall woman and the lap-dog to the ship, and left the
little, low-set Swaddler alone on the island. He was
travelling, and ever moving right on before him. In the
dusk of the evening he saw a small dwelling-house, with
a light in it, by the road-side. He entered and found a
large fire burning, but there was no one before him.
However, he was not long waiting and listening when a
tall man returned home and said, " What news has the
little low-set Swaddler?" He replied that he had no
news, unless he got any from the tall man who had
come home.

" My news are but sorrowful," said the tall man, " for
my beautiful sister, who used to put me in the bath

when I returned home from fighting the battle, and made me as cheerful as ever to go to battle and combat the next day, has been taken away, and is lost and astray from me."

"If that was all she could do," said the little low-set Swaddler, "perhaps I may do it myself;" and he took him and washed him in the washing-bath, so that he never felt more refreshed or joyful.

Another brother now returned home, and said when he entered the house, "What news has the little, low-set Swaddler?"

"I have neither little nor much of any news," said he, "unless I may get some from yourself."

"The burden of my news is but sad," this brother said, "for my beloved sister, who put me in the washing-bath at eve, after the battle, so that next day I was as well as ever, has been taken away with the little, brown, fat lap-dog that followed at her heel."

"If she could only do that," said he, "I may myself be able to do it;" and he put this tall brother in the bath and washed and cleaned him, so that he was as fresh as he ever was, next day, to go to fight.

Another tall brother came home soon after, and said the self-same words with the others, "What news has the little low-set Swaddler?"

"I have no manner of tale to tell," he replied, "but what the big, strong man who came in has better."

"My share of the story is but poor," said the third brother, "for my handsome sister, who bathed me on my return from battle, and next day I was better than ever to go to combat, has been taken away, and I shall now be without strength or counsel."

"If that is all," said the Swaddler, "I may try to do it myself;" and he took him to the farthest-off part of the house and washed and bathed him, so that next day he was better prepared than ever to engage in battle and combat.

The little Swaddler then said, " Will you allow me to go to the battle to-night in your place?"

One of the brothers replied to him, " Miserable being, what could you do there alone, when they keep three of us fighting?"

" But will you not tell me how many are coming to trouble you?" said the little man.

Another of the brothers then answered, " That there was a regiment of soldiers, and although he beheaded every one of them, a tall old woman came after him with a life-restoring stoup in her hand, and when she dipped her finger in the life-restoring stoup and put it in the mouths of the men, every one of them sprang up alive."

" Will any others come?" asked the Swaddler.

" There will come then," resumed the next of the brothers, " another regiment of soldiers, with musical harpers at their head, and they will set you to sleep."

" Will none other than these come?" said he.

" Then will come," said the third brother, " a tall old man of terrific and gruesome appearance, who will take your life unless you can keep combating him all night. After him, a tall, old woman will come, and if you let her get near you her breath will kill you."

The Swaddler then asked if any others would come. The brothers told him that none else would come.

He obtained permission to go away that night to the battle. When he reached he saw the first regiment approaching, and he hid himself until they had passed ; he then came up behind and killed every one of them. He now saw a great, enormous old woman coming with a life-restoring stoup in her hand. When he saw that she was near, he laid himself down in the row among the dead men. She put her finger out of the life-restoring stoup in the mouth of the man nearest to him, and he started up alive. She then put her finger in his mouth, and he took it off from the knuckles. She cried out :

" Of all those lying there, may you be the last man of your mother's race to rise!"

" No, but I shall be the second man to rise," and he rose up, and threw off both of their heads together.

He was there but a short time after he got that battle over when he heard the musical harpers drawing near, and the next regiment hurrying towards him. He was overcome with fatigue and was dropping asleep. To keep himself awake, he placed the hilt of his sword on the upper part of his foot and the point to his eyebrow, and whenever he began to nod the sword kept him awake. When the band of soldiers passed near him he came up after them and killed them all.

He now thought the Tall Old Man would not be long of appearing, and he began to dig a wide, deep hole in the earth, and to cover it with wood, grass, and moss. When the pitfall was nearly finished, in the gathering twilight the terrific and incomparably dreadful Big Grey Man came, and he and the little Swaddler began to fight a battle. They attacked one another roughly and fiercely. In the heat of the conflict they drew near the opening that was in the ground, and the terrible Great Man fell in. Then the little Swaddler took the advantage of him, and cut off his head.

Shortly after this fight was over, the Old Woman, whose size was large and great, appeared. As she came close to him, her breath was weakening him; he endeavoured as much as he could to keep her from him, and they fought almost all night. At the break of day, when one of the brothers awoke, he said to himself: " I must rise, for I am certain that the man who went to fight in my place is long since dead."

Another of the brothers said: " That part is not the worst of it for you, but that your kingdom will be destroyed." The third brother said to them all : " We had better go together to the place where the battle is being fought.'

They then set off, and when they arrived at the place
of battle, they found the Enormous Old Wife and the
little Swaddler both together, quite exhausted. One of
the brothers then said : " Oh ! will you not give me the
sword, that I may cut off the wretched Old Woman's
head ?"

" Since I finished the foot measure," said the little
Swaddler, " I will undertake the inch measure ; but do
you put your finger in that little Life-restoring Stoup
over there, and then place it in my mouth."

When the little Swaddler had this done to him, he
rose, swept the head of the Old Woman, and killed her.
The Tall Men then carried him home on their shoulders,
and they continued to live together.

One day, when the little Swaddler went to the hill
to look abroad, he saw the darkening of a shower coming
from the north-west, out of which came a rider on a
black steed, who fiercely attacked the little Swaddler ;
but he drew his sword, and cut off the head of the rider
of the black steed. Then the little Swaddler, finding
that he was quite dead, tried to get the valuables he possessed ; but on searching him, he found only two combs
and a slim, silken purse, in which were Fionn Mac-
Cumhail's six teeth. He took possession of them, and
returned home.

One of the brothers asked him what he saw to-day
(that day) on his travels. He said that he did not see
anything that gave him pleasure, but the gloom of a
shower from the north-west, out of which came a rider
on a black horse. " He tried to cut off my head ; but I
drew my sword and separated his head from his body,"
said the little Swaddler.

" What treasure have you found upon him ?" they
asked.

" I only found two combs and a slim, silken purse, in
which there were six teeth," said he.

"Alas! alas!" said the tallest brother, "you never did any good for us before that is not equalled by the evil you have done us to-day. You have killed our father's only brother, who went abroad once a year, through every kingdom of the Universe to its remotest bounds, and returned to give us a history of everything that was taking place."

What the little Swaddler said to them was : "If the act that I performed is not pleasant to you, I will play the selfsame trick on yourselves."

Another of the brothers then said : " It has been long foretold that it would be the restorer of Fionn Mac-Cumhail's loss who would give us deliverance from all our warfare and conflicts."

The little Swaddler now said that he thought he would leave them, as he had found Fionn's Ransom. In reply, the brothers said they would give him a Black Steed that would ride the green ocean as though it were the fair grassy land. " And you will bring to our sister news of us, and make her your lawful wife."

The Little Man with the Steed then directed his face for Féinne Land, and in the dusk and twilight of that evening was with Fionn MacCumhail, to inquire from him and his foster brothers whether they had found the Ransom.

They all answered that they had not found it. He then drew out the slim, silken purse, with the Six Teeth contained in it, and said to Fionn : " Your Ransom is there, but your foster brothers did not get it for you."

EIRIG FHINN.

Aon uair chaidh Fionn 's a thriuir cho-dhaltan, an Ridire Dearg, Ridire 'Chuirn, 's Ridire 'Chlaidheimh, do 'n bheinn sheilg 's shuidh iad air cnocan boidheach breac, a ghabhail seallaidh, am fasgadh na gaoithe, 's fa chomhair na greine.

far am faiceadh iad fhéin h-uile duine 's nach fhaiceadh duine iad fhéin. Mar bha iad tacain 'nan suidhe an sin, thuirt Ridire 'Chlaidheimh, "Saoil mi an do choisich e talamh na 'n d' imich e an t-athar, fear aig an robh chridhe tàir na tarcuis a dheanamh air Fionn Mac Cumhail 's a thriuir cho-dhaltan còmhladh ris."

Mu 'n gann a so bha facal air radhainn, chunnaic iad dubhradh froise tighinn as an Aird 'n iar thuath, as an d' thainig fuaim siubhail seachad 's marcaiche steud' dhubh'. Rinn e direach far an robh Fionn 's bhuail e mu 'n bheul e, 's chuir e tri fiaclan as gu h-ard 's gu h-iosal. Dh' éirich Ridire 'Chlaidheimh sin, 's thuirt e gu'n deanadh an talamh lag 'na bhonn 's an t-athar nead 'na cheann, 's nach bu cheum tilleidh dha, "Gus am faigh mi Eirig Fhinn." Thubhairt an da cho-dhalta eile, an t-aon ceudna. Ghabh iad sin sios gu cladach, 's thòisich iad air uidheamachadh luing air son falbh. Cha robh iad fada aig an obair so 'nuair a chunnaic iad Fear Beag Iosal Lapanach a' teannadh air an aite 'san robh iad. Dh' fhàiltich iad e; 's dh' fharraid esan sin do Ridire 'Chlaidheimh am faigheadh e cead no comas falbh leo air an luing. Fhreagair Ridire 'Chlaidheimh:

"Cha'n fhaigh. De feum dheanadh duine leibideach coltach riutsa dh' fhalbh leinne le luing?"

Dh' fharraid e sin do Ridire 'Chuirn an robh doigh aige-san air gu 'm faigheadh e dol leo air an turus, ach thubhairt Ridire 'Chuirn, nach robh feum aca air duine mi-choltach mar bha esan air luing.

Chuir e sin a' cheist cheudna ris an Ridire Dhearg, 's fhreagair esan, gu 'm bu mhi-iomchuidh leithid sin do cheist a chur air-san.

"Co bhitheadh co dana 's gu 'n d' thoireadh iad ablach do chreutair lachduinn, leibideach coltach riutsa leo air luing gu cuan."

Dh' fhalbh e so gu Fionn 's dh' innis e dha gu 'n do dhiult iad sid uile e, 's dh' fharraid e dheth an leigeadh esan comhladh ris e.

"Leigidh," orsa Fionn; "'s fhearr thu na clach co dhiu."

Chuir iad mach an long. Thug iad toiseach ri muir 's

deireadh ri tìr; thog iad na siùil bhreaca bhaidealach an aghaidh
nan crannaibh fada, fulangach, fiùtha le soirbheas, beag, lagach
ciuin a bheireadh duilleach bharr chraoibh, seileach bharr bheann,
's fraoch òg as a bhun 's as a fhreumhaichean, 'cur na fairge
fiolcanaich falcanaich an leathoir chéin 's an leathoir fhaisg, 's an
fhaochag bheag cham chiar a bha seachd bliadhna air an aigeal
'toirt chuige chnag air a beul mòr, 's sad air a h-ùrlair. 'Se bu cheòl
's bu chànran doibh, sgiamhail easgann sgreadail fhiaclan, a'
bheist a bu motha ag itheadh na beist a bu lugha 's a 'bheist a bu
lugha 'deanamh mar a dh' fheudadh i. Ghearradh i an coinl-
ean coiree aig a ro-thoseach le feabhas a stiuirimiche 's dheanadh
Fionn Mac Cumhail iul 'na toiseach, stiuir 'na deireadh, 's
beairt 'na buillsgean, 's shuidhich iad a cùrsa air Rioghachd nam
Fear Mòra.

Mar bha iad da latha aig seòladh dh' iarr Fionn air Ridire
Chlaidheimh sealltuinn o 'n chrann am faiceadh e fearann.
Chaidh Ridire 'Chlaidheimh so astar beag suas, 's thill e nuas,
's thuirt e nach robh roinn no carrann ri fhaicinn. Dh' iarr
Fionn so air Ridire 'Chùirn dol dh' fheuchainn am faigheadh
esan sealladh air fearann 's chaidh esan suas astar goirid 'sa
chrann, 's thill e nuas, 's thuirt e nach robh sgathadh do thalamh
na do thuar 's an fhradharc. Dh' iarr an so Fionn air an
Ridire Dhearg sealltuinn uaithe am faiceadh e fearann, 's
cha deachaidh esan suas ach gle bheag astair 'sa chrann dar
a theirinn e, 's thuirt e nach robh fearann na fonn ri fhaicinn
's nach robh 'san t-sealladh ach muir 's athar. Dh' éirich so am
Fear Beag Iosal Lapanach, 's thuirt e riutha, "Mur deanadh
sibh na b' fhearr na sid bha e cheart co math dhuibh fuireach
far an robh sibh," 's leum e 's rainig e barr a' chroinn, 's mar
thill e air ais thuirt e ri Fionn:

"'Tha e mòr a dh' fheannaig, 's beag dh' fhearann; ach cum
romhad mar tha thu."

An latha 'r 'n ath mhaireach bha iad 'sa chaladh 'an Rioghachd nam Fear Mòra.

Mar ràinig iad an acairseid cha 'n fhaigheadh iad air tìr.
Bha tri Gathan Teinnteach 'cuairteachadh a 'chalaidh.

Sin chuir am Fear Beag Iosal Lapanach, sgiath bhucaideach, bhacaideach air a laimh chli 's air a laimh dheis, 's thug e

leum nan tri Eang a 's bha e air tir. Mar fhuair e fhein gu tir thug e Fionn 's a thri co-dhaltan ann cuideachd. Ghabh iad sin gu siubhal an Eilein 'nan ceathrar. Mar bha iad 'dol roimhe thachair riutha boirionnach mòr 's measan donn, builgeanta aig a sàil, 's h-uile h-uair a shealladh am measan air Fionn bhiodh na fiaclan 'dol ann mar bha iad riamh, 's mar 'thionndaidh am measan a chulthaobh bha na fiaclan falbh a Fionn. Shaoil an so na co-dhaltan aig Fionn gu 'n robh Eirig Fhinn aca, agus ghoid iad leo an Té Mhòr 's am Measan do 'n long, 's dh' fhag iad am Fear Beag Iosal Lapanach 's an Eilean.

Bha esan 'siubhal 's a 'sior imeachd roimhe, 's 'an dorchadh na h-oidhche chunnaic e bothan beag 's solus ann. Chaidh e stigh 's bha teine mòr ann an sin, ach cha robh duine roimhe. Cha robh e bheag 'sam bith a dh' ùine 'feitheamh 's ag eisdeachd mar thainig Duine Mòr dhachaidh 's thuirt e:

"Gu de naigheachd an Fhir Bhig Iosail Lapanaich?" Thuirt esan, nach robh naigheachd 'sam bith mur fhaigheadh e aig an Fhear Mhòr a thainig stigh i.

"Cha 'n 'eil mo naigheachd fhein ach bochd," ors' am Fear Mòr. "Tha mo phiuthar àluinn a nigheadh mi 'sa bhallan ionnlaid 'nuair a thiginn dhachaidh o chur a 'chath 's a bhithinn co sunndach an latha 'r 'n mhaireach dhol chur chath 's chomhraig 's a bha mi riamh, air toirt air falbh 's i air chall 's air seachran orm."

"Mur deanadh i ach sin dhuit," ors' Fear Beag Iosal Lapanach, "ma dh' fhaoidte gu'n dean mi fhein e," 's ghabh e sios 's nigh e 'sa bhallan-ionnlaid e, 's cha robh am fear ud riamh na b' aoibhneiche na bha e sin.

Thainig nis brathair eile dhachaidh, 's thuirt e 'nuair bha e stigh, "De naigheachd an Fhir Bhig Iosail Lapanaich?"

"Cha 'n 'eil bheag na mhòr do naigheachd agamsa," ors' am Fear Beag Iosal Lapanach, "mur faigh mi uait fhein i."

"Cha'n 'eil fath mo naigheachdsa ach trom," ors' am fear so. "Tha mo phiuthar ghradhach a nigheadh mi 'sa bhallan-ionnlaid 'san fheasgar an deighinn a chath, 's bhithinn an latha 'r 'n mhaireach co math 's a bha mi riamh, air toirt air falbh 's a measan donn builgeanta aig a sàil."

"Mur deanadh i ach sin," ors' am Fear Beag Iosal Lapanach,

"feudaidh mise amuis air," 's chuir e 'm Brathair Mòr so 'sa bhallan ionnlaid, 's nigh 's ghlan e e, 's an latha 'r 'n mhaireach bha e cheart co ùr dhol an chath 's a bha e riamh.

Thainig an ath-fhear dhiu sin rithist dhachaidh, 's thuirt e cheart seanachas a thuirt a bhràithrean.

"De sgeul an Fhir Bhig Iosal Lapanaich?"

"Cha 'n eil innseadh sgeoil 'sam bith agamsa," ors' esan. "Nach 'eil na 's fhearr aig an Fhear Mhòr làidir a thainig dhachaidh."

"Cha 'n eil mo chuid sgeoil-sa ach truagh," thuirt esan. "Tha mo phiuthar cheutach a nigheadh mi 'sa bhallan-ionnlaid dar thillinn o chur a' chath, 's bhithinn an la 'r 'n mhaireach na b' fhearr na bha mi riamh gu dol air m' ais a chath 's a chomhrag, air a toirt air falbh, 's bithidh mi nis gun chlì gun chomhairle."

"Mur deanadh i ach sin duit feudaidh mi fhein feuchainn ris," ors' am Fear Beag Iosal Lapanach, 's thug e do cheann eile an tighe e 's nigh 's ghlan e 'sa bhallan-ionnlaid e, 's an la 'r 'n mhaireach bha e na bu deise na bha e riamh roimhe air son cath 's comhrag a chumail.

An sin thuirt am Fear Beag Iosal Lapanach, "An leig sibh mise chur a' chath an nochd air 'ur son?"

Thuirt fear de na Braithrean ris, "A dhuine thruaigh! 'De tha thusa dol a dheanamh ann leat fhein dar tha iad cumail ruinne 'nar triuir?"

"Ach nach innis sibh dhomh gu de na bheil tighinn a chur dragh oirbh?" ors' am Fear Beag.

Fhreagair sin fear dhiu gu'n robh reisimeid shaighdearan 'tighinn 's ged chuireadh e an ceann bharr h-uile h-aon diu gu'n robh cailleach mhòr a thigeadh as a dheighinn, 's stòpan Ath-bheothachaidh aice, 's 'nuair a chuireadh i a meur as an stopan Ath-bheothachaidh 'nam beul, gu 'n èireadh h-uile aon diu beo.

"An dig ach sin?" ors' esan.

"Thig," ors' an Ath-fhear, "reiseamaid eile, 's cruitearan ciuil air an ceann, 's cuiridh iad sin 'nad chadal thu."

"An dig ach sin?" ors' esan.

"Thig," ors' Fear eile dhiu, "Bodach Mòr Uamhbhanta Gàbhanta a leagas tu 's a bheir uat do bheatha, mur cum thu cath oidhche ris, 's Cailleach mhòr 's ma gheibh i dluth dhuit marbhaidh a h-anail thu."

" An dig ach sin ?" ors' esan.

Thuirt iadsan nach tigeadh, 's fhuair e cead falbh an oidhche sin thun a' bhatail.

Mar ràinig e chunnaic e a'cheud reiseamaid 'tighinn, 's chaidh e 'm falach gus an deachaidh iad seachad, 's thainig e air an cùl thaobh 's mharbh e h-uile h-aon riamh dhiu. Chunnaic e nis Cailleach Mhòr, thar tomhais 'am meudachd, 'tighinn 's stòpan Ath-bheothachaidh 'na laimh, 's mar chunnaic esan i tighinn leig e e-fhein 'na shineadh 'san streath 'san robh na daoine marbh. Chuir ise a corrag as an stòpan Ath-bheothachaidh ann am beul an Fhir a bha laimh ris, 's leum e beo. Chuir i 'na bheul-san an ath-uair i, 's thug e dhith a' chorrag o 'n rudan. Ghlaodh ise :

" Gu'm bu tu Fear mu dheireadh de shliochd do mhathair dh' éiricheas de na bheil 'nan laidhe sin."

"Cha mhi, ach 's mi an darna Fear a dh' éiricheas," 's dh' éirich e 's thilg e na cinn dhiu le cheile, agus cha robh e sin ach uine ghoirid an deighinn am blar sin chur seachad tra chual' e na Cruitearan Ceolmhor sin tighinn 's an ath-reiseamaid casadh air. Bha e air a chlaoidh thairis 's e 'tuiteam 'na chadal; 's g'a chumail fhein 'na fhaireachadh, chàraich e ceann a chlaidheimh ri uchdan a choise 's a bharr ri 'mhalaidh, 's h-uile cnotach cadail a bha 'tighinn air, bha an claidheamh 'ga chumail 'na dhùsgadh ; 's mar thainig a' Bhuidheann Shaighdearan fagasg dha, ghabh e air an culthaobh 's mharbh e uile iad. Smaoinich e so nach biodh am Bodach Mòr ro fhada gun tighinn, agus thòisich e air deanamh toll farsuinn domhain anns an talamh, 's gu 'chur thairis le fiodh, 's le feur, 's le còinneich.

Dar bha e gu bhi cùrnaichte, 'an croma-ciar 's 'an trath-dhorcha an fheasgair thainig am Bodach Uambhanta Gabhanta mi-chuimseach mi-choimeasach ud, 's thoisich e fhein 's am Fear Beag Iosal Lapanach air cur a 'chath. Theann iad ri cheile gu garbh, gàbhaidh, 's àm 'san ruith dhluthaich iad air an fhosgladh a bha 'san làr, 's chaidh am Fear Mòr ann, 's fhuair esan cothrom air a cheann a thoirt dheth.

Beagan uine an deighinn so thainig a 'Chailleach bu Mhotha 's bu mhòr. 'Nuair bha i gu bhi laimh ris, bha a h-anail 'ga lagachadh ; dh' fheuch e co math 's a b' urrainn dha cumail uaithe, 's bha iad cluich chathadh chuid bu mhotha do 'n oidhche. Ann am briseadh soillcireachd an latha, mar dhùisg Fear do na Bràithrean, thuirt e ris fhein, "Feumaidh mis' eiridh, tha mi cinnteach gu bheil am Fear a chaidh a chur chath' air mo shon marbh o cheann fhada."

Thuirt Fear eile, "Cha 'n e sin 's duilghe dhuit ach gu'm bi do Rioghachd air a sgrios." Ach thuirt an treasa brathair riu uile : "'S fhearr dhuinn dol far am bheil iad 'cur a 'chath" 's a mach ghabh iad 's thug iad orra far an robh iad a' cluich bhatailibh. Air dhoibh ruigheachd, fhuair iad a' Chailleach mhòr 's Fear Beag Iosal Lapanach air toirt thairis, taobh air thaobh.

Thuirt Fear de na Braithrean, "O! nach d' thoir thu dhomh an claidheamh, feuch an cuir mi an ceann bharr na beiste."

Bho'n rinn mi fhein an troidh, ni mi an t-òirleach," ors' am Fear Beag Iosal Lapanach : "Ach cuir thusa do mheur anns an stòpan Ath-bheothachaidh ud thall, as cuir 'am bheul-sa sin i." Rinn e so, 's dar fhuair am Fear Beag Iosal Lapanach so, ghluais e 's sguab e 'n ceann bharr na Cailliche : 's bha i marbh !

Thog na Fir Mhòra leo dhachaidh e sin air an guaillean. Bha iad fuireach comhladh.

Aon latha chaidh am Fear Beag Iosal Lapanach mach air chuairt feadh a' mhonaidh, 's chunnaic e dubharadh froise 'tighinn as an Aird 'n iar thuath, as an d' thainig Marcaiche Steud dhubh, 's thug e garbh ionnsuidh air an Fhear Bheag Iosal Lapanach, ach tharruing esan a chlaidheamh 's chuir e 'n ceann de mharcaiche na steud dhubh. 'Nuair fhuair e marbh e, dh' fheuch e sin gu de na fiachan bha e giùlan. 'Nuair rannsaich e cha do thachair ris ach da chir, sporan seang, sìoda 's sia Fiaclan Fhinn 'ic Cumhail ann. Thill e dhachaidh 's sid aige.

Dh' fharraid Fear do na Braithrean, 'De chunnaic e 'n diugh air chuairt. Thuirt esan nach fhaca ni sam bith a thug toileachadh dha, ach dubhradh froise as an Aird 'n iar thuath as an d' thainig marcaiche steud dubh, "'S dh' fheuch e ris a' cheann a thoirt bharramsa ach tharruing mise mo chlaidheamh as sgar mi dheth-san an ceann," ors' am Fear Beag Iosal Lapanach.

"De fhuair thu 'na luib ?" ors' iadsan.

"Cha d' fhuair ach da chir, 's sporan seang sioda anns an robh Sia Fiaclan," ors' esan.

"Och! och!" ors' am Bràthair Mòr, "cha d' rinn thu do mhath riamh dhuinn nach d' rinn thu do chron an diugh, dar mharbh thu aon Bhrathair ar n-Athar a bha 'cur cuairt uair 'sa bhliadhna air uile Rioghachdan an Domhain diomhair 's a thigeadh a thoirt dhuinne eachdraidh air gach ni mar bha 'dol." 'Se thuirt am Fear Beag Iosal Lapanach riutha sin, "Mur 'eil an gniomh a rinn mi taitneach leibh, ni mi cheart chleas oirbh fhein."

Sin thuirt fear eile de na Braithrean, "'S fhada bho'n tha e 'san tailgneachd gur e Fear a thigeadh a thogail Éirig Fhinn 'ic Cumhail a bheireadh saorsa dhuinne ás gach cath as còmhrag.'

Thuirt am Fear Beag Iosal Lapanach gu'n robh e smaointeachadh air falbh nis bho 'n fhuair e Éirig Fhinn. Mu choinneamh sin thuirt na Bràithrean ris, gu'm faigheadh e uapa-san Steud dhubh a mharcaicheadh an cuan glas mar machaire geal sgiamhach, "'S bheir thu ar naigheachd-sa do 'r piuthar 's bitheadh i agad fhein 'na mnaoi phòsda."

Thug esan 's an Steud an aghaidh air an Fhéinn 's am bial an athaidh 's an fheasgair, bha e le Fionn Mac Cumhail a dh' fharraid dheth fhein 's de 'cho-dhaltan an d' fhuair iad an Eirig, 's fhreagair iadsan, nach d' fhuair. Thug esan mach an sporan seang sioda 's na Sia Fiaclan ann, 's thuirt e ri Fionn, "Tha d' Éirig an sin, 's cha d' rinn do cho-dhaltan 'fhaighinn dhuit."

NUMBERING OF DUVAN'S MEN.

(AIREAMH FIR DHUBHAIN.)

ACCORDING to popular lore, Duvàn (*Dubhan*) was a man
somewhere far away in the North (it is noticeable that
whenever the locality of a place is unknown, if it existed
at all. it is said to be in the Far North), and Fionn was
asked to his house. A plot was laid to destroy Fionn
and his men, and on this coming to the knowledge of
the daughter, she made an arrangement by which every
one of Dubhan's men were got out of the house, and
Fionn's men only were left in. The men were set in a
circle, and continuously counting, every ninth man was
made to rise and go out. This is a curious arithmetical
problem, and its existence, wherever it is to be found,
will be an important item in the question of races, and
where this class of tales had their origin.

The numeration is as follows :—

> " Four wild white men, at the beginning,
>   And five black next to them,
>   Of Duvàn's tall fighting men,
>   Two from MacCumal, anew ;
>   One from Dewan of reddish comeliness,
>   Three from Fionn of fairest appearance,
>   One from Devan of secret purposes.
>   Fionn will not sit in the Fair Fort
>   Without two black ones on one hand,
>   And two white ones by his side
>   Of the family of the King of Alban.
>   Two black ones about determined Duvàn,
>   One white one in their company,
>   Two smart black ones near these,
>   Two from Fionn and one from Duvàn."

" Ceathrar fear fionn fiadhaich air thùs,
Mar chòigear dhubha 'nan dail,
Do dh' fhearaibh àrd fir chogaidh Dhubhain,
Dithis o Mhac Cumhaill a nuadh,
Fear o Dhubhan dreach ruadh,
Triuir o Fhionn 's àillidh dreach,
Fear o Dhubhan diuramach,
Cha suidh Fionn anns a 'Bhrugh Bhàn,
Gun dithis dhubh' air a leth laimh,
'S gun dithis fhionna air a léis,
Do theaghlach Righ Albainn.
Dithis dhubh' mu Dhubhan dhil,
Aon fhear fionn 'na fhochair sin,
Da lasgair' dhubh 'nan dàil,
Dithis o Fhionn 's fear o Dhubhan."

Albainn is the present name of the kingdom of
Scotland, as distinguished from Ireland or England.
The terminal syllable seems merely to denote a region,
and the initial syllable "Alb" is perhaps connected with
Alpine, denoting a wild or mountainous region, and was
probably applied at first to some region bordering upon
the Highlands and Lowlands. Breadalbane means only
the heights of Alban; the word *braigh* denotes the
upper part of districts, the *d* being only accessory and
intercalated.

THE LAD WITH THE SKIN COVERINGS;

OR,

CEUDACH, SON OF THE KING OF THE COLLA MEN.

WHITE DEW, son of the King of Gold, and White
Hand, son of the King of France, and Ceudach, son of
the King of the Colla Men, were companions. Ceudach,
son of the Colla King, was a poor lad, but had every
accomplishment and gift befitting a King's son. One
day, when the three companions were returning home
driving a ball (shinty, or football playing, it does not
appear which) before them, the ball by chance went into
the house of a woman whose occupation was working at
silver-work, and destroyed the work. The scheme pro-
posed and agreed to by the three boys was, that he who
was standing nearest the door should go in to get the
ball. White Hand, son of the King of France, went
in, and roughly demanded the ball to be thrown out,
but the woman refused until she got payment from him
for the loss of the silver-work, saying to him, " More
than asking it is necessary, young man ; come in and
pay it." But he said to her, " You will keep it a long
time before I pay it."

White Dew, King of Gold's son, went in the same
way, and was equally unsuccessful in recovering the
ball. Then Ceudach went in gently where the woman
was bending over the fragments of her labour, and asked
modestly and cheerfully, with the utmost grace and
polish, that the ball be given back. It was returned to
him with a handful of gold and silver for his civility.
She then laid the three under crosses and spells, " That
you will fall back to back in the same battle."

"Up and down with your crosses and spells!" they said.

"Neither up nor down, but that same," she replied.

They then left, and were wandering about for some time, when they parted with each other amidst great sorrow and lamentations. On the hillock where they parted, they promised to meet again. In the long run, the promise was made good, and it was then agreed amongst them that they should go for the daughter of the King of the Iron City to be wife to White Dew, son of the King of Gold. The others were armed, but not Ceudach. When they reached the city, they found that it was surrounded by a wall with several gates on it. They were told that in front of the King's house there were twenty-score poles with a head on each pole with the exception of three, and that a great beast was guarding the palace. White Hand, son of the King of France, said he would go to see what the beast was like. He did not go very near it, when he hastily returned, and his companions asked what like it was. He said that its appearance was frightful, and no one could go near it. Then White Dew, son of the King of Gold, said he would go, that he was an armed warrior, and should not be daunted by any man or thing. He went, and if he did not keep further away, he did not go any nearer to the monster. Then Ceudach said he would go whatever would happen to him; they said, it was not very likely that he would succeed, unarmed, when they, in full panoply, could not go near. Ceudach said, he was never with a master who would not let him try what he could do. They said that their confidence in his success was but weak, but since he was so strong in his own opinion, he could go and try. Then he got the armour of White Hand, son of the King of France. When he reached the place he found the beast sleeping, and was stepping across it, when it awoke, and said to

him, " You must be a bold man to try and get past me
without asking leave ; it is not in that way you will get
in.　Well I know the object of your journey and travel ;
there are twenty-score posts in the fence before the
house, and only three of them empty ; many a human
countenance I have destroyed, and your head will be on
one of the posts to-night ; you will get no respite from
me ; take care of yourself." With that the Beast arose,
shook itself, and they attacked each other with such
fury that the sound of the wild slapping of the onslaught
was to be heard at a good distance.　The King's
daughter was at the window with sixteen of her attendant maidens, and on hearing the sounds of the
combat, she put her head out of the window, and was
watching what was going on.　In one of the throws,
Ceudach threw off the head of the great Beast, but it
was no sooner off than it flew on again.　The King's
daughter then called out, that when he got the head off
the next time, he was to hold the sword to the marrow-
bone of the Beast till the blood froze, and the head
would not go back on its neck again, and that would
kill it.

" Many a day," said the Beast, " I have been guarding
you, and if that is all the reward I am to get for defending
you so long, I will take off his head first and then
yours."

What happened was, that the head was swept off the
Beast and never went back on its neck again, and it
filled the three empty poles, or stobs, that were in the
fence before the house.

The other two came now to see what happened, or
what their chances were of getting the King's daughter.
She would only follow the one that killed the Beast, but
to prevent any ill-feeling amongst them, she took a fine
way, and made them a law that whoever of them would
enter at the same door with her would be the one that

she would follow, and in spite of all evil and mishaps, it
so chanced that Ceudach went in at the same door after
her. He had a knowledge of the "black art", and it was
by means of it that he was able to know the door at
which she had entered, rather than any of the other doors,
and they were married. The others were going to leave,
full of pride at being rejected by the King's daughter.
She said to them, at parting, that she was laying them
under crosses and spells, and the nine cow-spancels of the
fairy woman, the bald tricky calf (1), worse than its name,
to take off their heads without warning if they would not
meet together at the end of a year and a day, whether
they were alive or dead. When the others went away,
he thought of going to Fionn, where the Fians were idle,
but she advised him to remain where he was that night,
and before daylight she had a dress of skins without flaw
or fault ready for him (2).

When he put on the dress, she said, "May you enjoy
and wear your dress : your name will be The One with
the Skin Coverings" (3).

They went away together, and when they were
close upon the place where Fionn and his men were,
she asked to be allowed to make terms with Fionn.
He said that he had nothing to say against that (4).
When they reached, Fionn came to meet them, and asked
her what work her husband was good at. She answered,
that he could undertake to do one work well and three
badly, and that he was best at cookery. Fionn then
asked what wages he would want. He said that was
that his wife should get in amongst the Fian women.
Fionn then said to him, "I hold you in much esteem and
respect," and asked him his name. He said he was the Man
with the Skin Coverings (5). He began his work; there
were seven-score fires to be attended to (6) and nine tables,
with nine times nine men sitting at each table, and
Fionn's table over and above, and he was not missed at

any time. When he asked help for one who was able to give it, two would be worthless. Fionn went round the fires three times, and said he never saw better work.

One of the days a coracle was seen coming to the harbour in which there was only one woman, who on landing struck a challenge-note on a shield to send Fionn Mac Cumal instantly and smartly down to where she was, as she had a shirt that took her seven years and seven days to make for him. One of the attendants, some say it was Thinman (*Caoilte*), went down, and the shirt was tried on him. It fitted, and she asked if he was Fionn. He said, "Without doubt I am now." She then stuck a small knife in the prow of the coracle, and said to him, " If you can turn three times, standing on your heel, on the point of that knife, you are undoubtedly Fionn MacCumal." That one tried, but he was only able to make a half-turn, and she said, " I knew myself that you were not Fionn ; go up at once and quickly send down Fionn MacCumal here, that I may try on him the shirt that I have been so long making for him."

The Lad with the Skin Coverings was sent down this time (7) ; the shirt was tried on and it fitted very well.

" But if you are Fionn, stand on your heel, on the point of that small knife there, and turn round three times."

That one tried it, but he only turned round twice. " You are not Fionn, yet," she said ; " go up quickly, quickly, and send Fionn here, that I may try on him the shirt I have been so long making for him."

When it was told Fionn that she would take no denial, he said, "Whatever is to be done must be done."

When she saw Fionn she knew him at once ; she tried on the shirt, and it fitted him perfectly, then she told him to stand on the knife and turn round three times. He did this easily. " Without any doubt, you are Fionn," she said, and laid him under crosses and spells that he would go to her father's kingdom three times under these spells

and three times against them. She then went away, and
Fionn returned home and began to make ready.

In a year and a day the whole fleet of the Fians was
fitted out, and Fionn then cut down a tree, and made two
masts for a coracle ; when it was ready he went to the
wife of the Lad with the Skin Coverings and asked her
to allow her husband to go with them. " What request
could you make that would not be granted?" she said,
and that she would let him go away with him, on condition that he would bring him back alive or dead. When
she was parting with her husband, she said :

"You are going in search of the woman. I know and will
tell you who she is ; she is the daughter of a King Avack
Glùn Du, from the city of Camlisk, under Druidic spells.
You will be the one to guide them ; you will go in Fionn's
own ship, and when you are a day's sailing, you will go up
to the top of the mast and will see at some distance from
you the land of the Tutor of the Son of Avack Black
Knee, and on a white beach of sand,

> 'A little thickset man
> In a russet coat, bounding three times.'

He will have a magic keg upon his shoulder, and will be
casting it into the sea. You are not to be afraid of him,
but put your hands on your hips, jump ashore, and you
will of a certainty reach land ; then catch hold of the little
man, take from him the magic keg, and strike him down
to the waist in the soft sand; his death is not under the
heavens but in that way. You will take with you the
magic keg, and one who will steer you to the Kingdom
of Avack Black Knee (8), and when you reach the land,
the ships of the Tutor of the Son of Avack Black Knee
will come, then you will throw out the magic keg, and the
whole of the ships will be destroyed."

In this way everything occurred, and the Tutor's ships
were lost. Fionn then went away, he and his men of

war, to the King's Palace, and he struck a challenge note
on his shield. The King looked out and said, " Fionn
has come, and if he is on our side we will be the better
of it, but if he is against us it will be worse for us." The
King's daughter met them, and said, "You have come
sooner than we expected you."

"It is a good thing," Fionn said, "that everything that
is expected does not occur, otherwise I and my men
would have been lost to-day. I am here, as I was bound
to be ; and as you sought to take my life, I will now
take yours. Death is above you."

She then knelt to him, and asked him to spare her
life. He asked what she would give as a ransom (9) for
her life. She said that would be that she would assist him
any time when he was in danger or difficulty ; he
had only to remember her, and if he spared her life,
she would stand by him in right or wrong for ever.
Fionn said, " It is better to avoid wrong. Avoid
evil, and evil will avoid you," and that he would
spare her life, though she had not deserved much
kindness at his hands. He then turned away, he and
his men.

They had hardly left the harbour, when two ravens appeared above the boat in which he was. The Lad with the
Skin Coverings jumped up along with them, but it was
only after they were sailing some time that they missed
him. Fionn turned his ship and went in search of him ;
he sought him everywhere, not only once but twice ; the
third time he found him and the two others lying back
to back, dead, on a green sward, among the stones of
the shore, in the Kingdom of Avack Black Knee. Fionn
took him with him and returned to the place where the
Fians were resting. When he reached the shore the
Lad with the Skin Coverings' wife was before them.
She said to Fionn, " Have you him with you alive or
dead ?" He said, " It is his death I have."

" It is good to have him even in death," she said, and when she saw his dead body what she said was :

> " I would know you, though not by your dress,
> But by your goodly waving locks,
> And unless I tell lies,
> You are Ceudach, Son of the King
> Of the Colla men." (10)

Fionn then said, " I might easily have known that he was the only son of my father's brother."

She asked Fionn to leave him with herself, and she watched all night. At the dawn of the morning she saw a small coracle coming with two men in it, one in the bow and one in the stern, each with a sword throwing the other's head off; and when they were near the shore one of them said to the other, " Look at the dead man in front of the woman who is sitting on the rock." They came to land where she was, and she said to them, " Will you not try the small game of old on the man lying here?" (11) On this one of them threw the head off the body with his sword, and the dead man rose up alive and well as before. They recognised each other then, that they were those who went away together. Fionn with the whole host of the Fians met them and carried them shoulder high to Fionn's house, and the rejoicing on the occasion was the second greatest entertainment ever held among the Fians, and lasted seven days and seven nights.

GILLE NAN COCHLA CRAICIONN.

Bha Ceudach mac Righ nan Collach, 's Driuchd Gle-gheal mac Righ an Òir, 's Lamh Gle-gheal mac Ri na Frainge 'nan tri chompanaich. Cha robh ann an Ceudach mac Righ nan Collach ach duine bochd, ach bha h-uile oilean a dh' fheumadh a bhi aig mic righrean aige. Latha bha sin dar bha an triuir tighinn dachaidh ag iomain rompa, chaidh a' chniad stigh thaobh

tuiteamas do thigh te aig an robh obair airgid, agus bhristeadh
an obair airgid. 'Se an lagh rinn iad, 'nan triuir a so, am fear bu
teinne air an dorus gur esan rachadh stigh a dh' iarraidh na cniad.
Chaidh Lamh Gle-gheal mac Righ na Frainge stigh 's dh' iarr
e gu doirbh a' chniad chur a mach, ach, dhiult an té so a
dheanamh gus am faigheadh i paidheadh air son an obair airgid,
'se thuirt i ris, " Feumaidh tu tuille 's iarraidh dheanamh 'ille ;
thig stigh 's paidh e." 'Se thuirt esan rithe, " Cumaidh tu i
treis mu 'm paidh mise e."

Chaidh Driuchd Gle-gheal mac Righ an Oir stigh 'sa cheart
ruith, 's cha d' éirich dha ni na b' fhearr 's cha d' fhuair e 'chniad.
An sin chaidh Ceudach gu siobhalta stigh far an robh i crom
sealltuinn air na bloighean de 'n obair aice, is dh' iarr e gu
modhail suilbhir, 's gu ceannalta uasail, am faigheadh e a'
chniad air ais. Thug i dha air ais i 's làn aid' a dh' òr 's a dh'
airgiod air son a mhodhalais. Chuir i sin an triuir aca fo
chroisean 's fo gheasan, " Gu 'n tuit sibh cùl ri cùl 'san aon
chath."

" Sios 's suas do 'd gheasan," thuirt iadsan.

" Cha sios 's cha suas ach mar sid," thuirt ise.

Dh' fhalbh iad sin 's bha iad 'siubhal 's ag imeachd greis,
's dhealaich iad a' tuireadh 's a' caoidh. Air a 'chnoc air an
do dhealaich iad rinn iad cumhnanta gu 'n tachaireadh iad
a ris. Ri ùine thachair so. Chuir iad sin an cinn ri cheile
gu 'm falbhadh iad a dh' iarraidh nighean Righ na Cathrach
Iaruinn air son a bhi 'na bean do Dhriùchd Gle-gheal mac
Righ an Òir. Bha armachd aig an dithis eile ach cha robh
aig Ceudach. Dar rainig iad am baile mòr, bha e air
chuairteachadh le balladh air an robh geatachan. Chaidh
innseadh dhoibh gu 'n robh fichead a dh' fhicheadan stob air
beul-thaobh tigh an Righ agus ceann air h-uile stob dhiu
sin ach tri, 's gu 'n robh Béist mhòr a' cumail dion air an tigh.
Thuirt Lamh Gheal mac Righ na Frainge gu 'n rachadh esan a
shealltuinn co ris a bha a' bhéist coltach. Cha deachaidh esan
ro theann oirre 'nuair thill e ann an cabhaig, 's dh' fheoraich
a chompanaich dheth co ris a bha i coltach. Thuirt e riu gu 'n
robh coltas uamhasach oirre 's nach b' urrainn h-aon 'sam bith
dol mar astar dhith. Thuirt Driuchd Gle-gheal mac Righ an

Oir gu 'n robh e 'na ghaisgeach fo armachd 's nach bitheadh eagal air roimh ni no neach. Dh' fhalbh e 's mur e a b' fhaide dh' fhan uaipe cha'n e bu teinne a chaidh oirre. Thuirt Ceudach so gu'n rachadh esan ann 'de 'sam bith dh' éireadh dha. Thuirt iadsan nach robh e ro-choltach gu 'm buaidheachadh esan 's e gun airm 'sam bith dar nach b' urrainn iadsan 's iad fo lan armachd dol g' a còir. Thuirt Ceudach, nach robh e riamh le maighstir nach leigeadh leis fheuchain 'de b' urrainn da dheanamh. Thuirt iadsan nach robh am beachd mu dheighinn ach fann, ach bho'n bha e co daingean 'na bheachd fhein gu feudadh e dol ann 's fheuchain. Thug Lamh Gle- gheal mac Righ na Fraing dha armachd fhein sin. Dar rainig e 'n t-aite fhuair e 'n Uile-bheist 'na cadal, 's dar bha e toirt ceum thairis oirre dhuisg i 's thuirt i ris, " Feumaidh gu bheil thu misneachail dar tha thu feuchain ri faighinn seachad ormsa gun chead iarraidh, cha 'n anns an doigh sin a gheibh thu stigh : 's math 's aithne dhomhsa ceann do sheud 's do shiubhail. Tha fichead a dh' fhicheadan stob anns an rathad mu choinneamh an tighe, 's cha 'n 'eil ach tri dhiu falamh ; 's iomadh gnuis a mharbh mise riamh, 's bithidh do cheannsa air fear do na stuib am màireach ; cha 'n fhaigh thu fathamas 'sam bith bhuamsa ; bi deanamh air do shon fhein."

Leis a sin dh' éirich an Uile-bheist 's chrath i i fhein, 's chaidh iad an caramh a cheile co searbh 's gu 'n robh slachd- artaich na comhraig ri chluinntinn fad as cian air astar. Bha nighean an righ le sia deug g' a maighdeanan coimheadach aig an uinneig, 's dar chualaic i farum na h-iorghuill chuir i a ceann mach, 's bha i 'ga fheitheamh. Ann an h-aon do na ionnsuidhnean thilg Ceudach an ceann bharr a' Bheist mhòir, ach cha bu luaithe bha e dhith na leum e air rìs. Ghlaodh nighean an Righ ris dar gheibheadh e an ceann deth an ath uair e chumail a' chlaidheamh fhuar ris an smìor-chailleach aig an Uile-bheist gus an reodhadh an fhuil, 's nach rachadh an ceann air amhaich tuille, 's gu marbhadh sin e. " 'S iomadh latha tha mi 'gad dhion, ma 's e sin an duais a tha mi dol a dh' fhaighinn air a shon, bheir mi an ceann dheth-san an toiseach, 's sin bheir mi dhiotsa e."

'Se mar thachair gu 'n deachaidh an ceann thoirt thar an

Uile-bheist 's cha deachaidh e tuille air an amhaich. Lion e na
tri stuib a bha falamh air beul-thaobh an tighe, 's thainig so an
dithis eile a ghabhail sealladh air mar bha cùiscan dol na co de'n
triuir a dh' fheudadh ise fhaighinn. Cha ghabhadh ise ach am
fear a thug an ceann bhar na Uile-bheist, 's chum 's nach biodh
mi-thlachd air fear seach fear dhiu, ghabh i doigh ghrinn ; rinn
i lagh dhoibh, gur e fear 'sam bith rachadh stigh air an dorus air
an rachadh ise, gur e sin am fear a leanadh i, 's dh' aindheoin
gach uile 's sgiorradh mar thachair 'se Ceudach chaidh stigh 'na
deighinn. Bha an Sgoil Dubh aige-san 's leis so bha fios aige
air an dorus air an deachaidh ise stigh, seach aon de na dorsan
eile, agus chaidh am pòsadh. Bha an fheadhainn eile so 'dol a
dhealachadh ris, lan àrdain nach d' fhuair iad fhein nighean
an righ. Thuirt ise sin 'san dealachadh gu 'n robh i 'gan cuir fo
chroisean 's fo gheasan 's fo naoi buaraichean na mna sìth,
laogh maol carach na 's miosa na 'ainm, a thoirt chinn gun
chosnadh dhiu mur coinnicheadh iad comhla an ceann latha
's bliadhna c'dhiu bhiodh iad beo no marbh. Dar dhealaich an
dithis eile, smaointich esan air dol dh' ionnsuidh Fhinn far an
robh an Fheinn 'nan tamh, ach dh' iarr ise air fuireach far an
robh e 'n oidhche so, 's mu 'n d' thainig fàire na maduinn,
bha deise chraicnean gun mhear gun uireasbhuidh aice deas dha.
Dar chuir i air an deise thuirt i ris, " Gu' m meal 's gu 'n caith
thu do dheise ; 's tu fear nan Cochulla Craicinn." Dh' fhalbh
iad comhla, 's dar bha iad teann air an aite 'san robh Fionn 's a
chuid dhaoine, dh' iarr ise gu' m faigheadh i fhein cumhnant a
dheanamh ri Fionn. Thuirt esan nach robh esan 'cur dad an
aghaidh sin. Dar rainig iad thainig Fionn 'nan coinneamh
's dh' tharraid e 'de an obair bha an duine aice math air, 's
fhreagair i gu'n gabhadh e os laimh aon obair a dheanamh gu
maith 's tri gu dona, 's gur e còcaireachd a b' fhearr e air. Dh'
fharraid Fionn so gu de an duais a bhiodh e 'g iarraidh, 's thuirt
e gu'm b'e gu'm bitheadh uaigneas mnathan na Feinne da mhnaoi.
Thuirt Fionn ris, " 'S mòr do mhiadh 's do mheas agam," 's
dh' fharraid e 'ainm. Thuirt esan gum b' e Fear nan Cochulla
Craicinn. Thòisich e air obair. Bha seachd fichead teine
aige ri fhreasdal dhoibh, agus naoi bùird 's naoi naoinear
'nan suidhe aig h-uile bòrd, agus bòrd Fhinn air chul-thaobh

sin, 's cha d' fhairich iad uapa aig àm 'sam bith e. 'Nuair dh' iarradh e cuideachadh air son h-aoin a bheireadh, bha dhà nach b' aithne. Chaidh Fionn mu 'n cuairt nan teineachan tri uairean 's thuirt e nach fhaca e obair riamh a b' fhearr.

Latha do na laithean chunnaic iad curachan beag tighinn do 'n chaladh 's cha robh innte ach aon bhoirionnach, 's dar thainig i air tir bhuail i beum sgèithe, Fionn Mac Cumhaill a chur nuas gu tapanta far an robh ise, gu'n robh leine aice a bha i seachd lathan 's seachd bliadhna 'deanamh air a shon. Chaidh fear de na gillean fridhealaidh sios, 's chaidh an léine fheuchain air, 's fhreagair i dha, 's dh' fharraid ise dheth am b' esan Fionn.

Thuirt esan, " 'S mi gun teagamh a nis." Chuir ise sin sgian bheag ann an toiseach a' bhata, 's thuirt i ris, " Ma chuireas tu tri chuir dhiot air shàil air barr na sgéine sin, 's tu gun teagamh Fionn Mac Cumhaill."

Dh' fheuch am fear ud ri sud a dheanamh, 's cha do chuir e dheth ach bloigh cuir, 's thuirt ise, " Thuig mi fhein nach bu tu Fionn ; rach suas gu luath 's cuir nuas gu tapanta Fionn Mac Cumhaill 's gu 'm feuchainn uime an léine tha mi co fada deanamh air a shon."

'N uair so chaidh Fear nan Cochulla Craicinn chur sios 's chaidh an léine fheuchain uime, 's fhreagair i gle mhath dha. " Ach ma 's tu Fionn seas air do shail air an sgian bheag sin a sin, 's cuir car tri uairean dhiot." Dh' fheuch am fear ud 's cha do chuir e ach da char dheth. " Cha tu," ors' ise, " Fionn fhathast ; rach suas gu ealamh, ealamh 's cuir nuas Fionn Mac Cumhaill so 's gu 'm feuchainn-sa air an léine a tha mi co fada deanamh air a shon." Dar dh' innis iad do dh' Fhionn nach gabhadh i diùltadh, thuirt e, " Na tha ri dheanamh feumaidh e dheanamh." Dar chunnaic ise Fionn dh' aithnich i 'am priobadh na sùl e ; dh' fheuch i an léine air 's fhreagair i dha gun mhear gun uireasbhuidh, 's dh' iarr i air seasamh air an sgian 's trì chuir chur dheth air a shàil. Rinn e so gu réidh.

" Gun teagamh 's tusa, Fionn," 's chuir i fo chroisean 's fo gheasan e gu'n rachadh e do rioghachd a h-athar " tri uairean air mo bhuadhas 's tri uairean air mo dhimeas!" Leis a sin dh' fhalbh i, 's thill Fionn dhachaidh 's thòisich e air deanamh deas.

An ceann latha 's bliadhna bha cabhlach na Féinne 'na h-uidheam. Leag Fionn sin craobh 's chuir e da chrann 'sa cauarachan. Dar bha i deas chaidh e dh' ionnsuidh bean fear nan Cochulla Craicinn, a dh' iarraidh oirre a leigeil air falbh comhla ris. Thuirt i ris, " Tha thu dol air tòir na mnà, tha fios agamsa 's innsidh mi dhuit co i, is i nighean Abhaig Ghlùn Dubh, a Cathair na Camluisg fo dhruidheachd ; 's tusa ni iùl dhoibh ; bithidh tu 'san aona bhàta ri Fionn, 's dar bhitheas tu latha aig seòladh togaidh tu fearann Oide Abhaig Ghlùn Dubh 's air an traigh gheal ghaineamhaich,

> ' Fear beag iosal lapanach
> Le cota lachdunn nan tri eang,'

's inneal druidheachd aige air a ghualainn' ga chaitheamh' san fhairge ; na biodh eagal 'sam bith agad roimhe, ach cuir do lamhan an ceanna do leis, 's leum air tir agus 's cinnteach gu 'n ruig thu ; 's beiridh tu air an fhear bheag 's bheir thu uaithe an inneal druidheachd 's càiridh tu e ann an comhair a chinn gus an teis meadhon anns an t-sughanaich ghaineich, cha 'n eil a bhàs fo adhar ach 'san doigh sin. Bheir thu sin leat am buideal druidheachd, 's fear a stiuireas tu gu rioghachd Abhaig Ghlùn Dubh, 's dar bheir thu mach fearann thig soithichean Oide Abhaig Ghlùn Dubh, 's caithidh tu mach an inneal druidheachd, 's bithidh iad uile air an call."

'S ann mar sin thachair dhoibh air a' cheanna mu dheireadh, 's chaidh soithichean Oide Abhaig Ghlùn Dubh a chall. Mach ghabh Fionn 's a chuid feachd gu tigh an Righ. Bhuail e beum sgeithe. Sheall an Righ mach 's thuirt e, " Tha Fionn air tighinn 's ma 's ann leinn a bhitheas e, 's fheairde sinn e, 's ma 's ann' nar n-aghaidh, 's misde sinn e."

Thainig nighean an righ 'nan còmhdhail 's thuirt i, " Thainig sibh na bu luaithe na bha fiughair ribh."

" 'S math," ors' Fionn, " nach tachair na bheil fiughair ris, air neo bhithinn-sa 's mo chuid dhaoine air ar call an diugh, tha mi so mar dh' fheumainn a bhi 's ma tha thusa air son mo bheatha thoirt dhiom bheir mise nis dhiotsa do bheatha, ' Bàs os d' chionn.'" Chaidh ise air a glùn dha dh' iarraidh air a beatha 'chaomhnadh dh' i. Dh' fharraid esan gu de éirig a beatha, 's

thuirt i gu'm b' e sin gu 'm bitheadh i leis uair sam bith a bhiodh
e 'n càs no 'n éiginn, 's na 'm mathadh e a beatha dhi nach biodh
aige ach cuimhneachadh oirre 's gu 'n seasadh i e 'n còir 's an
eacoir gu bràth. Thuirt Fionn gum b' fhearr an t-olc sheachn-
adh, "seachuinn an t-olc 's seachnaidh an t-olc thu," 's gu
'm mathadh e a beatha dhi ged nach do choisinn i moran
caoimhneas uaith-san. Thill Fionn air falbh, e fhein 's a chuid
dhaoine, 's cha robh iad ach air togail o 'n chaladh dar nochdadh
dà fhitheach os cionn a' bhata anns an robh e. Leum fear nan
Cochulla Craicionn suas comhla riu, 's 'sann dar a bha iad
tacan aig seòladh 'sann dh' fhairich iad 'gan dith e, 's
thill Fionn an soitheach mu 'n cuairt, 's chaidh e air a thòir, 's
dh' iarr e 'sa h-uile ait' e fo h-aon 's fo dhà. An treas uair
fhuair e e fhein 's an fheadhain eile cùl ri cùl marbh air lianag
ghorm, 'an clachan a 'chladaich ann an Rioghachd Abhaig Ghlùn
Duibh. Thug Fionn leis e 's thill e thun an aite 'san robh an
Fhéinn 'nan tàmh. Dar rainig iad an cladach bha 'bhean aig
Fear nan Cochulla Craicionn air thoiseach orra, 's thuirt i ri
Fionn, " A 'bheil a bheo no 'mharbh agad dhomh?"

"Se a bhàs a th' agam," thuirt esan.

" 'S math marbh fhein," thuirt ise, 's dar chunnaic i marbh e
'se thuirt i,

> " Dh' aithn'inn thu 's cha b' ann air éideadh,
> Ach 'sann air chùl ceudach clannach,
> 'S mur athris mi na breugan
> 'S tu Ceudach mac righ nan Collach."

Thuirt Fionn sin, " B' fhurasd' dhomh aithneachadh gur e
aon mhac bràthar m' athar a th' ann."

Dh' iarr ise air Fionn 'fhagail aice fhein, 's dh' fhuirich i sin
fad na h-oidhche. Ann an soilleireachadh an latha chunnaic i
curachan beag 'tighinn 's dithis dhaoine innte. Bha fear 'san
toiseach 's fear 'san deire, 's claidheamh an t-aon aca 's iad 'tilgeil
nan ceann bhar a 'cheile. Dar thainig iad teann air a' chladach,
thuirt an darna fear ris an fhear eile, "Seall," ors' esan, " an
duine marbh a th' air beul-thaobh a' bhoirionnaich a tha 'na
suidhe air a' chreig."

Thainig iad air tir far an robh i, 's thuirt i riu, " Nach feuch
sibh an cleas beag o chian air an fhear a tha 'na laidhe so?"

Aige so thilg fear dhiu an ceann òhar na coluinn leis a
chlaidheamh 's dh' éirich an duine marbh suas beo slan mar bha
e roimhe.   Dh' aithnich iad a cheile, gur an fheadhainn a dh'
fhalbh comhla bh' ann.   Thainig Fionn 's a chuid dhaoine 'nan
coinneamh, 's thog iad air bharraibh an guaillean iad suas gu
tigh Fhinn, agus b' i sin an darna cuirm bu mhotha bha 'san
Fhéinn riamh, 's mhair i seachd lathan 's seachd oidhchean.

An imperfect version of the foregoing story, "The Sons
of the Three Kings", which the writer has, says they were
White Dew, son of the King of Gold, Lion, son of the
King of France, and Ceudach, son of the King of the
Colla men.   When the school was dismissed, they were
in the habit of playing shinty, and Ceudach said he
would drive the ball against all the rest of the school.
The ball was of gold and the clubs of silver.   A match
was played, and Ceudach won.   They played for several
days, and every game was won by him, without their
being able to turn one stroke of his.   A woman who
had been standing watching the play, came to him and
said:

"I lay you under crosses and charms that you will
never marry anyone but myself."

"Lift off me your crosses and charms," he said: "I
cannot keep you, and I do not want you."

She would not loosen him.   Upon this he went to a
tailor, and got a suit of skin made for himself, to see if
she would not leave him when she saw him meanly clad.
She would not, however, part with him, and said:

"May you enjoy your name, My Lad with the Skin
Covering."

He then went to Fionn MacCumhaill, of whom he
heard that he would give employment to anyone with

suitable qualifications. When he reached they welcomed each other (*bheannaich esan Fionn, 's bheannaich Fionn e*). Fionn asked his news; he said he had none, but was seeking employment. Fionn asked him what trade he followed and what work he could do. He said he would leave the Féinn with one stocking and one shoe on, and he would be so long before them in the farthest-off point of Ireland that he would have meat and tents ready for them when they reached. Fionn then asked what wages he wanted.

"That I be the first person to whom you will tell what causes you trouble or anxiety, and that my wife will be in the best company of wives of the Féinn, and that when the men arrive I take the other shoe off them."

On a good day soon after this, Fionn said:

"We will make trial whether you can perform what you said."

The Lad with the Skin Covering left the Féinn with one shoe and one stocking on, and when they reached the farthest-off point of Ireland they found tents ready before them, and meat. He went to take the shoe off, and took off the foot along with the shoe.

— —   — —

Notes.

(1.) The terms of the spell call for attention, the prominence given to the calf appears in several noticeable cases. The instance among the Jews of the descent of Moses after receiving the law of finding the people engaged in worshipping a golden calf is well known; it was not the gold that attracted the people's adoration, but the calf. Among the ancient Egyptians, the ox was an object of worship, and it is matter worthy of inquiry and speculation whether this spell does not bear traces of the same origin, and, if so, why?

(2.) Some say the dress was made of every sort of skin, others say it was made of sheep-skin only, and others of goat-skin.

(3.) In the Highlands it is not deemed fortunate for the wearer of a dress, when it is newly put on, that it should be a woman who would wish him first the usual compliment of his enjoying and wearing it. In Tiree, even at the present day, when a person puts on a new suit for the first time, a woman meeting him says: " Have they said it to you?" ("*An d' thuirt iad riut e?*"), meaning, Has the compliment been already paid by a man? When the suit is tried on by the tailor, and found fitting, the tailor himself, if he is up to his work, will say it, as his own work is completely finished. In this story all the evils that afterwards followed are ascribed to the woman's having been too forward in using the expression. It is said in some places that a married woman, whose firstborn is a son, can use the expression harmlessly with the addition of " I may say it" ("*Faodaidh mise a rádhain*").

(4.) In one version, it is said, he put on a dark skin-dress, so that he might not be recognised by Fionn (*Bha e air son e fhein chumail do-aithnichte do dh' Fhionn*).

(5.) It is said he was a near relative of Fionn's.

(6.) Another version says there were twenty score fires and twenty score men round each fire.

(7.) Some also say that Dermid was the one sent the second time.

(8.) Black Knee is a name that occurs also in the history of the MacGregors.

(9.) The word Eirig, which is here translated Ransom, and which occurs several times in these stories about Fionn, denotes a recompense, or the equivalent payment for which one's liberty is given to him, or by which his character is vindicated from any stain or reproach, or injury done to it, or aspersion thrown on it. In the Book of Job the equivalent is redemption, denoting merely freedom from the trials and misunderstandings that afflicted that estimable and sorely tried old man.

(10.) This was the first time that Fionn heard who he was. The King of the Colla men was his own father's brother, and this Ceudach would be his own cousin-german.

There is another story called " The Lad with the Skin Covering", which has no connection with the Fians. It has been thought best, however, to retain the name used by the reciter of the tale here given. In making inquiry about this section of the Fian host, the name closely resembles the name given to the inhabitants of the neighbouring island of Coll, and a person of whom inquiry was made regarding the tale said :

" The Coll men with a King !—they never had and never will
have a King to themselves."

(11.) Another version says, "Will you not let me see the game of
ancient?" ("*Nach leig thu fhaicinn dhomh an cleas o chian?*").

As to extracting anything historical from these tales
and poems, or even to fix the time of the Fians, the
attempt would be useless. One cannot but be struck by
the prominence given to sword exercise, and the limit-
less extent of territory over which the Fians had scope.
The Gaelic proverb forces itself upon one's mind, that
suppositions are not sound sense (*cha chiall na saoilsinnean*).
One thing is clear, that the Fians were of heathen belief,
and the mind is set wondering as to how Christianity
made its way so early to so remote a place as Ireland,
and how Irish manuscripts are so superior. If Jonah
was for taking ship to fly out of the known limits of the
world, that is, beyond the Straits of Gibraltar to Tarshish,
or the land north of Spain, it is by no means improbable
that persecution made Christianity at the very earliest
time spread itself abroad. An ancient name for Ireland
is Inisfail, and Innis, though rendered in dictionaries 'an
island', means, in ordinary names, 'a place of shelter', such
as were used near villages and growing towns for the
milking of cattle.

In Ardnamurchan, in the woods, and untouched by
water, there is a place called *Innis-na-feoraig*, the
squirrel's place of shelter ; and the celebrated Insh of
Perth is not caused by the winding of the Tay and must
have derived its name from the place having been used
for the milking of cattle, when Perth was a growing
village. To fall back upon the Irish name, the last
account we have of Paul from his own writings is that
he intended next summer to go to Spain. The religious

persecutions have made men cross angry seas, and betake themselves to remote situations, even when not so severe as we hear of in early Christian times. We are told that under the Roman Emperors Christians were smeared over with tar, and set on fire at street-corners to make the streets clear at night. It is therefore not at all unlikely that men of wealth and means fled or made their way to places the most remote, to avoid such terror and cruelty. That they should be accompanied by scribes or people whose profession it was to increase copies of the law by handwriting, is not an unlikely supposition. When Iceland was discovered by the Norsemen in the year 874, copies of books, bells, and other ecclesiastical articles were found by them, which they ascribed to people from Ireland, or the Western Islands, having visited the place (see Mallet's edition of *Percy's Northern Antiquities,* p. 189). Bad news proverbially travels fast, and any report of the cruelties inflicted on the early Christians would make people fly to the earth's remotest bounds. Even in modern times the smaller, and comparatively harmless, persecutions made people cross to America or Pennsylvania. In this way the early Christian refugees may have taken shelter in Ireland, and from thence spread the tenets of their religion. Some Irish families are said to derive their origin from Palestine.

That the Fians ended their existence with the introduction of Christianity is clear and evident whence or whenever they originated, and Ossian's daughter being married to Patrick of the Psalms is a confirmation of the opinion. The date of this Patrick, who he was, or where he came from, is not a matter on which much weight can be placed.

Before parting with this subject, it is but just to speak highly of Macpherson, by whom these compositions were first brought before the attention of the world. Without entering at all upon the controversy which the authenticity and genuineness of the work he published raised, he himself was possessed of high literary talent ; and if, nowadays, his works seem overstrained and " foolish", it was only that he followed the fashion of the times. Macpherson was himself a native of Badenoch, which was one of the most inaccessible, rugged, and wild districts in the Highlands. He is accused of ignorance of Gaelic, but unjustly. His having broken down all prejudices, and attracted the attention of the most learned men, and those of finest taste and most acute judgment, shows him to have been possessed of no mean gifts. That he was buried in Westminster Abbey at his own request, and that he said he would be ashamed to imitate what he could not compose, is capable of different interpretations, and might lead one into the heat of the controversy.

All that the writer has to say on the subject is that the work here published is entirely from oral sources, without any straining to make it resemble the works of either Greece or Rome, or any other work, ancient or modern.

BIBLIOGRAPHICAL NOTES.

[In the following notes, MacInnes, refers to Vol. II of the present series : "Argyllshire Folk and Hero Tales," edited by the Rev. D. MacInnes, with Notes by Alfred Nutt : L. na F., refers to "Leabhar na Feinne", heroic Gaelic ballads collected in Scotland chiefly from 1512 to 1871, arranged by J. F. Campbell ; MS. Mat., to E. O'Curry's "MS. Materials for Irish History" : M.C., to the same author's "Manners and Customs, etc."; D'Arbois de Jubainville, to the "Essai d'un catalogue de la littérature épique de l'Irlande". All references to Campbell alone are to the "West Highland Tales".]

P. 6. Conlaoch and Cuchullain. Four versions in *L. na F.*, pp. 9-15 : (*a*) Dean of Lismore's Book ; (*b*) Kennedy ; (*c* Gillies ; (*d*) Irvine. The present version is closest to Gillies. The only other complete translation of any of the Gaelic texts is in Miss Brookes, pp. 9-23. See D'Arbois de Jubainville, p. 16, for a list of the Irish MSS. The oldest Irish text is in prose, in the 14th-15th cent. MS. H. 2, 16, col. 955-57, and there Conlaoch is called Enfir Aife. The 10th century Irish poet, Cinaed hua Artacain, mentions Oinfer Aife in his poem on the heroes of Erin, *Book of Leinster*, p. 31.

Our story forms a kind of continuation to that of Cuchullain's education as it is found in the Tochmarc Emer, or Cuchullain's Wooing of Emer. In the oldest redaction we have of this text, edited and translated by Prof. Kuno Meyer, *Rev. Celt.*, xi, 433 *et seq.*, and ascribed by him to the eighth century, we read as follows concerning Aife : "Then she said she was pregnant. She also said that it was a son she would bear, and that the boy would come to Erin that day seven years. And he left a name for him" (p. 451). The second redaction of the Tochmarc Emer, ascribed by Prof. Meyer to the 11th century, and translated by him in the first volume of the *Archæological Review*, adds : "Cuchullain left a golden finger-ring for him, and said to her that he should go and seek him in Erinn when the ring would fit on his finger. And he said that Conla was the name to be given to him, and told her that he should not make himself known to anyone, that he should not go out of the way of any man, nor refuse combat to any man" (*A. R.*, i, p. 352). I think there is no reasonable ground for doubting that the story of

Cuchullain and Conlaoch, substantially as related in the later
texts, was current in Ireland prior to Cinaed hua Artacain,
i.e., in the early 10th century; for my own part, I believe the
story to be as old at least as the oldest redaction of the
Tochmarc Emer, *i.e.*, to date back to the eighth century on
Irish ground; but this is an inferential belief only.

The combat between father and son is found on Teutonic
soil at the latest in the eighth century; the MS. date of the
fragment of Hildebrand and Hadubrand is *circa* 800, and
the fragment presupposes an older written copy, which itself
presupposes a ballad orally transmitted (Kögel, in *Paul's
Grundriss*, ii, p. 180). But the situation is by no means
similar to that in the Irish story; for instance, Hadubrand
imagines that his father is dead. On the other hand, the
situation in our text resembles that in the episode of Sohrab and
Rustem in the *Shahnameh* (accessible to all in Matthew Arnold's
exquisite version). Firdusi, born 939, died 1030, compiled the
Shahnameh from older traditions. It seems impossible to
admit direct influence of the Persian upon the Celtic version,
and I see no reason for doubting that the three stories (Persian,
Teutonic, Celtic) are variants of a pan-Aryan heroic legend.
Full references to the spread of the father and son combat
in the romantic literature of the Middle Ages will be found in
Warnke's edition of *Marie de France* (Halle, 1885), R. Köhler's
note to *Milun*, p. xcvi *et seq.*

As Milun and the lay of Doon, which resembles it very
closely, are the only two other instances on Celtic soil of this
theme which are of anything like the same antiquity as the
story of Cuchullain and Conlaoch, they deserve some attention.
Milun, like the other lays of Marie de France, must be ascribed
in its present form to the last quarter of the twelfth century.
Marie herself places the *locale* in the British Isles, and describes
Milun as a South-Welsh prince; and it seems reasonable to
hold that she heard the story in Wales. Milun loves a lady
secretly, when they part he leaves a ring with her. She bears
a son, and, later on, he meets his father in a tournament, over-
throws him, recognition follows by means of the ring, and the
three personages are reunited. Dates alone forbid the supposition that the Irish story is due to Marie's lay, even if the
latter were obviously not a weakened version of the theme,
which the Gaelic story represents, on the contrary, in its full
tragic power. I do not think one can say more at present than
that the combat of father and son was a favourite subject
among both branches of the Celtic race; but if there has been
borrowing on the one side or the other, the Gaels have a far
better claim to be considered the lenders than the Kymry.

P. 8. Deirdre. A translation of the modern folk-tale printed in the *Transactions of the Inverness Soc.*, xiv, may be found in the *Celtic Mag.*, xiii. Of the old Irish heroic tale two forms are known : (*a*) the text of the *Book of Leinster*, compiled in the middle of the 12th cent. from older MSS., printed by Windisch in the first series of the *Irische Texte* (pp. 67-82), and translated into French by M. Ponsinet, *Revue des Traditions populaires*, iii, pp. 201-7. A text, printed and translated by T. O'Flanagan (*Transactions of the Gaelic Society of Dublin*, 1808, pp. 146-177), agrees substantially with this. (*b*) The text printed and translated in *Irische Texte*, ii, 2, pp. 109-178, by Mr. Whitley Stokes, from a 15th cent. MS. O'Flanagan gives a very similar version (*l.c.*, pp. 16-135). Cf. my *Grail*, p. 233, and for a full list of the MSS. of the Irish text, D'Arbois de Jubainville, p. 10.

P. 11. Dunbar's reference to Finn. The interest and importance of this reference have never been sufficiently appreciated. It shows that in the 15th century (Dunbar, born about 1450, died 1525) there were current about Finn tales of the kind now associated with Conan (see *supra*, p. 73), but which have entirely died away from the popular memory, and which also have, to the best of my knowledge, left no traces in the extensive Gaelic MS. literature of the last three centuries—a fact, by-the-bye, which shows what little reliance can be placed upon the argument *ex silentio*. These tales represented either Finn or Conan as a harrier of hell. It is impossible not to connect this feature with that spirit of defiant paganism which I have noted as characteristic of the ballad form of the later Fenian saga, a spirit which differentiates it so completely from the Irish fourteenth-century prose texts. Now the feature must have been very prominent in the Fenian legend of the Middle Ages for it to have impressed an alien Lowlander, as Dunbar was, as the most characteristic trait of the hero's personality. Can it be connected with anything in the pre-eleventh century Fenian texts? It so happens that a poem in the *Book of Leinster*, edited and translated by Mr. Whitley Stokes, *Rev. Celt.*, vii, 289, describes the visit of Finn and his men to the land of monstrous beings, with whom they strive all night, and who disappear with the incoming daylight. Such an incident may well have got transformed into a visit to hell, but it is important to note, it is in its origin and essence totally different, and must be much older than any purely Christian legendary conceptions. The development of the incident, however, as well as the anti-Christian tone of the ballad form of the Fenian texts, would certainly seem to show that these ballads took shape at a period and among conditions of struggle between Christianity and paganism. The commonly received theory, which makes Finn a third-century man—*i.e.*, places the formative period of the cycle in the fourth-sixth centuries—would fit in with the facts ; but so would Prof. Zimmer's theory, which makes the legend grow up among the pagan Norse invaders and semi-paganised Irish of the ninth century. In any case it is not a little remarkable that not only the "clerical" spirit of the Irish fourteenth-century prose texts, but also the special Christian transformation of the incident of Finn's visit to the otherworld, vouched for by Dunbar's reference and by the proverbs about Conan, have both utterly died away out of the folk-mind. When, thirty years ago, Campbell of Islay noted the tale of Finn's enchantment it was closely akin to the poem preserved by the twelfth-century *Book of Leinster* (see the tale, *Rev. Celt.*, i).

Pp. 12, 13. Brugh Farala. Six versions in *L. na F.*, pp. 175-80 : (*a*) Fletcher's ; (*b*) Kennedy's : (*c*) Kennedy's ; (*d*) Irvine's ; (*e*) Staffa Coll. : (*f*) ditto.

P. 14. Fenian Topography. Cf. Mr. Stuart Glennie's essay on Arthurian localities, prefixed to vol. iii of the Early English Text Society, Merlin.

P. 16. Fionn Mac Cumhail. I have examined the story of Finn's birth and rearing in my paper : "The Aryan Expulsion and Return Formula among the Celts," *Folk Lore Record*, vol. iv, pp. 1-36. The oldest version closely connected with the traditions summarised in the text is the "Boyish Exploits of Finn", printed and translated (incompletely) from a 15th cent. MS. by O'Donovan, *Oss. Soc.*, iv, pp. 281 *et seq.*, printed completely by Kuno Meyer, *Rev. Celt.*, v, p. 195 : but the substance of the story, though shorn of its supernatural incidents and setting, appears in the "Fotha Catha Cnucha" (The Cause of the Battle of Cnucha), a text of the *Leabhar na h'Uidhre*, a MS. copied at the end of the 11th century from older MSS., and probably representing a harmony of old Gaelic legend made in the first quarter of the 11th century. This text was edited and translated by the late W. M. Hennessy, *Revue Celtique*, ii, pp. 86-91.

I have not anywhere else met the tradition, noted 23-24, of the luring of Cumhal. The whole of this section should be compared with Kennedy's account, printed in *L. na F.*, pp. 35-37.

It is remarkable that of this extensive series of prose traditions, extending from the 15th century Boyish Exploits (and presumably from the 11th century Battle of Cnucha) to the present day, and still flourishing vigorously, there is not a single metrical version. One set of incidents about Finn seems to have been told in prose, another in verse, as far back as we can go.

Cf. my notes, MacInnes, pp. 404 and 415.

P. 33. The Battle of Gabhra. Another version printed, *Transactions of the Ossianic Society*, vol. i, with English translation; also *L. na F.*, pp. 180-195, eight versions: (*a, b*) Dean of Lismore; (*c*) Mac Diarmaid (1762-69); (*d*) Mac Nicol; (*e, f*) Kennedy; (*g*) Gillies; (*h*) Irvine. See also *West High. Tales*, iii. p. 304, and D'Arbois de Jubainville, p. 70, for a list of the Irish MSS., the oldest of which is dated 1715, *i.e.*, none are as old as the Lismore version. Mons. d'Arbois also refers to the older form of the tradition, the *Book of Leinster* poem, attributed to Oisin, printed and translated by O'Curry, *Oss. Soc.*, vol. i. Cf. my notes to MacInnes, p. 405.

P. 49. Goll. See *MS Mat.*, p. 302, for the earliest Irish references to Goll. Cf. *L. na F*, p. 164, where versions are printed from MacNicol, Kennedy, and Irvine. According to these, Goll kills Coireal, so that the latter cannot be Oscar, yet Campbell equates him with Oscar. I have not met with the tradition noted in our text elsewhere.

Mr. Campbell is incorrect in his interpretation of Dunbar's verse about Goll being shorn out of his mother's womb. The operation was necessary on account of his size. This feature is a commonplace in the heroic legend, not only of the Middle Ages, but generally; *e.g.*, Rustem, the hero *par excellence* of Persian legend, had to be cut from his mother's body, and this was performed with the help of a feather given to Rustem's father, Sal, by the eagle Simurg, who, upon the feather being cast into the fire, appears, renders the mother insensible, and afterwards heals her. I quote this instance from Persian legend out of the numberless ones that could be cited, as it is interesting to find this second parallel between Iranian and Gaelic saga. Moreover, a similar incident to that of the eagle's being summoned apparently occurs in the Etana legend, an old Babylonian heroic tale which can hardly be less than 3,500 years old (see Dr. E. Harper's letter to the *Academy*, May 30), and it is not unreasonable to assume that the remainder of the episode likewise formed part of this legend, so that the Cæsarean heroic birth-incident, as it may be called, goes back to the remotest antiquity. In Teutonic legend it is associated with Volsung, the eponymous ancestor of the Volsung race.   See also Grimm, *Deutsche Mythologie*, sect. 361.

P. 52. Dermid. Compare my note, MacInnes, p. 403, for the oldest Irish mention of Diarmaid. The story of his flight with Grainne was known in Ireland at the very latest in the first quarter of the eleventh century, as it is mentioned in the story-list of the *Book of Leinster* (*MS. Mat.*, p. 590). Mons. d'Arbois de Jubainville indicates two fifteenth-century Irish versions (p. 35); see also p. 249 for a list of the later MSS. An episode of the flight, the *Uath beinne Etair*, or Hiding of the Hill of Howth, has been printed and translated from a fifteenth-century MS. by Prof. Kuno Meyer, *Rev. Celt.*, xi, 125 et seq. This tale figures likewise in the *Book of Leinster* story-list (*MS. Mat.*, p. 587). Mr. Standish Hayes O'Grady has printed and translated an eighteenth-century prose Irish version, *Oss. Soc.*, vol. iii, which has been reprinted as one of the text-books issued by the Society for the Preservation of the Irish Language. Campbell, *L. na F.*, pp. 152-164, prints thirteen poems from the Diarmaid cycle, from Dean of Lismore, Kennedy, Irvine, and MacNicol; also Kennedy's English Summaries, which should be carefully compared with the versions in our text. Cf. also *West Highland Tales*, vol. iii, p. 39.

P. 64. See my note, MacInnes, pp. 404-406, for the earliest Irish mentions of Caoilte. In the stage of the legend represented by the fourteenth-fifteenth century *Agallamh na Senoraib* (Dialogue of the Elders), Caoilte occupies the place taken in the ballads by Oisin, he is the witness *par excellence* to the departed glories of the Fenian age. Here, again, we note a marked difference between the prose and the verse accounts.
Campbell, *L. na F.*, pp. 52-56, gives seven poems about Caoilte, from MacNicol, Fletcher, Kennedy, and Irvine; also Kennedy's English summaries. Versions of the poem in our text are printed *L. na F.*, pp. 65-68, from Kennedy, Gillies, and current tradition; also Kennedy's English Summaries. Cf. also *West High. Tales*, iii, p. 379.

P. 76. End of the Feinne. Cf. for other versions of the incident mentioned on this page, *L. na F.*, pp. 158-64.

P. 79. Ossian's deer mother. See my note, MacInnes, p. 470; also Hyde's *Beside the Fire*, p. 178. There are several versions of the song in our text. *L. na F.*, pp. 198-199.

P. 82. Ossian after the Fians. This series of traditions is
well represented in Ireland, *Oss. Soc.*, vol. iv ; see also *L. na F.*,
p. 197, for Kennedy's version of Oisin's death, and pp. 38-51
for version of Oisin's stay with Patrick, and the various
episodes connected therewith. A prose version of the last
hunt, corresponding to p. 83 of our text, is on pp. 38-39 from
Staffa's collection, and five versions from current tradition in
West High. Tales, vol. ii, p. 102 *et seq.* See also my note,
Hyde, *Beside the Fire*, p. 179.

P. 86. "The end of the Fians was the going of Fionn to
Rome." This statement should have been mentioned in the
section "Brugh Farala" (*infra*, p. 164). It was after Finn had
been wounded by Oscar, when the latter beheaded Garaidh,
as therein related, that he went to Rome to be healed, and it
was during his absence that the state of affairs arose which
culminated in the slaughter of Gabhra, and in the destruction
of nearly all the Fenian heroes. See Kennedy's Summary of
the Cycle, printed *L. na F.*, p. 36, col. 2. The passage in the
text is a fragment divorced from its proper context.

P. 91. The Red Cataract. See *L. na F.*, p. 127, for a discussion of this cycle. The oldest Irish text is one bound up
with *H.*, 2, 17, a MS., portion of which dates back to the four-
teenth century, but the greater part of which is of the fifteenth
and sixteenth centuries (D'Arbois de Jubainville, p. lxv).
Campbell calls this MS. the *Book of Leacan* by mistake.
Campbell prints versions, *L. na F.*, pp. 127-137, from Dean of
Lismore, Staffa's coll., MacNicol, Kennedy, Gillies, Fletcher,
and current tradition. See more especially Kennedy's English
Summaries, pp. 131 and 132. D'Arbois de Jubainville, pp.
45 and 118, gives a list of the Irish MSS., all, save the above
mentioned, *H.*, 2, 17, of the eighteenth and nineteenth centuries. See my Introduction to vol. iii of present series for a discussion of the mythological interpretation of the Fenian poems.

P. 106. Manus. English version, Miss Brookes, pp. 37-65.
Campbell, *L. na F.*, pp. 71-83, prints versions from MacNicol,
Kennedy, Irvine, MacDonald, and a fragment from Dean of
Lismore. See Kennedy's English Summaries, pp. 74 and 76.
See also *West High. Tales*, iii, p. 346, and D'Arbois de
Jubainville, p. 164, for a list of the Irish MSS., none of which
are anterior to the eighteenth century. I have discussed the
prose tale of Manus, MacInnes, pp. 482-85.

P. 113. Alvin. Campbell, *L. na F.*, pp. 95-104, prints

versions from MacNicol, Fletcher, Kennedy, and Irvine. See more especially Kennedy's English Summaries, pp. 98 and 100.

P. 121. Conn, Son of the Red. The Dearg cycle is discussed by Campbell, *L. na F.*, p. 107. Versions of our text are printed, pp. 113-121, from MacNicol, Fletcher, Kennedy, Gillies, Irvine, and current tradition. Kennedy's English Summary, p. 117. D'Arbois de Jubainville, p. 161, quotes several Irish eighteenth-century texts of "Laoidh an Dearg mhic Dhroithchill", and "Laoidh Chuinn mhic an Deirg".

P. 131. The Muileartach. Four other versions printed, *L. na F.*, p. 59, from MacNicol, Fletcher, Irvine, and current tradition. See also *West High. Tales*, iii, p. 122.

The hag is described much as is the mother of the three giants, with whom, in many Gaelic tales, the hero has to wage his hardest fight (*e.g*, in Campbell's No. 52, "The Knight of the Red Shield"). A similar description occurs in a thirteenth-century French romance, Gerbert's continuation of the Conte del Graal. I have discussed this question, *Grail*, pp. 165 *et seq.*

P. 159. Lay of the Smithy. See *L. na F.*, pp. 65-68, for a composite version, and for Kennedy's with English argument. See also *West. High. Tales*, iii, p. 378.

P. 162. This lament for Caoilte is wrongly placed here. It does not belong to the Smithy Lay at all, but should be classed with the poems printed *L. na F.*, pp. 47-50, "Oisin's Lament for his Comrades."

P. 164. Brugh Farala. See note on p. 12, and compare Kennedy's Summary, *L. na F.*, p. 36. The death of Fionn seems peculiar to the version in our text.

P. 175. Fin Mac Coul in the Kingdom of Big Men. I know no parallel to this story as a whole. Cf. for the skilful companions, my note, MacInnes, pp. 445-48.

P. 192. How Fionn found his Missing Men. Fionn and his Men. These two tales, which are close variants, may be compared with *L. na F.*, p. 89-92, where five versions of the "Lay of the Black Dog" are given from Staffa, MacNicol, Fletcher, and Kennedy. Mr. Standish Hayes O'Grady, in the list of tales common in late Irish MSS. prefixed to his edition of Diarmaid

(*Oss. Soc.*, iii, p. 18), notes Laoidh na con diubhe.   See vol. i
of the present series, p. 7, and Hyde's *Beside the Fire*, pp.
178-79.

P. 204.   How Fionn found Bran.   There is a fragmentary
version in vol. ii of the series—No. II : "Feunn MacCitail and
the Bent Grey Lad."   See my notes to the same, MacInnes, pp.
445-452.   In vol. iii of the present series there is a good version
—No. I : "How Finn kept his Children for the Big Young
Hero of the Ship, and how Bran was Found."

P. 225.   Ceudach, son of the King of the Colla Men.   Eachtra
Cheadaigh Mhoir (Adventures of Ceudach the Big), are men-
tioned in Mr. Standish Hayes O'Grady's already cited list of
Irish MS. tales (*Oss. Soc.*, iii, p. 21).   There is a frag-
mentary version of the tale, differing in many important
respects, in vol. ii of the present series, entitled "Leomhan
Cridheach and Ceudamh".   See my notes on the same, Mac-
Innes, p. 489.   The tale is still current in Ireland.

P. 239.   Fionn's Ransom.   This is a variant of Campbell,
No. 52, "The Knight of the Red Shield".

P. 260.   The Lad with the Skin Covering.   Partly a variant
of Ceudach (p. 225 in this vol.).   This one is more like the
MacInnes version.   So far as I am aware, there are no similars
to this tale as a whole in print.

RUNS.

LONDON : WHITING AND CO., 30 AND 32 SARDINIA STREET, W C.

www.ingramcontent.com/pod-product-compliance
Lightning Source LLC
Chambersburg PA
CBHW021120270326

41929CB00009B/971